Lecture Notes in Artificial Intelligence 1570

Subseries of Lecture Notes in Computer Science
Edited by J. G. Carbonell and J. Siekmann

Lecture Notes in Computer Science

Edited by G. Goos, J. Hartmanis and J. van Leeuwen

Springer

Berlin
Heidelberg
New York
Barcelona
Hong Kong
London
Milan
Paris
Singapore
Tokyo

Frank Puppe (Ed.)

XPS-99:
Knowledge-Based Systems

Survey and Future Directions

5th Biannual German Conference
on Knowledge-Based Systems
Würzburg, Germany, March 3-5, 1999
Proceedings

 Springer

Series Editors

Jaime G. Carbonell, Carnegie Mellon University, Pittsburgh, PA, USA
Jörg Siekmann, University of Saarland, Saarbrücken, Germany

Volume Editors

Frank Puppe
Universität Würzburg, Institut für Informatik
Allesgrundweg 12, D-97218 Gerbrunn, Germany
E-mail: puppe@informatik.uni-wuerzburg.de

Cataloging-in-Publication data applied for

Die Deutsche Bibliothek - CIP-Einheitsaufnahme

Knowledge based systems : survey and future directions ;
proceedings / XPS-99, 5th Biannual German Conference on
Knowledge Based Systems, Würzburg, Germany, March 3 - 5, 1999.
Frank Puppe (ed.). - Berlin ; Heidelberg ; New York ; Barcelona ;
Hong Kong ; London ; Milan ; Paris ; Singapore ; Tokyo : Springer,
1999
  (Lecture notes in computer science ; Vol. 1570 : Lecture notes in
  artificial intelligence)
  ISBN 3-540-65658-8

CR Subject Classification (1998): I.2

ISBN 3-540-65658-8 Springer-Verlag Berlin Heidelberg New York

© Springer-Verlag Berlin Heidelberg 1999
Printed in Germany

Typesetting: Camera-ready by author
SPIN 10703016   06/3142 – 5 4 3 2 1 0   Printed on acid-free paper

Preface

A special year like 1999 invites one to draw a balance of what has been achieved in the roughly 30 years of research and development in knowledge based systems (still abbreviated as XPS following the older term "expert systems") and to take a look at what the future may hold. For the 5ᵗʰ German conference on knowledge-based systems we therefore asked current and former speakers of the four working groups (FG's) in the subdivision of knowledge-based systems (FA 1.5) of the German association of Informatics (GI) to present a survey of and future prospects for their respective fields: knowledge engineering, diagnosis, configuration, and case-based reasoning.

An additional 14 technical papers deal with current topics in knowledge-based systems with an equal emphasis on methods and applications. They are selected from more than 50 papers accepted in the 4 parallel workshops of XPS-99: a) Knowledge Management, Organizational Memory and Reuse, b) various fields of applications, c) the traditional PuK Workshop (planning and configuration), and d) the GWCBR (German workshop on case-based reasoning). The other papers presented at these workshops are not included in this volume but are available as internal reports of Würzburg university together with the exhibition guide that emphasizes tool support for building knowledge based systems.

We are indebted to many people who helped to make the conference a success. First of all, I would like to thank the coordinators of the workshops, Rudi Studer, Dieter Fensel, Jana Koehler, Erica Melis and Thomas Wetter and the members of the respective program committees for reviewing the papers. As there can be no conference without submissions we thank all authors – successful or not – for submitting to XPS-99. Thanks also go to the many people who helped organize the conference, in particular to Petra Braun and all the other members of my research group at Würzburg university. Finally, we thank Springer-Verlag and especially Alfred Hofmann for their support in producing these proceedings.

January 99   Frank Puppe

XPS-99

Conference Chair

Frank Puppe, Würzburg

Workshop Chairs

Dieter Fensel, Karlsruhe
Jana Koehler, Freiburg
Erica Melis, Saarbrücken

Rudi Studer, Karlsruhe
Thomas Wetter, Heidelberg

Programm Committee Members

Klaus Althoff, Kaiserslautern
Franz Baader, Aachen
Brigitte Bartsch-Spörl, München
Michael Beetz, Bonn
Klaus Bena, Zürich
Ralph Bergmann, Kaiserslautern
Susanne Biundo, Ulm
Andreas Böhm, Darmstadt
Hans-Ulrich Buhl, Augsburg
B. Chandrasekaran, Ohio (USA)
Roman Cunis, Hamburg
Stefan Decker, Karlsruhe
Jürgen Dorn, Wien
Oskar Dressler, München
Ute Gappa, Frankfurt
Ulrich Geske, Berlin
Mehmet Göker, Ulm
Andreas Günter, Bremen
Michael Heinrich, Berlin
Knut Hinkelmann, Kaiserslautern

Hubert Keller, Karlsruhe
Dieter Landes, Ulm
Mario Lenz, Berlin
Gerd Mann, Neuherberg
Peter Mertens, Erlangen
Wolfgang Nejdl, Hannover
Bernd Neumann, Hamburg
Gerd Pews, Kaiserslautern
Christoph Ranze, Bremen
Ulrich Reimer, Zürich
Michael M. Richter, Kaiserslautern
Jürgen Sauer, Oldenburg
Gregor Snelting, Braunschweig
Benno Stein, Paderborn
Peter Struss, München
Thomas Uthmann, Mainz
Christoph Wargitsch, Erlangen
Stefan Wess, Kaiserslautern
Bob Wielinga, Amsterdam
Wolfgang Wilke, Kaiserslautern

Table of Contents

Invited Papers

Technical Papers: Methods

Technical Papers: Applications

Knowledge Engineering: Survey and Future Directions

Rudi Studer[1], Dieter Fensel[1], Stefan Decker[1], and V. Richard Benjamins[2]
[1]Institute AIFB, University of Karlsruhe, 76128 Karlsruhe, Germany
{studer, decker, fensel}@aifb.uni-karlsruhe.de
http://www.aifb.uni-karlsruhe.de

[2]Dept. of Social Science Informatics (SWI),
University of Amsterdam, Roetersstraat 15, 1018 WB Amsterdam, The Netherlands
richard@swi.psy.uva.nl, http://www.swi.psy.uva.nl/usr/richard/home.html

Abstract. This paper provides an overview of important developments in the field of Knowledge Engineering. We discuss the paradigm shift from a transfer to a modeling approach and discuss two prominent methodological achievements: problem-solving methods and ontologies. To illustrate these and additional concepts we outline several modeling frameworks: CommonKADS, MIKE, PROTÉGÉ-II, and D3. We also discuss two fields which have emerged in the last few years and are promising areas for applying and further developing concepts and methods from Knowledge Engineering: Intelligent Information Integration and Knowledge Management.

1 Introduction

In its early days, research in Artificial Intelligence was focused on the development of formalisms, inference mechanisms and tools, for operationalizing Knowledge-based Systems (KBS). Typically, the development efforts were restricted to the realization of small KBSs in order to study the feasibility of new approaches.

Although these studies brought forth rather promising results, the transfer of this technology for building commercial KBSs failed in many cases. Just as the software crisis resulted in the establishment of the discipline Software Engineering, the unsatisfactory situation in the construction of KBSs made clear the need for more methodological approaches. Thus the goal of Knowledge Engineering (KE) is similar to that of Software Engineering: constructing KBSs in a systematic and controlable manner. This requires an analysis of the building and maintenance process itself and the development of appropriate methods, languages, and tools suitable for developing KBSs.

Subsequently, we will first give an overview of some important achievements in KE: we discuss the paradigm shift from the so-called *transfer approach* to the so-called *modeling approach*. This paradigm shift is occasionally also considered as the transfer from first generation expert systems to *second generation expert systems* [22]. In addition, we will discuss the notion of *problem-solving methods* and *ontologies*. In Section 3 we will present some modeling frameworks which have been developed in recent years: D3 [78], CommonKADS [81], MIKE [4], and PROTÈGÈ-II [77]. This section concludes with a brief description of the IBROW[3] framework for configuring problem-solvers on the Web. In Section 4 and 5 we will discuss two new fields that have emerged during the last years: Intelligent Information Integration and Knowledge

Management. Both fields provide promising perspectives for the future development of KE methods.

In KE much effort has also been invested in developing methods and supporting tools for knowledge elicitation (compare [29]). In the VITAL approach [82], e.g., a collection of elicitation tools, like repertory grids (see [43]), are offered for supporting the elicitation of domain knowledge. However, a discussion of the various elicitation methods is beyond the scope of this paper. A more detailed description of some concepts and approaches discussed in this paper may be found in [85].

2 Achievements

In this section we will discuss some major concepts which were developed in the KE field in the last fifteen years. We will first outline the paradigm shift from the transfer to the modeling approach and then discuss two fundamental concepts in that modeling framework: Problem-Solving Methods and Ontologies.

2.1 Knowledge Engineering as a Modeling Process

In the early 1980s the development of a KBS was seen as a *process* of transfering human knowledge to an implemented knowledge base. This transfer was based on the assumption that the knowledge which is required by the KBS already exists and only has to be collected and implemented [67]. Typically, this knowledge was implemented in some type of production rules which were executed by an associated rule interpreter.

A careful analysis of the various rule knowledge bases has shown, however, that the rather simple representation formalism of production rules did not support an adequate representation of different types of knowledge [18]. Such a mixture of knowledge types, together with the lack of adequate justifications of the different rules makes the maintenance of such knowledge bases very difficult and time consuming. Therefore, this transfer approach was only feasible for the development of small prototypical systems, but it failed to produce large, reliable and maintainable knowledge bases. Furthermore, it was recognized that the assumption of the transfer approach, that is that knowledge acquisition is the collection of already existing knowledge elements, was false due to the important role of tacit knowledge for an expert's problem-solving capabilities.

These deficiencies resulted in a paradigm shift from the transfer approach to the *modeling approach*. This paradigm shift was also inspired by Newell's *Knowledge Level* notion [70]. This knowledge level proposes the modeling of knowledge independent from its implementation and to structure knowledge models with respect to different knowledge types.

In the modeling framework constructing a KBS means building a computer model with the aim of realizing problem-solving capabilities comparable to a domain expert. Since an expert is not necessarily aware of some knowledge that is part of his or her skills, this knowledge is not directly accessible, but has to be constructed and structured during the knowledge acquisition phase. This knowledge acquisition process is therefore seen as a model construction process [20].

Some observations can be made about this modeling view of the building process of a KBS:

- Like every model, such a model is only an *approximation* of reality.
- The modeling process is a *cyclic* process. New observations may lead to a refinement, modification, or completion of the already constructed model. On the other hand, the model may guide the further acquisition of knowledge.
- The modeling process is dependent on the subjective interpretations of the knowledge engineer. Therefore this process is typically *faulty* and an evaluation of the model with respect to reality is indispensable for the creation of an adequate model.

2.2 Problem-Solving Methods

Originally, KBSs used simple and generic inference mechanisms to infer outputs for provided cases. The knowledge was assumed to be given "declaratively" by a set of Horn clauses, production rules, or frames. Inference engines like unification, forward or backward resolution, and inheritance dealt with the dynamic part of deriving new information. However, human experts use knowledge about the dynamics of the problem-solving *process* and such knowledge is required to enable problem-solving in practice and not only in principle [40]. [18] provided several examples where knowledge engineers implicitly encoded control knowledge by ordering production rules and premises of these rules which together with the generic inference engine, delivered the desired dynamic behaviour. Making this knowledge explicit and regarding it as an important part of the entire knowledge contained by a KBS, is the rationale that underlies *Problem-Solving Methods (PSMs)*. PSMs refine the generic inference engines mentioned above to allow a more direct control of the reasoning process. PSMs describe this control knowledge independent from the application domain, enabling reuse of this strategic knowledge for different domains and applications. Finally, PSMs abstract from a specific representation formalism as opposed to the general inference engines that rely on a specific representation of the knowledge. In the meantime, a large number of such PSMs have been developed and libraries of such methods provide support in their reuse for constructing new applications.

Reuse is a promising way to reduce development costs of software and knowledge-based systems. The basic idea is that a KBS can be constructed from ready-made parts instead of being built up from scratch. Research on PSMs has adopted this philosophy and several PSM libraries have been developed. In the following, we sketch several issues involved in developing such libraries:

- There are currently several libraries of PSMs. They all aim at facilitating the knowledge-engineering process, yet they differ in various ways. In particular, libraries differ along dimensions such as universality, formality, granularity, and size. The type of a library is determined by its characterization in terms of these above dimensions. Each type has a specific role in the knowledge engineering process and has strong and weak points.
- There are several alternatives for organizing a library and each of them has

consequences for indexing PSMs and for their selection. Determining the 'best' organizational principle for such libraries is still an issue of debate.

- Whatever the organizational structure of the library, PSMs are used to realize tasks (tasks describe the *what*, PSMs describe the *how*) by applying domain knowledge. Therefore, there are two possible reasons why a PSM cannot be applied to solve a particular problem: (1) if its requirements on domain knowledge are not fulfilled, or (2) if it cannot deliver what the task requires, that is, if its competence or functionality is not sufficient for the task. Methods for weakening and strengthening PSMs are discussed in [87].

- Traditionally, PSMs are described in an operational style. They are described as decomposing a task into a set of subtasks by introducing their dataflows and knowledge roles and by defining some control on how to execute the subtasks. However, these are not the most important aspects from the standpoint of reuse. As mentioned earlier, two main aspects decide about the applicability of a PSM in a given application: whether the competence of the method is able to achieve the goal of the task and whether the domain knowledge required by the method is available. [6] discussed the characterizations of PSMs by their functionality where the functionality is defined in terms of assumptions over available domain knowledge. Meanwhile several papers have appeared providing declarative characterizations of PSMs (e.g. [9], [39], [21]) and thus dealing with an important line of future work on PSMs.

Offering brokering services for accesing Web-based PSM libraries and configuring KBSs from these libraries is the goal of the IBROW³ project [10] (cf. Section 3.5).

2.3 Ontologies

Since the beginning of the 1990s ontologies have become a popular research topic and have been investigated by several Artificial Intelligence research communities, including KE, natural-language processing and knowledge representation. More recently, the notion of ontology is also becoming widespread in fields such as intelligent information integration, intelligent information retrieval on the Internet, and knowledge management (see Sections 4 and 5). The reason that ontologies have become so popular is in a large part due to what they promise: a shared and common understanding of a domain that can be communicated across people and computers.

Many definitions of ontologies have been given in the last decade, but one that, in our opinion, best characterizes the essence of an ontology is based on the definition in [50]: *An ontology is a formal, explicit specification of a shared conceptualization.* A 'conceptualization' refers to an abstract model of some phenomenon in the world by identifying the relevant concepts of that phenomenon. 'Explicit' means that the type of concepts used and the constraints on their use are explicitly defined. 'Formal' refers to the fact that the ontology should be machine readable, which excludes natural language. 'Shared' reflects the notion that an ontology captures consensual knowledge, that is, it is not private to some individual, but accepted by a group. Basically, the role of ontologies in the knowledge engineering process is to facilitate the construction of a domain model. An ontology provides a vocabulary of terms and relations with which a domain can be modeled.

Especially because ontologies aim at consensual domain knowledge, their development is often a cooperative process involving different people, possibly at different locations. People who agree to accept an ontology are said to *commit* themselves to that ontology.

Depending on their generality level, different types of ontologies that fulfil different roles in the process of building a KBS can be identified ([89], [53]). Among others, we can distinguish the following ontology types:

- *Domain ontologies* capture the knowledge valid for a particular type of domain (e.g. electronic, medical, mechanic, digital domain).

- *Generic or commonsense ontologies* aim at capturing general knowledge about the world and provide basic notions and concepts for things like time, space, state, event etc. ([75], [42]). As a consequence, they are valid across several domains. For example, an ontology about mereology (part-of relations) is applicable in many technical domains [12].

- *Representational ontologies* do not commit themselves to any particular domain. Such ontologies provide representational entities without stating what should be represented. A well-known representational ontology is the *Frame Ontology* [50], which defines concepts such as frames, slots and slot constraints allowing us to express knowledge in an object-oriented or frame-based way.

The ontologies mentioned above all capture static knowledge in a problem-solving independent way. KE is, however, also concerned with problem-solving knowledge, therefore the so-called *method* and *task ontologies* are also useful types of ontologies ([38], [84]). Task ontologies provide terms specific for particular tasks (e.g. 'hypothesis' belongs to the diagnosis task ontology) and method ontologies provide terms specific to particular PSMs [48] (e.g. 'correct state' belongs to the Propose-and-Revise method ontology). Task and method ontologies provide a reasoning point of view on domain knowledge. In this manner, these ontologies help to solve the 'interaction problem' [15], which states that domain knowledge cannot be independently represented from the way in which it will be used in problem solving and vice versa. Method and task ontologies enable us to make explicit the interaction between problem-solving and domain knowledge through assumptions ([9], [40]).

Part of the research on ontology is concerned with envisioning and constructing a technology which enables the large-scale reuse of ontologies on a world-wide level. In order to enable as much reuse as possible, ontologies should be small modules with a high internal coherence and a limited amount of interaction between the modules. This requirement and others are expressed in design principles for ontologies ([51], [52], [88]).

Assuming that the world is full of well-designed modular ontologies, constructing a new ontology is a matter of assembling existing ones. In [33] the Ontolingua server is described which provides different kinds of operations for combining ontologies: inclusion, restriction, and polymorphic refinement. The inclusion of one ontology in another, e.g., has the effect that the composed ontology consists of the union of the two ontologies (their classes, relations, axioms). The SENSUS system [86] provides a means for constructing a domain specific ontology from given commonsense ontologies. The basic idea is to use so-called seed elements which represent the most important domain concepts for identifying the relevant parts of a top-level ontology. The selected parts are then used as a starting point for extending the ontology with further domain-specific concepts. Another approach for the systematic reuse of commonsense ontologies is the KARO approach (Knowledge Acquisition Environment with Reusable Ontologies) [75] which offers formal, linguistic, and graphical methods for retrieving and adapting concept definitions from a given ontology. The supplementation of graphical methods with formal and linguistic means, i.e. with classification mechanisms and natural language processing features, achieves a flexible way for reusing ontologies. The SKC project (Scalable Knowledge Composition) [55] aims at developing an algebra for systematically composing ontologies from already existing ones. It aims at offering union, intersection, and difference as basic operations.

Various kinds of formal languages are used for representing ontologies, among others description logics (see e.g. LOOM [63] or CYCL [61]), Frame Logic [56], and Ontolingua [50], which is based on KIF (Knowledge Interchange Format) [45], and is basically a first-order predicate logic extended with meta-capabilities to reason *about* relations.

2.4 Specification Approaches in Knowledge Engineering

Over the last ten years a number of specification languages have been developed for describing KBSs. These specification languages can be used to specify the knowledge required by the system as well as the reasoning process which uses this knowledge to solve the task assigned to the system. On the one hand, these languages should enable a specification which abstracts from implementation details. On the other hand, they should enable a detailed and precise specification of a KBS at a level which is beyond the scope of specifications in natural language. This area of research is quite well documented by a number of workshops and comparison papers based on these workshops. Surveys of these languages can be found in [41], [34] provides a comparison to similar approaches in software engineering. [91] provide insights as to how these languages can be applied in the broader context of *knowledge management*.

As mentioned above, we can roughly divide the development of knowledge engineering into a knowledge transfer and a knowledge modelling period. In the former period, knowledge was directly encoded using rule-based implementation languages or frame-based systems. The (implicit) assumption was that these representation formalisms are adequate to express the knowledge, reasoning, and functionality of a KBS in a way which is understandable for humans and computers. Serious difficulties arose, however [19]:

- different types of knowledge were represented uniformly,
- other types of knowledge were not represented explicitly,
- the level of detail was too high to present abstract models of the KBS,
- and knowledge level aspects were constantly mixed with aspects of the implementation.

As a consequence, such systems were hard to construct and to maintain when they become larger or were used over a longer period of time. As a consequence, many research groups worked on more abstract description means for KBSs. Some of them were still executable (like the generic tasks [16]) whereas others combined natural language descriptions with semiformal specifications. The most prominent approach in the latter area are the KADS and CommonKADS approaches [81] that introduced a conceptual model (the *Expertise Model*) to describe KBSs at an abstract and implementation independent level. As explained below, the *Expertise Model* distinguishes different knowledge types (called layers) and provides different primitives for each knowledge type (for example, knowledge roles and inference actions at the inference layer) to express the knowledge in a structured manner. A semiformal specification language CML [79] arose that incorporates these structuring mechanisms in the knowledge level models of KBSs. However, the elementary primitives of each model were still defined by using natural language.

Using natural language as a device to specify computer programs has well known advantages and disadvantages. It provides freedom, richness, easiness in use and understanding, which makes it a comfortable tool in sketching what one expects from a program. However, its inherent vagueness and implicitness make it often very hard to answer questions as to whether the system really does what is expected, or whether the model is consistent or correct (cf. [54]). Formal specification techniques arose that overcome these shortcomings. Usually they were not meant as a replacement for semiformal specifications but as a possibility to improve the precision of a specification when required. Meanwhile, around twenty different approaches can be found in the literature ([41], [34]). Some of them aim mainly at formalization. A formal semantics is provided that enables the unique definition of knowledge, reasoning, or functionality along with manual or automated proofs. Other approaches aim at operationalization, that is, the specification of a system can be executed which enables prototyping in the early phase of system development. Here, the evaluation of the specification is the main interest. They help to answer the question as to whether the specification really specifies what the user is expecting or the expert is providing. Some approaches aim at formalizing and operationalizing (cf. e.g. the specification language KARL [35]), however they have to tackle conflicting requirements that arise from these two goals.

Specification languages for KBSs arose to formalize their conceptual models. They use the structuring principles of semiformal specifications and add formal semantics to the elementary primitives and their composition (cf. [27], [28]). As introduced above, the *Expertise Model* [81] describes the different types of knowledge required by a KBS as well as the role of this knowledge in the reasoning process of the KBS. Based on this, specification languages provide formal means for precisely defining:

- the goals and the process necessary to achieve them,
- the functionality of the inference actions, and
- the precise semantics of the different elements of the domain knowledge.

Definitions in natural language are supplemented by formal definitions to ensure unambiguity and preciseness. The structure of the conceptual models organizes the formal specification in a natural manner, improving understandability and simplifying the specification process.

3   Modeling Frameworks

In this section we will describe different modeling frameworks which address various aspects of model-based KE approaches: D3 [78] introduces the notion of configurable role-limiting methods, CommonKADS [81] is noted for having defined the structure of the Expertise Model, MIKE [4] puts emphasis on a formal and executable specification of the Expertise Model as the result of the knowledge acquisition phase, and PROTÉGÉ-II [31] exploits the notion of ontologies.

It should be clear that there are further approaches which are well known in the KE community, like e.g VITAL [82] and EXPECT [49]. However, a discussion of these approaches is beyond the scope of this paper.

3.1   D3: Configurable Role-Limiting Methods

Role-Limiting Methods (RLM) [64] were one of the first attempts to support the development of KBSs by exploiting the notion of a reusable problem-solving method. The RLM approach may be characterized as a shell approach. Such a shell comes with an implementation of a specific PSM and can thus only be used to solve a type of tasks for which the PSM is appropriate. The given PSM also defines the generic roles that knowledge can play during the problem-solving process and it completely determines the knowledge representation for the roles such that the expert only has to instantiate the generic concepts and relationships which are defined by these roles. Therefore, the acquisition of the required domain specific instances may be supported by (graphical) interfaces which are custom-tailored for the given PSM.

In order to overcome this inflexibility of RLMs, the concept of configurable RLMs has been proposed. *Configurable Role-Limiting Methods* (CRLMs) as discussed in [76] and implemented in D3 [78] exploit the idea that a complex PSM may be decomposed into several subtasks where each of these subtasks may be solved by different methods. In [76], various PSMs for solving classification tasks, like *Heuristic Classification* or *Set-covering Classification*, were analysed with respect to common subtasks. This analysis resulted in the identification of shared subtasks like „data abstraction" or „hypothesis generation and test". Within the CRLM framework a predefined set of different methods are offered for solving each of these subtasks. Thus a PSM may be configured by selecting a method for each of the identified subtasks. In that way the CRLM approach provides a means for configuring the shell for different types of tasks. It should be noted that each method offered for solving a specific subtask has to meet the knowledge role specifications that are predetermined for the CRLM shell, i.e. the CRLM shell comes with a fixed scheme of knowledge types. As a consequence, the introduction of a new method into the shell typically involves the modification and/or extension of the current scheme of knowledge types [76]. Having a fixed scheme of knowledge types and predefined communication paths between the various components is an important restriction which distinguishes the CRLM framework from more flexible configuration approaches such as CommonKADS (see Section 3.2).

The D3 system places strong emphasis on supporting graphical knowledge acquisition methods that allow domain experts to build up domain models themselves [7]. D3 offers a variety of form-based or graphical editors covering the basic types of editors which are needed for knowledge acquisition:

- *Object Forms* are used to specify single objects together with their attributes and their respective values.

- *Object-Attribute Tables* are similar to relational database tables and allow entering a collection of objects which all have the same atomic attributes.

- *Object-Object Tables* are tables in which both rows and columns are labeled by objects. These tables support the specification of simple relations between objects.

- *Object-Relation Tables* are complex tables in which rows are labeled by object attributes and columns by relations. This type of table provides a means for entering relations between several attributes of an object.

- *Hierarchies* are used for entering taxonomic relations between objects or for specifying decision tables.

All these different editors are integrated in a uniform user interface supporting a flexible switching between the different editor types. Of course, grapical means cannot conveniently cope with arbitrary n-ary relations between objects. Therefore, D3 includes graphical abstractions, which visualize such complex relations, but result in some type of information loss [7].

In order to reduce the effort for implementing such graphical interfaces D3 includes META-KA (Meta Knowledge Acquisition System) which generates the required graphical editors from declarative specifications [44]. META-KA is based on the object oriented representation of the knowledge types that are used for the system internal knowledge representation. This internal representation is enriched by information concerning the layout of the tables or the navigation structure that defines, e.g., the menus and dialogue buttons which are offered to the user.

D3 was used in several application projects for developing KBSs. Examples are medical diagnosis and tutoring systems or service-support systems for printing machines (see [78] for more details).

3.2 The CommonKADS Approach

A well-known knowledge engineering approach is *KADS* [80] and its further development to *CommonKADS* [81]. A basic characteristic of KADS is the construction of a collection of models, where each model captures specific aspects of the KBS to be developed as well as its environment. In CommonKADS we distinguish the *Organization Model*, the *Task Model*, the *Agent Model*, the *Communication Model*, the *Expertise Model* and the *Design Model*. Whereas the first four models aim at modeling the organizational environment the KBS will operate in and the tasks that are performed in the organization, the expertise and design model describe (non-) functional aspects of the KBS under development.

Subsequently, we will briefly discuss each of these models and then provide a detailed description of the Expertise Model:

- Within the *Organization Model* the organizational structure is described together with a specification of the functions that are performed by each organizational unit. Furthermore, it identifies the deficiencies of the current business processes and possibilities for improving these processes by introducing KBSs.

- The *Task Model* provides a hierarchical description of the tasks which are performed in the organizational unit in which the KBS will be installed. This includes a specification of which agents are assigned to the different tasks.

- The *Agent Model* specifies the capabilities of each agent involved in the execution of the tasks at hand. In general, an agent can be a human or some kind of software system, e.g. a KBS.

- Within the *Communication Model* the various interactions between the different agents are specified. Among other things, it specifies which type of information is exchanged between the agents and which agent is initiating the interaction.

A major contribution of the KADS approach is its proposal for structuring the *Expertise Model*, which distinguishes three different types of knowledge required to solve a particular task. Basically, the three different types correspond to a static view, a functional view and a dynamic view of the KBS to be built. Each type of knowledge is modeled in a different layer of the *Expertise Model*:

- *Domain layer*: At the domain layer the domain specific knowledge needed to solve the task at hand is modeled. This includes a conceptualization of the domain in a domain ontology (see Section 2) and a declarative theory of the required domain knowledge. One objective for structuring the domain layer is to model it as reusable as possible for solving different tasks.

- *Inference layer*: At the inference layer the reasoning process of the KBS is specified by exploiting the notion of a PSM. The inference layer describes the *inference actions* of which the generic PSM is composed as well as the *roles* which are played by the domain knowledge within the PSM. The dependencies between inference actions and roles are specified in what is called an *inference structure*. Furthermore, the notion of roles provides a domain independent view of the domain knowledge.

- *Task layer*: The task layer provides a decomposition of tasks into subtasks and inference actions, including a goal specification for each task and a specification of how these goals are achieved. The task layer also provides a means for specifying the control over the subtasks and inference actions that are defined at the inference layer.

CML (Conceptual Modeling Language) [79], a semi-formal language with a graphical notation, is offered to to describe an *Expertise Model*. CML is oriented towards providing a communication basis between the knowledge engineer and the domain expert during the model construction process.

The clear separation of the domain specific knowledge from the generic description of the PSM at the inference and task layer enables, in principle, two kinds of reuse: on the one hand, a domain layer description may be reused for solving different tasks by different PSMs, on the other hand, a given PSM may be reused in a different domain by defining a new view of another domain layer. This reuse approach is a weakening of the strong interaction problem hypothesis [15]. In [81] the notion of a *relative interaction hypothesis* is defined to indicate that some kind of dependency exists between the structure of the domain knowledge and the type of task which is to be solved. To achieve a flexible adaptation of the domain layer to a new task environment, the notion of layered ontologies is proposed: *Task* and *PSM ontologies* may be defined as viewpoints of an underlying domain ontology. Within CommonKADS a library of reusable and configurable components, which can be used to build up an *Expertise Model*, has been defined [13].

In essence, the *Expertise Model* and *Communication Model* capture the functional requirements for the target system. Based on these requirements the *Design Model* is developed, which specifies among other things the system architecture and the computational mechanisms for realizing the inference actions. KADS aims at achieving a *structure-preserving design*, i.e. the structure of the *Design Model* should reflect the structure of the *Expertise Model* as much as possible [81].

All the development activities which result in a stepwise construction of the different models are embedded in a cyclic and risk-driven life cycle model similar to Boehm's spiral model [11].

The knowledge models of CommonKADS can also be used in a Knowledge Management environment for supporting the knowledge acquisition process and for structuring the knowledge according to different knowledge types [91]. This is a nice example of how methods from KE may contribute to new fields like Knowledge Management.

3.3   The MIKE Approach

The *MIKE approach* (*Model-based and Incremental Knowledge Engineering*) (cf. [4], [5]) provides a development method for KBSs covering all steps from the initial elicitation through specification to design and implementation. MIKE proposes the integration of *semiformal* and *formal specification techniques* and *prototyping* into an engineering framework. The integration of prototyping and support for an incremental and reversible system development process into a model-based framework is actually the main distinction between MIKE and CommonKADS [81]:

- MIKE takes the *Expertise Model* of CommonKADS as its general model pattern and provides a smooth transition from a semiformal representation, the *Structure Model*, to a formal representation, the *KARL Model*, and further to an implementation oriented representation, the *Design Model*. The smooth transition between the different representation levels of the *Expertise Model* is essential for enabling incremental and reversible system development in practice.

- In MIKE the executability of the *KARL Model* enables the validation of the *Expertise Model* by means of prototyping. This considerably enhances the integration of the expert in the development process.

In MIKE, the entire development process is divided into a number of subactivities: *Elicitation*, *Interpretation*, *Formalization/Operationalization*, *Design*, and *Implementation*. Each of these activities deals with different aspects of the system development.

The knowledge acquisition process starts with *Elicitation*. Methods like structured interviews [29] are used for acquiring informal descriptions of the knowledge about the specific domain and the problem-solving process itself. The resulting knowledge, expressed in natural language, is stored in so-called *knowledge protocols*.

During the *Interpretation* phase the knowledge structures which are identified in the *knowledge protocols* are represented in a semi-formal variant of the *Expertise Model*: the *Structure Model* [69]. All structuring information in this model, like the data dependencies between two inferences, is expressed in a fixed, restricted language while the basic building blocks, e.g. the description of an inference, are represented by unrestricted texts. This representation provides an initial structured description of the emerging knowledge structures and can be used as a communication basis between the knowledge engineer and the expert. Thus the expert can be integrated into the process of structuring the knowledge.

The *Structure Model* is the foundation for the *Formalization/Operationalization* process which results in the formal *Expertise Model*: the *KARL Model*. The *KARL Model* has the same conceptual structure as the *Structure Model* whereby the basic building blocks, which have been represented as natural language texts, are now expressed in the formal specification language *KARL* [35]. This representation avoids the vagueness and ambiguity of natural language descriptions and thus helps to obtain a clearer understanding of the entire problem-solving process. The *KARL Model* can be directly mapped to an operational representation because KARL (with some small limitations) is an executable language.

The result of the knowledge acquisition phase, the *KARL Model*, captures all functional requirements for the final KBS. During the *Design* phase additional non-functional requirements are considered [60]. These non-functional requirements include efficiency and maintainability, but also the constraints imposed by target software and hardware environments. Efficiency is already partially covered in the knowledge acquisition phase, but only to the extent that it determines the PSM. Consequently, functional decomposition is already part of the earlier phases in the development process. Therefore, the design phase in MIKE constitutes the equivalent of detailed design and unit design in software engineering approaches. The *Design Model* which is the result of this phase is expressed in the language *DesignKARL* [58]. DesignKARL extends KARL by providing additional primitives for structuring the *KARL Model* and for describing algorithms and data types. DesignKARL additionally allows the description the design process itself and the interactions between design decisions.

The *Design Model* captures all functional and non-functional requirements posed to the KBS. In the *Implementation* process the *Design Model* is implemented in the target hardware and software environment.

The result of all phases is a set of several interrelated refinement states of the *Expertise Model*. All these different model variants are explicitly connected to each other via different types of links and thus ensure traceability of (non-)functional requirements

The entire development process, i.e. the sequence of knowledge acquisition, design, and implementation, is performed in a cycle guided by a *spiral model* [11] as process model. Every cycle produces a prototype of the KBS which may be evaluated by testing it in the real target environment. The results of the evaluation are used in the next cycle to correct, modify, or extend this prototype.

The MIKE approach as described above is restricted to modeling the KBS under development. To capture the embedding of a KBS in a business environment, the MIKE approach has been extended by new models which define different views of an enterprise. Main emphasis is put on a smooth transition from business modeling to the modeling of problem-solving processes [24].

3.4 The PROTÉGÉ-II Approach

The *PROTÉGÉ-II approach* [31] aims at developing a tool set and methodology for the construction of domain-specific knowledge-acquisition tools [30] and knowledge-based systems from reusable components, i.e. PSMs and knowledge bases.

In PROTÉGÉ-II a PSM comes with a so-called *method ontology* (cf. [31], [84]): such a method ontology defines the concepts and relationships that are used by the PSM for providing its functionality. The *Board-Game Method* [31], e.g., uses among other things the notions of 'pieces', 'locations', and 'moves' to provide its functionality, that is to move pieces between locations on a board. In this way, a method ontology corresponds to the generic terminology as introduced by the collection of knowledge roles of a PSM (compare Section 2).

A second type of reusable components are domain knowledge bases which provide the domain specific knowledge to solve a given task. Knowledge bases are accompanied by *domain ontologies* that define the concept and relationships which are used within the domain knowledge base.

Both PSMs and domain ontologies are reusable components for constructing a KBS. However, due to the interaction problem the interdependence between domain ontologies and PSMs with their associated method ontologies has to be taken into account when constructing a KBS from reusable components. Therefore, PROTÉGÉ-II proposes the notion of separate *mediators* [90] to adapt PSMs and knowledge bases to each other [47]. In contrast to PSMs and knowledge bases, mediators are specifically for solving an application task since they are tailored towards adapting a PSM to a knowledge base to solve a particular task.

Rather recently, PROTÉGÉ-II has been embedded in a CORBA environment [73] in order to make the different components accessible across different software environments. In essence, each of the three components comes with an *interface definition* specified in the CORBA Interface Definition Language. Thus components which run on different software platforms may communicate with each other and may therefore be reused for building up a KBS.

Mediators may provide either a static or a dynamic mediation between PSMs and knowledge bases. *Static* mediation means that all the knowledge that is needed by the PSM is made available by the mediator when the first 'LoadKB' request is issued by the PSM. Thus all further knowledge requests can be handled by the mediator without any further access to the underlying knowledge base. *Dynamic* mediation allows for access to the knowledge base at run-time. Such a flexible mediation may be needed in cases in which the kind of knowledge that is needed by the PSM is dependent on user-provided run-time inputs.

The PROTÉGÉ-II approach has a long tradition in generating knowledge-acquisition tools from ontologies [30]. For generating a knowledge acquisition tool one first has to specify an ontology, i.e the concepts and their corresponding attributes. PROTÉGÉ-II takes such an ontology as input and generates as output a knowledge-acquisition tool that allows domain specialists to enter instances of the domain concepts, i.e. domain facts. The PROTÉGÉ-II component for generating knowledge-acquisition tools is comparable to the META-KA component of D3 (see Section 3.1): META-KA offers more types of graphical editors, its degree of automation in generating a tool is, however, lower compared to PROTÉGÉ-II.

3.5 IBROW³: An Intelligent Brokering Service for Knowledge-Component Reuse on the World-Wide Web

The World Wide Web is changing the nature of software development to a distributive plug & play process. This requires a new method for managing software by so-called *intelligent software brokers*. The European IBROW³ project developed an intelligent brokering service that enables third party knowledge-component reuse through the WWW [10]. Suppliers provide libraries of knowledge components adhering to some standard, and customers can consult these libraries -- through intelligent brokers -- to configure a KBS suited to their needs by selection and adaptation. For achieving these goals, IBROW³ integrates research on heterogeneous databases, interoperability, and web technology with knowledge-system technology and ontologies. The broker can handle web requests for classes of KBS by accessing libraries of reusable PSMs in the Web and by selecting, adapting, and configuring these methods in accordance with the domain at hand. The main focus of the current work is reasoning knowledge, i.e. PSMs. The development of the description language *UPML (Unified Problem-solving Method Description Language)* summarized a decade of research on specification languages for KBSs. The language relies on a newly developed architecture for KBSs that uses (stacks of) KBSs adapters to express component connection and refinement [36]. This architecture provides a structured way for developing, adapting, and reusing PSMs. The broker supports component selection, adaptation, and combination through a user-guided browsing process and deductive inferences that relate goal descriptions of tasks to competence descriptions of PSMs. Summing up in a nutshell, IBROW³ integrates the results of KE in the new computational environments that are currently arising.

4   Intelligent Information Integration and Information Services

The growth of on-line information repositories (such as the Internet) has made information presentation and access much simpler. However, it has also become a cliche to observe that this growth has vastly complicated tasks involving the finding and synthesizing of precisely that information which someone is looking for. A tourist planning a trip to Paris, for example, can not simply use a Web browser today to call up a map showing the Italian restaurant closest to the Eiffel Tower. And the tourist is likely to become even more frustrated upon realizing that the Web in fact contains all the necessary information: maps of Paris, lists of restaurants and tourist sites, etc. The problems is not one of information distribution, but of information integration.

Constructing tools to simplify access to the wealth of available information constitutes a significant challenge to computer science [68]. One specific challenge to be addressed is the development of methods and tools for integrating partially incompatible information sources. In that context the notion of mediators is proposed as a middle layer between information sources and applications [90]. Among other things, mediators rely on the notion of ontologies for defining the conceptualization of the underlying information sources. Therefore, methods for constructing and reusing ontologies are directly relevant for developing mediators.

TSIMMIS [17] stands for The Stanford-IBM Manager of Multiple Information Sources. The goal of the TSIMMIS Project is to develop tools that facilitate the rapid integration of heterogeneous information sources that may include both structured and semistructured data. TSIMMIS uses a pattern-based approach to extract information from different sources. All extracted information is represented in OEM, a semi-structured data model which allows the user to cope with the varying structures found in different Web sources. Mediators that integrate information from different sources use these OEM structures as input and deliver OEM data as answers to queries.

[46] describes the *Infomaster system,* which is a generic tool for integrating different types of information sources, like e.g. relational databases or Web pages. Each information source is associated with a wrapper that hides the source specific information structure of the information sources. Internally, Infomaster uses the Knowledge Interchange Format for representing knowledge. Infomaster uses so-called base relations for mediating between the conceptual structure of the information sources and the user applications. The collection of base relations may be seen as a restricted domain ontology for integrating the different heterogeneous information sources.

Shopping agents [74] free the user from the need to search and visit several on-line stores when trying to buy a product via the WWW. At the request of the human client they visit several of these stores and use wrappers to extract the provided product information, and a mediator summarizes and integrates the results. These agents have become commercial products in the meantime and are integrated into the services of web search engines (cf. www.excite.com).

Ontologies are also used for supporting the semantic retrieval of information from the World-Wide Web. The *SHOE approach* [62] annotates Web pages with ontological information which can then be exploited for answering queries. Thus, the syntactic based retrieval of information from the Web, as is familiar from the various Web search engines, is replaced by a semantic based retrieval process. A further step is taken in the *Ontobroker project* ([37], [25]) which uses a more expressive ontology combined with a corresponding inference mechanism. Thus, the search metaphor of SHOE is replaced by an inference metaphor for retrieving information from the Web since the inference mechanism can use complex inferences as part of the query answering process.

Such systems will soon spread throughout the WWW based on newly emerging standards for information representation. The extendable Mark-up Language XML [93] provides semantic information as a by-product of defining the structure of the document. XML provides a tree structure to describe documents. The different leaves of the tree have a well-defined tag and a context through which the information can be understood. That is, structure and semantics of document are interweaved. The Metadata initiative of the W3C (the standardization committee of the WWW) developed the Resource Description Framework RDF[1] [66] which provides a means for adding semantics to a document without making any assumptions about the structure of this document. It is an XML application (i.e., its syntax is defined in XML) customized for adding meta information to Web documents. It is currently under development as a W3C standard for content descriptions of web sources and will be used by other standards like PICS-2, P3P, and DigSig. The Dublin Core [23] is a set of fifteen metadata elements intended to facilitate the discovery of electronic resources. Originally conceived for the author-generated description of Web resources, it has also attracted the attention of formal resource description communities such as museums and libraries. It corresponds to a simple ontology that fixes the content of meta-descriptions.

5   Knowledge Management and Organizational Memories

Knowledge Management (KM) receives more and more interest. Companies recognize that in the knowledge economy what organizations know is becoming more important than the traditional sources of economic power - capital, land, plants, and labor. It is important to recognize that KM is a multidisciplinary application area and that single solutions from one discipline do usually not work in a complex environment. Disciplines involved are e.g. management sciences, sociology, document management, ergonomics, computer supported cooperative work (cf. [26], [92] and Knowledge Engineering: Exploiting and protecting intellectual assets (cf. [71]) is obviously related to the aims of Knowledge Engineering. Usually, the task of KE is the „engineering" of knowledge with the construction of a KBSs in mind. This is not necessarily true in Knowledge Management: the outcome of a Knowledge Management Strategy may not be a KBS, not even a computer-based system. Even changes in the culture of an organization can support Knowledge Management. However, from an IT-point of view an *Organizational Memory Information System (OMIS)* (cf. [83], [1], [57]) plays an important role in KM.

---

1. See http://www.w3c.org/RDF.

5.1 Technological Support for Knowledge Management

Knowledge Engineering provides strong support for the tasks of building an OMIS, e.g. for elicitation of the content, for building and maintenance, and for knowledge retrieval and utilization. Thus it is no wonder that many knowledge elicitation tools and techniques exist which can be used inside an OMIS, e.g. for initial acquisition of knowledge or for an incremental use during the life-cycle of an OMIS. However, as mentioned before Knowledge Elicitation tools are not the only part of an OMIS, instead many other system components have to be integrated. To support these integration tasks and to enable, e.g., ontology-based knowledge retrieval [8] the construction of three different kinds of ontologies is suggested ([1], [91]):

- *Information ontology*: This ontology describes the information meta-model, e.g. the structure and format of the information sources. This supports the integration of information and is the lowest level ontology.

- *Domain ontology*: This ontology is used to describe the content of the information sources and can be used, e.g., for knowledge retrieval.

- *Enterprise ontology*: This ontology is used in modeling business processes. Its purpose is to model the knowledge needs in business processes so as to describe a process context, which enables active knowledge delivery.

These ontologies provide a basis for interoperability at several layers and enable more sophisticated use of the knowledge in an OMIS. The construction of these ontologies is itself a knowledge engineering task and can be supported by tools and techniques.

5.2 Knowledge Engineering vs. Knowledge Management

KE can provide a basis for Knowledge Management, but it is imporant to have the following differences between an OMIS and a KBS in mind:

- A KBS focuses on the solution of a single task. This is not true for an OMIS: it supports at least a collection of different business processes and thus has to support different tasks.

- A KBS contains knowledge at a high level of formalization, whereas an OMIS consists of knowledge at different formalization levels, e.g. documents, hypertext (cf. [32]), and formal knowledge bases. Typically, informally represented knowledge is usually much more important than formally represented knowledge. In KM the final consumers of the knowledge are human beings, not the system itself.

- An OMIS integrates different kinds of knowledge (e.g. „Best Practices" and „Experiences" (cf. [3], [59]), „Design Rationales" [14], Process Knowledge [65]] at different levels of representation. Because KBS aim at solving single tasks, their knowledge requirements are very homogenous.

- Groupware and knowledge dissemination techniques are usually not part of a KBS, but are essential for an OMIS because the knowledge inside the system has to be communicated to the employees. In addition an OMIS has to integrate many different preexisting *system components* and legacy applications, which are selected for a specific knowledge management strategy

A KBS can be part of an OMIS. Then it supports the knowledge-based solution of single business tasks. Furthermore several techniques developed in KE can contribute to a methodology for building an OMIS and supporting a *Knowledge Management Strategy* (cf. [24], [91]). The CommonKADS-Methodology, e.g., can help to identify and analyze a company's knowledge-intensive work processes. So we can conclude, that KE does not only provide tools and methodologies for building KBSs based on PSMs, but can also serve as to a great extend as a general framework for building an OMIS. For more details and references cf. [72].

6   Conclusion and Related Work

During the last decade, research in Knowledge Engineering resulted in several important achievements. Notable developments are:

- Within the framework of model-based Knowledge Engineering, model structures have been defined which clearly separate the different types of knowledge which are important in the context of Knowledge-based Systems (KBSs). The *Expertise Model* is the most prominent example of these models.

- The clear separation of the notions of task, problem-solving method, and domain knowledge provides a promising basis for making the reuse-oriented development of KBSs more feasible.

- The integration of a strong conceptual model is a distinctive feature of formal specification languages in Knowledge Engineering.

The notion of knowledge level models which evolved in Knowledge Engineering during the last decade is a promising general concept for modeling knowledge. Thus, other fields, like Knowledge Management or Intelligent Information Integration, that heavily rely on building up knowledge models may directly profit from these notions and the available modeling tools.

Reusing software components that are available in some kind of Web repositories becomes an interesting perspective for developing application systems. Again the Knowledge Engineering concepts of ontologies and problem-solving methods are a promising starting point for developing intelligent software brokering services. The framework of the IBROW[3] approach [10] is a first step in developing and implementing such brokering services.

Acknowledgement
Richard Benjamins was partially supported by the Netherlands Computer Science Research Foundation with financial support from the Netherlands Organisation for Scientific Research (NWO).

References
[1] A. Abecker, A. Bernardi, K. Hinkelmann, O. Kühn, and M. Sintek. Towards a Technology for Organizational Memories. *IEEE Intelligent Systems & Their Applications*,13:(3), 1998.

[2] A. Abecker and S. Decker, Organizational Memory: Knowledge Acquisition, Integration and Retrieval Issue, in: F. Puppe, ed., *Knowledge-based Systems: Survey and Future Directions, Proc. 5th German Conference on Knowledge-based Systems*, Wuerzburg, Lecture Notes in AI, Springer Verlag, 1999.

[3] K.-D. Althoff, F. Bomarius and C. Tautz, Using Case-Based Reasoning Technology to Build Learning Software Organizations, in: *Proc. of the 1st Workshop Building, Maintaining, and Using Organizational Memories (OM-98), 13th European Conference on AI (ECAI '98)*, Brighton, 1998. http://SunSITE.Informatik.RWTH-Aachen.DE/Publications/CEUR-WS/Vol-14/

[4] J. Angele, D. Fensel, D. Landes, and R. Studer, Developing Knowledge-Based Systems with MIKE, *Journal of Automated Software Engineering* 5, 4 (October 1998), 389-418.

[5] J. Angele, D. Fensel, and R. Studer, Domain and Task Modeling in MIKE, in: A. Sutcliffe et al., eds., *Domain Knowledge for Interactive System Design*, Chapman & Hall, 1996.

[6] H. Akkermans, B. Wielinga, and A.Th. Schreiber, Steps in Constructing Problem-Solving Methods, in: N. Aussenac et al., eds., *Knowledge Acquisition for Knowledge-based Systems, 7th European Workshop (EKAW'93)*, Toulouse, Lecture Notes in AI 723, Springer-Verlag, 1993.

[7] S. Bamberger, U. Gappa, F. Klügl, and F. Puppe, Komplexitätsreduktion durch grafische Wissensabstraktion, in: P. Mertens and H. Voss, eds., *Expertensysteme 97 (XPS'97), Proc. in Artificial Intelligence* 6, infix, St. Augustin, 1997.

[8] V. R. Benjamins, D. Fensel, and A. Gómez Pérez, Knowledge Management through Ontologies, in: *Proceedings of the 2nd International Conference on Practical Aspects of Knowledge Management (PAKM '98)*, Basel, Switzerland, October 1998.

[9] V. R. Benjamins, D. Fensel, and R. Straatman, Assumptions of Problem-solving Methods and Their Role in Knowledge Engineering, in: W. Wahlster, editor, *Proc. ECAI-96*, pages 408-412. J. Wiley & Sons, Ltd., 1996.

[10] V.R. Benjamins, E. Plaza, E. Motta, D. Fensel, R. Studer, B. Wielinga, G. Schreiber, Z. Zdrahal, and S. Decker: IBROW3: An Intelligent Brokering Service for Knowledge-Component Reuse on the World-Wide Web, in: *Proceedings of the 11th Workshop on Knowledge Acquisition, Modeling, and Management (KAW '98)*, Banff, Canada, April 1998. See http://www.swi.psy.uva.nl/projects/IBROW3/home.html.

[11] B.W. Boehm, A Spiral Model of Software Development and Enhancement, *Computer* 21, 5 (May 1988), 61-72.

[12] W. N. Borst and J. M. Akkermans, Engineering Ontologies, *International Journal of Human-Computer Studies*, 46 (2/3):365-406, 1997.

[13] J. A. Breuker and W. van de Velde, eds., *The CommonKADS Library For Expertise Modelling*, IOS Press, Amsterdam, 1994.

[14] S. Buckingham Shum, Negotiating the Construction and Reconstruction of Organisational Memories, *Journal of Universal Computer Science*, 3(8), *Special Issue on Information Technology for Knowledge Management*, Springer Science Online, 1997.

[15] T. Bylander and B. Chandrasekaran, Generic Tasks in Knowledge-based Reasoning: The Right Level of Abstraction for Knowledge Acquisition, in: B. Gaines and J. Boose, eds., *Knowledge Acquisition for Knowledge Based Systems*, Vol. 1, Academic Press, London, 1988.

[16] B. Chandrasekaran, Generic Tasks in Knowledge-based Reasoning: High-level Building Blocks for Expert System Design, *IEEE Expert* 1, 3 (1986), 23-30.

[17] S. Chawathe, H. Garcia-Molina, J. Hammer, K. Ireland, Y. Papakonstantinou, J. Ullman, and J. Widom: The TSIMMIS Project: Integration of Heterogeneous Information Sources, in: *Proceedings of IPSJ Conference, Tokyo, Japan, October 1994*, 7-18.

[18] W.J. Clancey, The Epistemology of a Rule-Based Expert System - a Framework for Explanation, *Artificial Intelligence* 20 (1983), 215-251.

[19] W.J. Clancey, From Guidon to Neomycin and Heracles in Twenty Short Lessons, in: A. van Lamsweerde, ed., *Current Issues in Expert Systems*, Academic Press, 1987.

[20] W.J. Clancey, The Knowledge Level Reinterpreted: Modeling How Systems Interact, *Machine Learning* 4, 1989, 285-291.

[21] F. Cornelissen, C.M. Jonker, and J. Treur; Compositional Verification of Knowledge-based Systems: A Case Study for Diagnostic Reasoning, in: E. Plaza and R. Benjamins, eds., *Knowledge Acquisition, Modeling, and Management, 10th European Workshop (EKAW'97)*, Sant Feliu de Guixols, Lecture Notes in Artificial Intelligence 1319, Springer-Verlag, 1997.

[22] J.-M. David, J.-P. Krivine, and R. Simmons, eds., *Second Generation Expert Systems*, Springer-Verlag, Berlin, 1993.

[23] The Dublin Core Initiative, *http://purl.org/metadata/dublin_core*.

[24] S. Decker, M. Daniel, M. Erdmann, and R. Studer, An Enterprise Reference Scheme for Integrating Model-based Knowledge Engineering and Enterprise Modeling, in: E. Plaza and R. Benjamins, eds., *Knowledge Acquisition, Modeling, and Management, 10th European Workshop (EKAW'97)*, Sant Feliu de Guixols, Lecture Notes in Artificial Intelligence 1319, Springer-Verlag, 1997.

[25] S. Decker, M. Erdmann, D. Fensel, and R. Studer: Ontobroker: Ontology-based Access to Distributed and Semi-Structured Information, in: *Proc. 8th IFIP 2.6 Working Conf. on Database Semantics (DS-8)*, Rotorua, January 1999.

[26] R. Dieng, O. Corby, A. Giboin and M. Ribière, Methods and Tools for Corporate Knowledge Management, in: *Proc. of the 11th Knowledge Acquisition, Modeling and Management for Knowledge-based Systems Workshop (KAW'98)*, Banff, 1998.

[27] H. Ehrig and B. Mahr, eds., *Fundamentals of Algebraic Specifications 1*, Springer-Verlag, Berlin, 1985.

[28] H. Ehrig and B. Mahr, eds., *Fundamentals of Algebraic Specifications 2*, Springer-Verlag, Berlin, 1990.

[29] H. Eriksson, A Survey of Knowledge Acquisition Techniques and Tools and their Relationship to Software Engineering, *Journal of Systems and Software* 19, 1992, 97-107.

[30] H. Eriksson, A. R. Puerta, and M. A. Musen, Generation of Knowledge Acquisition Tools from Domain Ontologies, *Int. J. Human-Computer Studies* 41, 1994, 425-453.

[31] H. Eriksson, Y. Shahar, S.W. Tu, A.R. Puerta, and M.A. Musen, Task Modeling with Reusable Problem-Solving Methods, *Artificial Intelligence* 79 (1995), 293-326.

[32] J. Euzenat, Corporate Memory through Cooperative Creation of Knowledge Bases and Hyper-documents, in: *Proc. of the 10th Knowledge Acquisition, Modeling and Management for Knowledge-based Systems Workshop (KAW'96)*, Banff, 1996.

[33] A. Farquhar, R. Fikes, and J. Rice, The Ontolingua Server: A Tool for Collaborative Ontology Construction, *International Journal of Human-Computer Studies*, 46:707-728, 1997.

[34] D. Fensel, Formal Specification Languages in Knowledge and Software Engineering, *The Knowledge Engineering Review* 10, 4, 1995.

[35] D. Fensel, J. Angele, and R. Studer, The Knowledge Acquisition and Representation Language KARL, *IEEE Transactions on Knowledge and Data Engineering* 10 (4), 527-550, 1998.

[36] D. Fensel; The Tower-of-Adapter Method for Developing and Reusing Problem-Solving Methods, in: E. Plaza et al., eds., *Knowledge Acquisition, Modeling and Management*, Lecture Notes in Artificial Intelligence 1319, Springer-Verlag, Berlin, 97-112, 1997.

[37] D. Fensel, S. Decker, M. Erdmann and R. Studer: Ontobroker: The Very High Idea, in: *Proceedings of the 11th International Flairs Conference (FLAIRS-98)*, Sanibel Island, 131-135, May 1998.

[38] D. Fensel and R. Groenboom, Specifying Knowledge-based Systems with Reusable Components, in: *Proceedings 9th Int. Conference on Software Engineering and Knowledge Engineering (SEKE '97)*, Madrid 1997.

[39] D. Fensel and A. Schönegge, Using KIV to Specify and Verify Architectures of Knowledge-Based Systems, in: *Proceedings of the 12th IEEE International Conference on Automated Software Engineering (ASEC-97)*, Incline Village, Nevada, November 1997.

[40] D. Fensel and R. Straatman, The Essence of Problem-Solving Methods: Making Assumptions for Efficiency Reasons, in: N. Shadbolt et al., eds., *Advances in Knowledge Acquisiiton*, Lecture Notes in Artificial Intelligence 1076, Springer-Verlag, Berlin, 1996.

[41] D. Fensel and F. van Harmelen, A Comparison of Languages which Operationalize and Formalize KADS Models of Expertise, *The Knowledge Engineering Review* 9, 2, 1994.

[42] N. Fridman-Noy and C.D. Hafner, The State of the Art in Ontology Design, *AI Magazine*, 18(3):53-74, 1997.

[43] B. Gaines and M.L.G. Shaw, New Directions in the Analysis and Interactive Elicitation of Personal Construct Systems, *Int. J. Man-Machine Studies* 13 (1980), 81-116.

[44] U. Gappa, Grafische Wissensakquisitionssysteme und ihre Generierung, Ph.D. Theses in Artificial Intelligence (DISKI 100), infix, St. Augustin.

[45] M.R. Genesereth and R.E. Fikes, Knowledge Interchange Format, Version 3.0, Reference Manual. Technical Report, Logic-92-1, Computer Science Dept., Stanford University, 1992. http://www.cs.umbc.edu/kse/.

[46] M.R. Genesereth, A.M. Keller, and O.M. Duschka, Infomaster: An Information Integration System, in: *Proc. ACM SIGMOD Conference*, Tucson, 1997.

[47] J.H. Gennari, H. Cheng, R.B. Altman, and M.A. Musen: Reuse, CORBA, and Knowledge-Based Sysems, *Int. J. on Human-Computer Studies* 49, 1998.

[48] J.H. Gennari, S.W. Tu, T.E. Rothenfluh, and M.A. Musen, Mappings Domains to Methods in Support of Reuse, *Int. J. on Human-Computer Studies* 41 (1994), 399-424.

[49] Y. Gil and C. Paris, Towards Method-independent Knowledge Acquisition, *Knowledge Acquisition* 6, 2 (1994), 163-178.

[50] T.R. Gruber, A Translation Approach to Portable Ontology Specifications, *Knowledge Acquisition* 5, 2, 1993, 199-221.

[51] T.R. Gruber, Towards Principles for the Design of Ontologies used for Knowledge Sharing, *International Journal of Human-Computer Studies*, 43:907-928, 1995.

[52] N. Guarino, Formal Ontology, Conceptual Analysis and Knowledge Representation, *International Journal of Human-Computer Studies*, 43(2/3):625-640, 1995.

[53] N. Guarino, ed., *Formal Ontology in Information Systems*, IOS Press, Amsterdam, 1998.

[54] F. van Harmelen and D. Fensel, Formal Methods in Knowledge Engineering, *The Knowledge Engineering Review* 9, 2, 1994.

[55] J. Jannink, S.Pichai, D. Verheijen, and G. Wiederhold; Encapsulation and Composition of Ontologies, in: *Proc. AAAI Workshop AI and Information Integration*, Madison, July 1998.

[56] M. Kifer, G. Lausen, and J. Wu, Logical Foundations of Object-Oriented and Frame-Based Languages, *Journal of the ACM* 42 (1995), 741-843.

[57] O. Kühn and A. Abecker, Corporate Memories for Knowledge Management in Industrial Practice: Prospects and Challenges, *J. of Universal Computer Science* 3, 8 (August 1977), Special Issue on Information Technology for Knowledge Management, Springer Science Online. URL: http://www.iicm.edu/jucs_3_8/corporate_memories_for_knowledge.

[58] D. Landes, DesignKARL - A Language for the Design of Knowledge-based Systems, in: *Proc. 6th International Conference on Software Engineering and Knowledge Engineering (SEKE'94)*, Jurmala, Lettland, 1994, 78-85.

[59] D. Landes, K. Schneider and F. Houdek, Organizational Learning and Experience Documentation in Industrial Software Projects, in: *Proc. of the 1st Workshop Building, Maintaining, and Using Organizational Memories (OM-98), 13th European Conference on AI (ECAI '98)*, Brighton, 1998.
http://SunSITE.Informatik.RWTH-Aachen.DE/Publications/CEUR-WS/Vol-14/

[60] D. Landes and R. Studer, The Treatment of Non-Functional Requirements in MIKE, in: W. Schaefer et al., eds., *Proc. of the 5th European Software Engineering Conference (ESEC'95)*, Sitges, Lecture Notes in Computer Science 989, Springer-Verlag, 1995.

[61] D. B. Lenat and R. V. Guha, *Representation and Inference in the Cyc Projec*, Addison-Wesley, 1990.

[62] S. Luke, L. Spector, D. Rager, and J. Hendler, Ontology-based Web Agents, in: *Proc. 1st Int. Conf. on Autonomous Agents*, 1977.

[63] R. MacGregor, Inside the LOOM Classifier, *SIGART Bulletin*, 2(3):70-76, June 1991.

[64] S. Marcus, ed., *Automating Knowledge Acquisition for Experts Systems*, Kluwer Academic Publisher, Boston, 1988.

[65] F. Maurer and B. Dellen; An Internet Based Software Process Management Environment, in: *Proc. ICSE 98 Workshop on Software Engineering over the Internet*, 1998.

[66] E. Miller, An Introduction to the Resource Description Framework, *D-Lib Magazine*, May 1998.

[67] M.A. Musen, An Overview of Knowledge Acquisition, in: J.-M. David et al., eds., *Second Generation Expert Systems*, Springer-Verlag, 1993.

[68] J. Myplopoulos and M. Papazoglou, Cooperative Information Systems, Guest Editors' Introduction, *IEEE Intelligent Systems* 12, 5 (September/October 1997), 28-31.

[69] S. Neubert, Model Construction in MIKE, in: N. Aussenac et al., eds., *Knowledge Acquisition for Knowledge-based Systems, Proc. 7th European Workshop (EKAW'93)*, Toulouse, Lecture Notes in Artificial Intelligence 723, Springer-Verlag, 1993.

[70] A. Newell, The Knowledge Level, *Artificial Intelligence* 18, 1982, 87-127.

[71] I. Nonaka and H. Takeuchi, *The Knowledge-Creating Company: How Japanese Companies Create the Dynamics of Innovation*, Oxford University Press, 1995.

[72] D. O'Leary, Enterprise Knowledge Management, *IEEE Computer*, 31(3):54-61, 1998.

[73] R. Orfali, D. Harkey, and J. Edwards, eds., *The Essential Distributed Objects Survival Guide*, John Wiley & Sons, New York, 1996.

[74] M. Perkowitz and O. Etzioni, Adaptive Web Sites: An AI Challenge, in: *Proceedings of the 15th International Joint Conference on AI (IJCAI-97)*, Nagoya, Japan, August 1997.

[75] Th. Pirlein and R. Studer, Integrating the Reuse of Commonsense Ontologies and Problem-Solving Methods, *Int. Journal of Expert Systems: Research and Applications*, 1999, in press.

[76] K. Poeck and U. Gappa, Making Role-Limiting Shells More Flexible, in: N. Aussenac et al., eds., *Knowledge Acquisition for Knowledge-Based Systems, Proc. 7th European Knowledge Acquisition Workshop (EKAW'93)* Toulouse, Lecture Notes in Artificial Intelligence 723, Springer-Verlag, 1993.

[77] A. R. Puerta, J. W. Egar, S. W. Tu, and M. A. Musen, A Multiple-Method Knowledge Acquisition Shell for the Automatic Generation of Knowledge Acquisition Tools, *Knowledge Acquisition* 4, 1992, 171-196.

[78] F. Puppe, U. Gappa, K. Poeck, and S. Bamberger: *Wissensbasierte Diagnose- und Informationssysteme*, Springer-Verlag, Berlin, 1996.

[79] A.Th. Schreiber, B. Wielinga, H. Akkermans, W. van de Velde, and A. Anjewierden, CML: The CommonKADS Conceptual Modeling Language, in: Steels et al., eds., *A Future of Knowledge Acquisition, Proc. 8th European Knowledge Acquisition Workshop (EKAW'94)*, Hoegaarden, Lecture Notes in Artificial Intelligence 867, Springer-Verlag, 1994.

[80] A.Th. Schreiber, B. Wielinga, and J. Breuker, eds., *KADS. A Principled Approach to Knowledge-Based System Development*, Knowledge-Based Systems, vol 11, Academic Press, London, 1993.

[81] A.Th. Schreiber, B.J. Wielinga, R. de Hoog, H. Akkermans, and W. van de Velde, CommonKADS: A Comprehensive Methodology for KBS Development, *IEEE Expert*, December 1994, 28-37.

[82] N. Shadbolt, E. Motta, and A. Rouge, Constructing Knowledge-based Systems, *IEEE Software* 10, 6, 34-38.

[83] E.W. Stein, Organizational Memory: Review of Concepts and Recommandations for Management, *International Journal of Information Management*, 15:17-32, 1995.

[84] R. Studer, H. Eriksson, J.H. Gennari, S.W. Tu, D. Fensel, and M.A. Musen, Ontologies and the Configuration of Problem-Solving Methods, in: *Proc. of the 10th Knowledge Acquisition for Knowledge-based Systems Workshop (KAW'96)*, Banff, 1996.

[85] R. Studer, R. Benjamins, and D. Fensel; Knowledge Engineering: Principles and Methods. *Data & Knowledge Engineering* 25 (1988), 161-197.

[86] B. Swartout, R. Patil, K. Knight, and T. Russ, Toward Distributed Use of Large-scale Ontologies, in: B. R. Gaines and M. A. Musen, editors, *Proceedings of the 10th Banff Knowledge Acquisition for Knowledge-Based Systems Workshop*, pages 32.1-32.19, Alberta, Canada, 1996. SRDG Publications, University of Calgary. http://ksi.cpsc.ucalgary.ca:80/KAW/KAW96/KAW96Proc.html.

[87] A. ten Teije and F. van Harmelen, Characterizing Approximative Problem-solving: from Partially Fulfilled Preconditions to Partially Achieved Functionality, in: *Proceedings of the 13th European Conference on AI (ECAI-98)*, Brighton, UK, August 1998.

[88] M. Uschold and M. Gruninger, Ontologies: Principles, Methods, and Applications, *Knowledge Engineering Review*, 11(2):93-155, 1996.

[89] G. van Heijst, A. Th. Schreiber, and B. J. Wielinga, Using Explicit Ontologies in KBS Development, *International Journal of Human-Computer Studies*, 46(2/3):183-292, 1997.

[90] G. Wiederhold and M. Genesereth, The Conceptual Basis for Mediation Services, *IEEE Intelligent Systems* 12, 5 (September/October 1997), 38-47.

[91] B.J. Wielinga, J. Sandberg, and G. Schreiber, Methods and Techniques for Knowledge Management: What has Knowledge Engineering to Offer, *Expert Systems with Applications* 13, 1 (1997), 73-84.

[92] K. Wiig, R. de Hoog and R. van der Spek, Supporting Knowledge Management: A Selection of Methods and Techniques, *Expert Systems With Applications* 13 (1997), 15-27.

[93] Extensible Markup Language (XML) 1.0, *http://www.w3.org/TR/REC-xml*.

Knowledge-Based Diagnosis – Survey and Future Directions

Oskar Dressler[*] and Frank Puppe[**]

[*] *OCC'M Software GmbH*, http://www.occm.de
[**] Würzburg University, Dept. of Computer Science, Am Hubland,
D-97074 Würzburg, puppe@informatik.uni-wuerzburg.de

Abstract: Diagnostic expert systems have long been considered an area where eventually a killer application might emerge[1]. Much time has passed since the first prototypes were demonstrated, but we have not yet seen it in the marketplace – despite many less spectacular success stories. Is the original idea doomed or will the technology finally live up to the expectations?
In this paper we survey the state of the art with an emphasis on highlighting specific values of individual methods as well as considering the context of their use. The ultimate goal is to identify conditions and matching methods that will lead to the kind of success that pragmatist customers will find convincing - and then and only then, a real market presence will result.

1. Introduction

Diagnostic reasoning was one of the first "knowledge-based" applications of computers and successful systems have been built as early as the late sixties, particularly in medical domains. For example, a Bayesian system diagnosing acute abdominal pain [de Dombal 72] or the heuristic system MYCIN determining probable organisms and an adequate antibiotic therapy for blood infections [Shortliffe 76] reached a competence level in their (narrow) domains comparable to medical experts. Intensive research during the past 30 years revealed a variety of problem solving methods and corresponding knowledge representation formalisms, making diagnostic problem

---

[1] The following citation from a prestigious medical journal illustrates the euphoria from the early years: "Indeed it seems probable that in the not too distant future the physician and the computer will engage in frequent dialogue, the computer continuously taking note of history, physical findings, laboratory data and the like, alerting the physician to the most probable diagnoses and suggesting the appropriate safest course of action. One may hope that the computer, well equipped to store large volumes of information and ingeniously programmed to assist in decision making will help free the physician to concentrate on the tasks that are uniquely human such as the application of bedside skills, the management of the emotional aspects of diseases and the exercise of good judgement in the non-quantifiable areas of clinical care." [Schwartz 70]

solving probably the best understood problem class in the field of knowledge-based systems.

Nevertheless, to look truth right into the eye, it is fair to say that while successful applications do exist, commercial success stories compared with the potential are rare. Simply consider that diagnosis applications are not a multi-billion Euro or Dollar business. This is true despite the fact that both the sub-domains of technical devices as well as medical decision support could probably support a business of that size.

Similar claims for other diagnostic domains lead to the conclusion that the field of diagnosis - in spite of the reported successes - is missing some essential ingredients to make it the kind of stellar success it could probably be. It is *not* the available computing power. Computer hardware is still imploding in terms of size and cost at an incredible speed while simultaneously exploding at an equally astounding rate in terms of functionality and performance. It is not software either, at least not alone.

For a real breakthrough in market demand there must be a *complete value chain* in place. With respect to technical devices, it must link the available technology via systems, products, and sales and support channels with those pragmatist customers that will buy when an order of magnitude advantage over current practices is defined, visible, repeatable, and available at a low cost, and when the technology integrates well with the organizational and technical systems already deployed. A 'whole' product from a customer's perspective is key.

Strictly viewing a proposed solution from a customer's perspective is frustrating for research-oriented people. Most of what is needed to really make it work for the customer apparently is not very interesting and requires resources which are not available. Some examples are import and export of data including interfacing with existing databases, generation of reports, a compelling graphical user-interface including the latest gimmicks as well as truly useful things like an 'undo' button and online context-sensitive help, integration with existing computing infrastructure some of which is really old "stuff", etc. An arguably minimally functional solution can strip off some of the above. Nevertheless, the 'whole product' is something else than only the pure diagnostic system.

Support and integration is needed at a level no single supplier can provide. This is what today's high tech markets expect. Only few deployed diagnosis systems have survived beyond an experimental stage in such harsh environments.

To make it work allies are needed that help to assemble the 'whole' product. If that happens repeatedly, a value chain has been formed. Open architectures and interfaces are key ingredients to allow that to happen. The emerging market for component-ware might be helpful. So far, however, we have mostly seen graphical widgets and report generators, where we can also imagine more of the hardcore problem solving components being offered as component-ware.

In this paper we take a step back. The goal is to identify promising domains or niches where individual methods are well-positioned and possess the *necessary* technical pre-requisites for and bear the chance of building up a complete value chain. We survey the available diagnosis problem solving methods from a technical viewpoint. We highlight specific, possibly unique advantages rather than disadvantages in comparison to other competing techniques. We provide a set of diagnosis problem characteristics and while describing individual methods, we will comment on how well these methods address those problem features and on how they provide adequate solutions in their niches. A complete treatment would also cover *sufficient* conditions for successfully building up a value chain. Unfortunately, we are not in the position to give that analysis as it includes far more than only technical aspects. Nevertheless, we will comment on implied technical aspects as well. For example, a recurring theme when discussing organizational integration of problem methods is the extent of re-use possible across applications within the same domain and across different, but nearby domains, and the possible re-use across different tasks involving similar knowledge. Questioning *when*, *where*, and *by whom* the knowledge will be re-used links the discussion of knowledge types involved in building diagnosis systems to the topic of knowledge management in a larger context. An understanding of knowledge types and problem characteristics is of vital importance to this discussion.

Before we embark on this endeavor we will cover some common ground and terminology for the different diagnosis problem solving methods, which will be the topic of the next section.

2. The diagnosis task

2.1. What is diagnosis ?

> Diagnosis is the task of *identifying* (classifying) an *object* to a *desirable_degree* given that *observations* about the object and potentially a set of *actions* that can be applied to the object are available.

The term 'object' is meant in a very broad sense. An object may be a physical object such as a technical device or process, but it may also be a more abstract entity such as the cash management in a company, e.g. a bank. With technical devices or processes observations will be about properties such as temperature, voltage, etc. In the case of a bank the relevant observations will be about cash and account values. An object's state is expressed through its properties' values.

The human body, a human's mental condition, ecological systems, a rock, a photocopier, a person seeking legal advice or a loan, a power transmission network, a company's cash flow, production lines in industry and biological systems, digital circuit boards, automotive systems, computer networks, etc. are all examples of *objects* in the aforementioned sense. You get a feeling of how many potential customers are out there.

The diagnosis goal is limited by the degree of details that should be uncovered about the given object. This takes into account that diagnosis always is performed in a larger context that sets the limits. Identifying faulted components in a device even within a smallest replaceable unit is not of interest, because the whole unit, e.g. a circuit board, will be replaced anyway. When the prescription for the range of diseases that are plausible given the available symptoms is the same for all of them, there is no reason for further investigations except for scientific purposes or the doctor's bank account.

Sometimes it is possible to stimulate the object by some action so that it will exhibit more aspects of its behavior. If appropriate a doctor will hit your knee in order to test your reflexes. Likewise in technical systems it is often possible to change external conditions so that the system's behavior can be observed under different conditions.

Please note, that the given definition does not resort to a distinction between normal and abnormal behavior, broken and correct components etc. This makes it very general, indeed. For example, it covers monitoring of devices and processes as a special case. Most medical and technical diagnostic applications, however, are concerned with identifying faults, diseases, and other *abnormal* properties in the object to be diagnosed. Nevertheless, with our definition, applications such as plant or rock identification, assessment for credit granting or legal advice, are still considered solving diagnosis tasks.

2.2. What is a solution ?

A solution is a description of the object to be diagnosed. As such it tells us about properties of the object. To really count as a solution the description needs to match further criteria that differ with the employed methods. In model-based diagnosis, for example, it is required that the solution is *consistent with* the observations (in a strict logical sense). In addition, it can be required that the solution entails (again, in a strict logical sense) 'output' observations, a subset of all observations. Other methods require that the diagnosis is plausible, rated with a certain confidence, is able of deriving symptoms, match the solution for a similar case, etc.

Due to the complexity of the objects to be diagnosed, a solution rarely consists of a complete description. Normally, it is abbreviated by listing the faulty components, diseases, etc. with the implicit convention that the given elements are characteristic for the description and imply all relevant detail about the object. If this is not possible, e.g. because even the normal state of the object is not completely known, the solution might imply only a partial description or simply indicate something useful to do.

In medical domains, a complete description of the patient is currently impossible due to the complexity of the human body. Even in most technical domains, the underlying processes are far too complex for a detailed description. Finding an appropriate level of detail always is key to successful applications.

2.3. The result of a diagnosis session

Usually it is not possible to identify the true state of an object with certainty. Therefore, the result of a diagnosis session normally is a *set* of solutions. Each solution gives a description of the object. It is detailed enough so that it is not confused with other solutions. It may *comprise one or more* solution elements, e.g. faults or diseases. Solutions are ordered according to some estimate of their probability, criticality, etc.

Hypothesizing a single solution element (e.g. a broken component) might be consistent with the available observations, but there is often a huge set of solution candidates with multiple solution elements available that are all consistent with the observations. In fact, assuming that everything is broken and operating in an unknown mode *always* constitutes a logically valid solution, although a very improbable one.

Before we continue the technical discussion we need to understand what went wrong with diagnosis expert systems in the marketplace and why a second attempt might now be feasible and fruitful.

3. A new value proposition to the customer

For a very brief period during the mid-eighties diagnostic expert systems as a forerunner of artificial intelligence had been given the chance of taking the 'market' by storm. The herd of pragmatist customers was ready to move, even stampede, and *invest*! They were all watching each other and waiting for the start signal, which - as history tells us - never came. Building on the hype - probably only comparable to the internet in recent years - software tool vendors such as Teknowledge and IntelliCorp, hardware makers such as LMI, Symbolics, Texas Instruments, were able to create a modest business by selling to AI *developers*. Unfortunately, however, the successes produced by these developers were *not* convincing to the pragmatist customer. Although not explicitly focused on diagnosis, but AI in general, the above mentioned companies have long moved on to others markets or are even out of business.

In marketing terms (e.g. [Moore 91]), the pragmatist target customers were not given a compelling reason to buy. At the time they could expect a strategic benefit which could also be achieved by other means (e.g. computer-support for viewing technical documents, a major improvement by then; or - even simpler - by using the fax machine to quickly distribute information about known good solutions to the field). This merely constituted a 'nice-to-have' or 'should-have' value proposition to the customer, whereas a 'must-have' value proposition would have implied strategic benefits at a level no other reasonably comparable means could have achieved.

Reviewing early success stories reveals that the value proposition made to the potential target customers at best fell into the 'should-have', *not* the 'must-have' category. With hindsight, none of the potential targets was harmed in any way because they did *not* use diagnostic expert systems. This would only have been possible if competitors had successfully adopted the technology, and based on it had outperformed the competition in a significant way, 'significant' meaning something similar to what e.g. Cisco and Dell do to their competition in making use of the internet these days.

Over the last fifteen years diagnostic expert system technology has certainly matured. Completely new approaches - like case-based and model-based diagnosis - have been introduced with the assessment of earlier approaches in mind. As we will show later on, from a technical point of view, the field is in much better shape to attack real world mission-critical business problems than ever before. But what is even more exciting is that new signs of commercial interest in medical and technical diagnosis expert systems are now showing up again. Each area can be used for a *must-have value proposition* - if carefully and thoroughly prepared!

Medical diagnosis: In all industrialized countries, the costs for medical care increase with a much higher rate than the GDP resulting e.g. in the USA in a jump from ca. 5% (1960) to 13% (1990)[2]. "It is no surprise that much is expected from using computers to control and stabilize the costs of health care. One of the proposed measures is the reinforcement of primary care in combination with providing physicians and nurses with computers. This would involve a shift from hospital care to primary care and home care. This implies collaboration between care providers supported by computer-based shared care and electronic interchange of patient data, computer supported tele-consulting by experts and decision-support systems, and the introduction of protocols and managed care. All this results in new responsibilities for clinicians and changes in the tasks of different care providers. It also means increased responsibilities for patients themselves, who could have a greater role in self-care if they were supported by computers" [Van Bemmel & Musen 97, p. 9]. Since medical care strongly depends on the correct diagnosis of the patient's problem, there is a huge potential for decision support by computers.

The key to a medical "value chain" is a standardized electronic patient record being used for documentation (including legal issues), diagnosis and therapy, quality and cost control, and research by all the different care providers including the patients themselves, who are the owner of their data. Since in nearly all medical domains lots of observations are necessary to classify the patient's state sufficiently well for selecting therapies, the reentry of data for stand-alone systems (whether for decision support or just for documentation or research) is simply too expensive for wide spread use.

Currently we can watch several pieces in this huge puzzle clicking into place. This provides the necessary infrastructure for value-adding, automated, intelligent systems with diagnostic expert systems occupying the pole position.

Technical systems diagnosis: *All* technical devices do break. Due to wear and tear, and inevitable decaying processes individual components necessarily *must* exhibit malfunction after some time. Add today's technical artifacts with their apparently ever increasing complexity which makes them vulnerable due to their inherent nature as physical objects. The more components they comprise the more likely they will fail to operate at some point in time. It is desirable to repair these technical artifacts rather than throw them away and replace them by new ones for several reasons, the least of which is *not* environmental correctness.

Within the last ten years complexity has crossed a threshold. It marks the point where no other reasonably means comparable to diagnostic expert systems can achieve similar benefits. For example, a European consortium of automotive companies and their suppliers including among others Daimler-Benz, Fiat, Volvo, and Bosch reported that 90% (!) of the electronic control units returned under guarantee were indeed functioning correctly ([VMBD 97]). While this speaks for the quality of the supplier's production processes, at the same time it means that in all these cases *the problems were misdiagnosed in the field*. Needless to say that this and similar cases translate into multi-million figures given that cars - besides allowing one to drive around - have been turned into networks of computers controlling every aspect of the 'ultimate driving machine'. Even if the number were only 5 or 10%, for the

---

[2] Source: OECD 1995.

companies in these businesses it identifies a *broken mission-critical business process*. It needs to be fixed before customers start questioning *their* value proposition: 'high tech cars with comfort, safety, environmental correctness, etc. all built in' do not match with unnecessary downtime and overpriced maintenance.

We suspect that for other sub-fields of diagnosis and industries similar opportunities are already there or are arising. The challenge, however, is only in part of technological nature. Success will only follow when the *right* method (or product for that matter) is used for the *right* application and the *right* customer. *Broken* mission-critical business processes hint at the right customers and applications. But they are not easy to find. Intimate knowledge about existing processes varying from organization to organization is needed here. Obviously, we can be of little help in that respect, but the next two sections will help in selecting the *right* method.

4. Problem Characteristics

A diagnostic system maps observations to solutions. The mapping quality crucially depends on the available knowledge. First and foremost this is an organizational issue. Who are the people or what are the systems in possession of the knowledge. Where are they? In large corporations, the organizational distance may be even more important than the distance in time and space. What other overlapping tasks do they accomplish by using that invaluable knowledge we are after? Only after addressing these and similar relevant organizational constraints does it makes sense to discuss more technical issues.

The major knowledge types are characterized by the terms 'cases', 'experience', and 'models'. Knowledge about *cases* captures observations about past behavior of systems and directly links it with known good solutions provided by humans. There is little to no abstraction beyond the raw data given by observations. *Experience* is gained by human experts over time while solving problem cases. Phenomenally, it links observations and solutions in abstract form. *Models* make explicit some of the background human experts use for deriving appropriate solutions. Examples include good engineering principles for specific domains, abstracting from more basic physical principles, and these 'first' principles as well.

For many domains not all knowledge types are available, e.g. empirical or case-based knowledge might be missing for diagnosing new technical devices, whereas for many biological systems causal understanding is often limited. If case-bases exist, their usefulness depends on their quantity, quality and formalization. Empirical knowledge might be inaccessible, if experts are unwilling or too occupied for formalizing it. Other factors influencing the choice of problem solving methods are:

- *Initial knowledge acquisition effort:* how much time is required for building an initial operational knowledge base?
- *Maintenance effort:* what resources - and especially human resources - are needed to keep the knowledge base operational in a changing environment?
- *Graceful degradation with faulty, incomplete or uncertain observations*: how sensitive is the employed method to the quality of supplied observations?

- *Graceful degradation with faulty or incomplete knowledge*: If it is not possible or economically feasible to build complete and correct knowledge bases, how does the quality of the solution degrade with the quality of the supplied knowledge?
- *Objectivity*: Can solutions be proven to be correct? This depends on assumptions about observations and the knowledge provided.
- *Explicability:* How well can the solutions be explained? Can humans judge the quality of the solution by checking the explanation? This is particularly important, if humans remain responsible for the quality of the solution.
- *Single fault assumption*: Is it theoretically or practically acceptable to diagnose one fault at a time? If there are multiple faults, do they typically interact? Do they trigger critical misdiagnoses if treated under the single fault assumption ?
- *Variants*: If the objects to be identified by diagnosis vary without belonging to totally different object classes, it is desirable to handle them with minor modifications of the knowledge base. What effort for variant modeling is implied?
- *Reuse of knowledge*: Is the knowledge used for diagnosis also applicable to other tasks?
- *Unanticipated solutions*: To what degree is it possible to diagnose faults not explicitly foreseen by the developers of the knowledge base?
- *Time dependency*: How important is the temporal change of observations and faults for finding solutions?
- *Variable observation / solution granularity*: What degree of observation and solution granularity is required? Does it need to vary during the diagnostic process? Will more precise observations translate into more accurate solutions?

For illustration of these characteristics, we discuss a few examples:

- *Medical diagnosis:* Empirical and case-based knowledge is usually available, model-based knowledge to a lesser extent. Probably the most severe bottleneck is data entry by physicians due to their hectic schedules. Data entry by patients circumvents this problem, but the quality of data is then much lower. Lots of observations (e.g. history, physical examination, interpretation of images or sounds) are inherently uncertain. Objectivity usually cannot be attained. Explicability is very important, because physicians remain responsible for the solutions. Variant modeling is not necessary. Unanticipated solutions, i.e. new diseases, are rare and reuse of data and knowledge outside the domain is limited, but possible (e.g. for intelligent documentation, accounting, training, research, therapy monitoring, document retrieval). Simplifications are feasible. The single fault assumption does not hold. Observations and solutions change over time and observations are often described on different granularity levels. Medical knowledge has a potential for extremely wide-spread use and does change comparatively slowly. Due to complexity and interdependency it does, however, require a large initial knowledge acquisition effort.
- *Technical systems diagnosis:* By definition, there are neither empirical knowledge nor cases available for *new* devices. New devices imply higher fault finding costs. These will drop as maintenance personnel gains experience with the

device over time. Towards the end of the devices' economic lifetime, again new types of faults occur that increase the fault finding costs up to the initial level. For a significant economic impact it is thus imperative to offer diagnostic capabilities that apply in the *early* and *late* phases of device lifetime. Fortunately, technical devices as designed artifacts lend themselves to using models. The device structure almost certainly is available in electronic form, if one can get organizational access to the design and engineering departments. This reduces the modeling effort to behavioral and/or functional modeling. The potential overlapping use of models for various tasks is apparent. On-board (embedded) and off-board scenarios can and often are very different with respect to availability and granularity of observations and required solution granularity. Depending on the distribution of the device (e.g. a few gas turbines vs. millions of cars) solving the variant problem may be a central concern or just a nice side effect.

- *Diagnostic Hotline Support:* The characteristics depend on whether handling an end-user or a system are in focus. Consequently, a mixture of the above examples applies. The quality of observations can vary widely as they solely depend on the hotline client who might be an expert or a naive dummy.

- *Object recognition:* Set-covering (abductive) and case-based knowledge is usually available, empirical knowledge sometimes, but typically no detailed model. Observations are often uncertain and incomplete. It is difficult to prove correctness. Other characteristics allow for simplifications: Explicability is less important. The single fault assumption typically holds, reuse is limited. There is no time dependency. Recognition of unanticipated solutions is impossible. Variable observation granularity may be important (e.g. depending on how close objects can be approached). Complete knowledge might not be available (e.g. if knowledge for recognizing rare objects is missing). The determining factor for the maintenance costs is the rate of change of the class of objects to be recognized.

- *Assessment:* Normative knowledge (e.g. guidelines for credit granting) or empirical and case-based knowledge are available. But observations are often uncertain, incomplete or even false (e.g. when a client seeks an advantageous rather than a correct assessment). Explicability is very important, otherwise the situation is similar to object recognition.

5. Survey of problem solving methods

The knowledge types that are used to link observations with solutions can be classified into three basic forms with many variants:

- Methods based on human experience:
  - Decision trees, where the internal nodes correspond to questions, the links to answer alternatives, and the leaves to solutions.
  - Decision tables consisting of a set of categorical rules for inferring solutions from observations[3].

---

[3] Instead of observations, intermediate conclusions or other solutions might be used as well in preconditions of rules. This holds for the other methods as well.

- Heuristic classification using knowledge of the kind "if <observations> then <solution> with <evidence>, the latter estimated by experts. Solutions are rated according to their accumulated evidence.
- Set covering or abductive classification using knowledge of the kind "if <solution > then <observation> with <frequency>", the latter estimated by experts. Solutions are rated according how well they cover (explain) the observed symptoms.
- Methods based on sets of cases with known solutions as their primary knowledge source:
  - Statistical classification (Bayes' Theorem, Bayesian nets) using knowledge about the a-priori probability of solutions $P(S)$ and the conditional probability $P(O/S)$ of observation O if solution S is present, where the probabilities are calculated from a representative case base.
  - Neural classification using a case base for adapting the weights of a neural net capable of classifying new cases. Important net topologies with associated learning algorithms for diagnostics are perceptrons, backpropagation nets and Kohonen nets.
  - Classification using a case base together with knowledge about a similarity measure. For a new case, the most similar cases from the case base are selected assuming their solutions being applicable to the new case as well.
- Methods based on generic knowledge about the function and behavior of systems in terms of constituents, e.g. processes, components, etc., and purpose.
  - Diagnosis can be done without modeling faulty behavior at all. Any observed behavior deviating from normal behavior or intended function is then considered faulty. If available, knowledge about faulty behavior can be exploited.

5.1. Methods based on (direct encoding of) human experience

In many domains human experts are quite successful in finding cost-effectively solutions to diagnostic problems. However, such experts are usually rare and therefore expensive and not always available. Since the beginnings of knowledge-based systems it has been a primary goal to capture their expertise in "expert systems". The two main problems were (1) finding effective representations of the knowledge being close to the mental models of the experts and (2) organizing the process of transferring the knowledge from the expert into the system. During the last 30 years, a variety of knowledge representations and corresponding problem solving methods with many variants have been developed, each with different draw-backs as well as advantages and success-stories. In particular, for all but the most difficult problems we can now offer adequate representations creating little overhead for building cost-effective systems. The best process of knowledge transfer is still controversial. While some argue for a knowledge engineer as mediator between expert and system, others propagate knowledge acquisition tools enabling experts to self-enter their knowledge. The latter is usually much more cost effective, but requires tailoring the knowledge representations and the acquisition tools to the demands of the experts [Gappa et al. 93]. If experts switch between different methods, they should be supported in reusing as much knowledge as possible [Puppe 98]. In this section, we present a variety of representations for direct encoding of human expertise allowing for rapid building of diagnostic systems (for more details, see [Puppe et al. 96]

The most straightforward and probably the most wide-spread representation are *decision trees* combining knowledge about data gathering and interpretation. They are very easy to understand and are often quite good in capturing the general practice of experts in routine cases. Typical examples are found in the manuals of many technical devices. Starting with an in-built error code, a list of questions is presented for localizing the fault, where the questions sometimes correspond to repair actions: Replace part x and check, whether the device works again. The sequence of questions is important, usually balancing probability of failures and costs for answering the question. In particular for small domains the initial knowledge acquisition effort may be rather low. Due to their importance, the main representation offered by some commercial diagnostic tools are therefore decision trees. However, some drawbacks require various extensions. Recognizing multiple faults is difficult, because the result of a decision tree is a single fault. For changing diagnostic knowledge, e.g. because of device improvements, adaptation of large decision trees can be very difficult (high maintenance effort). If the observations are uncertain, incomplete are even false, the user easily gets stuck in the decision tree or is unable to recover from a wrong branch. Of course, the expert can explicitly foresee such problems and create additional branches, but management of large and redundant decision trees is difficult. Redundancy can much better be encoded with other representations.

Decision tables are the next simple representation , inferring solution elements by categorical rules. They are easier to maintain than decision trees, because all rules are independent from each other (except contradictions, which can be detected automatically) but do not code data gathering knowledge - that would require separate tables. If several rules fire, their conclusions are all added to the list of solutions. In this way, multiple faults can be diagnosed if they are independent from each other. Otherwise, decision tables have similar characteristics as decision trees and in particular cannot deal very well with faulty, incomplete and uncertain observations and uncertain knowledge.

Next, we discuss a number of simple extensions for dealing with uncertainty. The first ones do not need any forms of probabilistic reasoning, while the latter ones require a model of combining uncertainties.

Redundancy, as already mentioned, plays an important role in diagnostics. Often, e.g. in many medical domains like rheumatology, for inferring a solution element, several criteria are available not all of which have to be met or checked. Since it is not convenient to express all combinations of e.g. 5 from 7 criteria with conventional rules (i.e. in disjunctive normal form), a formalism called *n-from-m rules* is very useful, where such rules are encoded directly. Sometimes, the criteria have a different relevance for the solution element. In simple cases, this can be encoded with main and auxiliary criteria, but in general, a weighting scheme is necessary, where each criterion is weighted with a number, and the sum of all observed criteria is compared with a threshold. Such *scores* are quite popular in many medical domains (see e.g. [Ohmann et al. 95]).

Another method is to represent *exceptions to a rule* and use belief revision techniques [Gardenfors 92]. This is especially useful for dealing with observations of variable granularity. If only general observations are available, default solutions are selected, but when more precise observations are known, they should be replaced with better solutions. The arrival of the precise observations are used as exceptions for the general rules, which are then substituted by the rules referring to the precise observations.

Riple down rules [Richards & Compton 98] are a knowledge acquisition methodology based on this idea. One starts entering general rules and continuously refines the rules based on test cases by adding context and exceptions, when a rule is applied wrongly. In a sense, rules are never removed or corrected, only added.

Categorical rules can also be extended with evidence values to reflect their probabilistic nature. There are still debates about the "right" reasoning scheme for combining evidence schemes. From a statistical point of view, the *theorem of Bayes* or *Bayesian nets* (see below) are the methods of choice. However, they require some independence assumptions and in particular, that evidence values can be estimated in accordance with the laws of statistics. Psychological experiments have shown, that humans are bad estimators of statistical probabilities, especially of very small ones, even if they are experts in their domains. Therefore, different reasoning schemes should be applied depending upon the nature of evidence value estimation (e.g. guessing by experts versus computation from case bases) While the latter situations are dealt with in section 5.2, the former situation requires reasoning schemes easily comprehendible by experts. Such *heuristic rules* are often combined with pseudo-probabilities (e.g. certainty factors, see MYCIN, above) or methods resembling the scoring schemes mentioned above, e.g. the evidence values used in the large INTERNIST/QMR diagnostic knowledge base for internal medicine [Masarie et al. 85]. Evidence values can complement either simple rules with only one-observation-one-conclusion or rather complex rules.

Internist/QMR combines heuristic with causal (set-covering) rules. While the former state how strong observations indicate solution elements ("evoking strength"), the latter represent, how often solution elements cause observations ("frequency"). Such causal relations are often reported in the literature and therefore reduce the knowledge acquisition effort. Instead of selecting solution elements with high evidence scores, the goal of set covering is to cover (explain) all observations [Reggia 83, Eshelman 88]. Set covering or abductive diagnosis lies in between empirical and model-based diagnosis, because the knowledge often comes from experts, but. - as will be seen later - the solution criterion can easily be expressed in the model-based diagnosis framework. Of course, all these mechanisms can be combined in a knowledge base, e.g. different solutions can be derived with different mechanisms depending on the complexity of the underlying knowledge. The same holds when the reasoning process uses intermediate conclusions, which are used similarly as observations for inferring other conclusions. Intermediate conclusions are also useful for a technique called reasoning by elimination or differential diagnosis. It can be used to represent a situation, where exactly one from a list of potential solution elements is required, so that the relatively best one can be selected. The selection of the best from a predefined set of alternatives can be done with different techniques, e.g. the Theorem of Bayes (see section 5.2) or exclusion of alternatives. Data gathering is often done either in a hypothetico-deductive manner, i.e. the current hypotheses (e.g. intermediate solutions, most probable hypotheses) determine what tests are done next, or with additional categorical knowledge.

In general, empirical methods with categorical knowledge are straightforward to build. If observations or knowledge are incomplete or uncertain, they can be extended in various ways to accommodate vagueness. Since empirical methods are modeled after human techniques, they allow for the generation of understandable explanations and have a graceful degradation curve, but it is difficult to prove correctness and completeness of the knowledge. Obviously, they cannot deal with unanticipated solutions. Large empirical knowledge bases are difficult to maintain, to reuse for other tasks and have difficulties in dealing with the variant problem. The technique of modeling large domains as a set of cooperating smaller agents (knowledge bases) lessens this problem (see section 6). Multiple faults can be recognized by most empirical methods, if the faults manifest themselves independently and do not mask each other. Recognizing time dependent observations requires preprocessing, which may be delegated to human users (e.g. classifying a disease as "acute" or "chronic"). Typically the knowledge is entered by humans, who should be supported by convenient knowledge acquisition editors (see above), but it can also be generated by inductive learning techniques from large sets of cases (see next section).

5.2. Methods based on case knowledge

A diagnostic case consists of a set of observations and the correct solution, e.g. a set of attributes (A) and values (V) together with a solution (S), i.e. $((A_1\ V_1)\ (A_2\ V_2)...$ $(A_n\ V_n)\ S)$ or in vector representation with a fixed order of attributes: $(V_1\ V_2\ ...\ V_n\ S)$.

A large set of cases with a standardized and detailed recording of observations represents a valuable source of knowledge, which can be exploited with different techniques: Case-based, statistical (Theorem of Bayes, Bayesian nets), inductive (e.g. ID3, star-methods) and neural classification (e.g. perceptrons and back-propagation, Kohonen nets). The main differences between these techniques lie in the assumptions made, the learning curve in relation to the number and quality of available cases, the explanation capabilities, and the necessity or opportunity to incorporate expert knowledge.

Cases provide factual knowledge about solutions to past problems, and these may be applicable to similar problems in the future. There are many different ways of generalizing the cases. Case-based classification uses no abstractions, since the cases remain unchanged. The theorem of Bayes, linear decision functions and perceptrons use simple abstractions with direct observation-solution correlations [Puppe 94]. Inductive reasoning techniques and back-propagation rely on more complex abstractions generating rules, decision trees, or changing weights of hidden units. Bayesian networks rely on complex abstractions using background knowledge in the form of the net topology. Background knowledge is also very useful within case-based classification for the similarity measure, which can be viewed as substitute for the generalizations of the other techniques. In a broader sense, all methods rely on additional knowledge for selecting or inferring the relevant observations, because using too low-level observations or too many very similar observations significantly decreases the performance of all techniques.

Case-based reasoning techniques have a number of attractive features: Maintenance is often a side-effect of using the system, requiring only good documentation of cases. Performance improves with every additional case. While some techniques like case-based classification already work with rather few cases, statistical and neural techniques can exploit large numbers of cases efficiently. In the face of uncertainty, statistical correlations may be the closest approximation to objective knowledge. The knowledge inside cases can also be generalized and thus reused for other tasks.

A severe problem for all case-based reasoning techniques is diagnosing multiple faults. Due to the combinatorics of multiple faults, one cannot expect to get much more than zero or one case for any individual combination of faults. Since most techniques work best with the single fault assumption, we use in this section the term solution instead of solution element. Combinatorial problems also lessen the ability of case-based methods to deal with variant modeling and time dependent observations. An inherent limitation is detecting new solutions.

The most exact techniques for exploiting knowledge in cases are statistical methods. While the theorem of Bayes can only deal with direct observation-solution relations and require conditional independence between the observations, Bayesian nets [Pearl 88, Russell & Norvig 95, Part V] can explicitly represent dependencies between observations and intermediate solutions in the net and have therefore a much broader spectrum of use. The biggest problem is to get enough cases, in particular for rare solutions. For example, if in the theorem of Bayes an observation-solution correlation is zero and the observation is given in a particular case, the solution gets the a-posteriori probability of zero. Substituting near-zero-probabilities with estimated values is very difficult, because expert knowledge is not particular reliable in that respect (see above).

Case-based classification [Bartsch-Spörl et al. 99] is better suited for dealing with the problem of relatively few cases. For example, they have a relatively good measure about their ignorance: if they cannot retrieve a sufficient similar case, they should present no solution instead of a (probably) wrong solution. In addition, presenting the user a similar case and pointing out relevant similarities and discrepancies is understandable for the user enabling him to bring to bear his own knowledge for validating the solution. Case-based classification can also profit from expert knowledge if available for improving the similarity measure or for filtering out inapplicable cases based on categorical rules. With a good similarity measure, case-based classification can also deal with the problem of variable solution granularity, being a serious problem for the other case-based methods. However, if many cases with subtle differences are available, case-based classification cannot generalize as well as statistical techniques.

Inductive reasoning techniques try to compile the cases into representations also used by experts to represent their empirical knowledge (section 5.1). Therefore, they complement those techniques of knowledge acquisition. The most popular learning method is the ID3-family [Quinlan 97], where a decision tree is generated from the cases by recursively selecting the most informative observation, whose values separate the cases into relatively homogenous subsets with respect to their solutions. The star method [Mitchel 97] recursively generates one rule after another, which can diagnose as much cases as possible correctly and as few as possible incorrectly. A problem of such techniques is to force them to generate the right level of generalization, e.g. preventing the star method to generate a rule for every case by and-connecting all their observations. Often, an upper limit for the complexity of the generated rule is predefined, e.g. a maximal number of conjuncts in a rule. The equivalent problem for decision trees is to have one branch for every case. Such overly large decision trees are pruned in a second phase based on whether the distinctions are statistically significant, e.g. using the chi-square test for a binary observation in a branch.

Neural classification [Kulikowski & Weiss 91] is a set of techniques making the fewest assumptions about the cases requiring no expert knowledge. Typical examples are recognition of spoken or handwritten words or object classification from pixels, where the other techniques are difficult to be used in a straightforward manner. The neural learning algorithms start with an arbitrary set of weights in the net, classify the training cases, compute an error vector from the misclassified cases and adjust the weights to reduce that error. This procedure is iterated until a (local) optimum is found. Typical problems are long training times or the danger – similar to the inductive reasoning techniques – not to find the right level of generalizing the cases. They can be lessened by adjusting some parameters in the learning algorithms or choosing an adequate net topology. However, it is still difficult to automate such procedures.

A large set of different algorithms for similar goals is often an indicator, that no one has a clear advantage over the others. This was indeed shown for case-based classification in the Statlog project [Michie et al. 94], where - among others - all of the above mentioned algorithms were compared with more than 20 large case sets from different domains. To avoid the typical bias of many studies, where the evaluators have different knowledge and experience with different algorithms, the algorithms were evaluated by different research groups being experienced with their techniques and interested in good results. Over the whole range of test case sets, no learning algorithm performed clearly better than the other ones.

5.3. Model-based Systems

Model-based reasoning aims at representing domain knowledge about "first principles" in a declarative and modular way in order to use it for different problem solving tasks, one of which is diagnosis. In a technical domain, this comprises engineering knowledge about the behavior of products and their parts, manufacturing processes etc. This has to be regarded in contrast to the aforementioned methods which basically capture empirical associations rather than the underlying physical and engineering principles and rigorous deductions based on them.

Model-based reasoning takes reductionism's view on systems, attempting to describe complex systems in terms of interactions of more basic ones. This allows for the separation of the

- *structural description* of a system (its "blueprint"), from the
- *behavioral description* of its constituent elements which are collected in model libraries.

The basic goals of model-based reasoning are then to *predict, analyze, and compare the behavior* of an aggregate system based on the knowledge about its structure and the constituents' behaviors.

This approach *intrinsically addresses the variant problem.* The structure may vary freely. Behavioral descriptions of constituent element *types* are re-used over and over. A maintenance and development effort is only necessary when substantially new and different constituent types occur.

Besides this basic required feature of *compositional modeling*, model-based systems are raising a number of other requirements:

- *Qualitative modeling*: the models should make *essential distinctions only*. This enables them to capture the behavior of *classes* of systems in *classes* of situations, thus enhancing re-usability of models across applications and tasks.
- *Functional modeling*: this allows for an abstract view of a system's behavior reflecting its role in a context and, particularly, the intended purpose in the view of a designer or user.
- *Multiple modeling* is concerned with the fact that special tasks may require different kinds of models of the same system for the sake of efficiency or cognitive adequacy. In order not to violate re-usability and to allow for the integration of different task-specific tools, different "incarnations" of a model have to be related in an explicit, formal way and, whenever possible, the translations and transformations between them should be carried out automatically.

Although these goals are quite ambitious and subject to on-going substantial research around the world, a set of principled methods, techniques, and industrial-strength tools have been developed that provide a solid foundation for application. This holds, in particular, for the most advanced field, *model-based diagnosis*.

The principle underlying model-based diagnosis exploits model-based behavior prediction by *comparing* the predicted (correct or faulty) behavior with the actual observations.

In a nutshell, a model-based diagnosis system works by cycling through the following five subtasks:

1. *Observations* of the actual behavior are entered either manually or automatically, e.g. via an on-line connection.
2. The *aggregate behavior model* computes conclusions about system parameters and variables (observed and unobserved), and thereby *predicts* the expected behavior.
3. If a *contradiction* is detected (i.e. conflicting conclusions / observations for a parameter or variable) the set of component modules involved in it indicates

which components possibly deviate form their intended behavior. This can be determined by the diagnosis system because the *aggregate behavior model* has structure. It reflects the device constituents that may incorporate faults.

4. *Solution candidates* are generated. They are called candidates because they must still withstand the consistency test in the next cycle to be true solutions.

5. Suggestions for useful *probes and tests* are generated. This is possible because the behavior model reveals where the diagnosis candidates entail distinctive features of behavior. This function can be used to reduce the costs in cases where observations are expensive and to act as a filter when the amount of information is overwhelming (see e.g. [Beschta et al. 93]).

In case *models of faulty components'* behavior are provided, the same approach (checking consistency of a model with the observations) can be used to discard particular faults on to exonerate components based on the tentative assumption that the set of fault models is complete or that an unknown fault is unlikely.

In step 3, conflict detection, it is possible to merely make use of the fact that a deviation exists or to take into account the size and form of the deviation. The former approach has been followed in AI [Hamscher et al. 92], the latter in process engineering [Frank 87, Patton & Chen 92, Isermann 84]. The AI approach has focused on qualitative models in order to capture classes of constituent behaviors. This has led to diagnosis systems capable of diagnosing multiple faults in *structurally complex* devices up to several thousand components (e.g. [de Kleer et al. 93]). The *constituent behavior descriptions*, however, *are rather simple*. The complex issue of feedback is avoided whenever possible. Feedback loops are encapsulated by providing appropriate models of the enclosing component. The process engineering approach (also called observer-based diagnosis) has been just the opposite: devices with a *small number of components*, but focusing on *the most detailed behavior description possible*. Typically, a device model consists of a set of higher order differential equations with a few parameters (in the order of 3 to 5) allowed to vary. Within this space combinations of parameter values are identified that will restore consistency between model and observed behavior.

From a research point of view a union of the approaches is long overdue and should cover some interesting middle ground. Whether there is any commercial interest in the investigation of this middle ground is an open question.

The focus on the most detailed model of the device as a whole, the consequential lack of compositional modeling and corresponding notion of model libraries, the relatively small number of components in a device, and the ability to diagnose feedback systems characterizes the niche for the process engineering approach. For the rest, structurally complex devices with adequate, qualitative models are the characterizing elements. An overview of consistency-based diagnosis can be found in [Dressler & Struss 96].

In step 4, candidate generation, solution candidates are generated that are *consistent with* the observations and the models as applied so far. An apparently small and subtle change in this step yields a significantly different approach. *Abductive* diagnosis requires that a solution candidate not only is consistent with the observations but actually *derives* deviating observations. This has major implications. For one, a formal treatment needs to divide the set of observations into inputs and outputs, thereby imposing a 'causal' direction on the models which may not be natural and is certainly not needed for the consistency-based approach. More importantly, in order to derive deviating observations one needs to supply a *complete* set of *complete* faults on a suitable abstraction level. Otherwise, the correctness of the diagnosis results cannot be guarantied. Therefore, [Console & Torasso 90] have introduced the notion of a continuum of diagnosis definitions ranging from consistency-based to abductive by varying the set of outputs that need to be derived. In practice, this requires that one pre-enumerates deviating observations. It is, however, possible to make use of abductive explanations by merely using them as preference criterion [Dressler & Struss 92]. This imposes none of the strict requirements above, but rather states that a solution is better than another if it explains more deviating observations.

Outside of model-based reasoning the abductive form of diagnosis has a long tradition, especially in medical diagnosis, where the method is sometimes called 'Set-Covering'. The definition of diagnosis in its abductive form is essentially identical in both fields. The distinguishing factor which puts them so far apart is compositional modeling. In medical diagnosis it is important that knowledge can be captured which does not require a detailed understanding of the human body and abstracts from the many nested feedback loops. It is thus crucial that diseases and observations (findings) can be related without deep physiological models. In the technical domain, however, from where the model-based approach derives its main motivation non-compositional linking of faults and observations comes at a prohibitive maintenance cost, if technical devices exist in many variants and designs change frequently.

The key principles of model-based diagnosis are fairly basic, simple, and straightforward. Nevertheless, they provide the foundation for diagnosis systems that address several key problems, especially problems arising in industrial contexts.

1. Diagnosing *new devices* becomes possible without available experience with them. This holds because and as long as they are assembled from components whose behavior models are contained in a model library.
2. *Unanticipated faults* and, in particular, multiple faults can be dealt with. This is based on the fact that the basic algorithm requires only the specification of models of correct behavior and, hence, makes no assumption about particular faults.
3. *New abnormalities*, i.e. any observation that manifests a deviation from normal behavior, even if encountered never before, will be detected as a contradiction and, hence, contribute to the generation of solution candidates.
4. The diagnosis procedure guarantees *completeness* and *correctness* of the results with respect to the phenomena captured by the models, the faults modeled, if any, and the observations provided.
5. There is a *formal theory* that characterizes the correct and complete output of these diagnosis systems [de Kleer et al 92]. Therefore, it is possible to provide provably correct diagnosis software for safety critical systems, in particular in the area of embedded systems where this requirement is often raised. Even if that level of software quality is not desired, the existence of the theory and a

simple test algorithm (Quine's algorithm for computing prime implicates from 1955) allows for automatic testing of diagnosis output based on test cases.

6. Model-based systems are *generated*, not programmed. As pointed out before, the only device-specific element is captured by the representation of the device structure. Often, it will be possible to import it from external, already existing sources, e.g. CAD systems. From this information and the elements of the domain-specific model library, a device behavior model can be derived automatically. The general diagnosis algorithm operating on this device model forms a diagnosis system tailored to the particular device. This means it is constructed without having to write a single line of code.

7. Since the diagnosis framework can be bought from the shelf, the entire effort of programming and knowledge-base construction is in the establishment and maintenance of the model library. This is essential for *solving the variant problem*. From a practical and economic point of view this is feasible.

8. Even if the actual runtime system is not a model-based one, model-based diagnosis can support programming diagnostics, for instance, for validation or as a starting point for the programmer who wants to violate the completeness of the model-based results in a controlled way. Also, the model-based technology can be used to generate the input to traditional types of diagnosis tools, e.g. by generating decision trees [Guckenbiehl et al. 99].

6. Discussion

Diagnostic expert system technology is good enough for business application - now. But although an impressive range of problem solving methods is available[4], success is not guaranteed. In fact, non-technical factors dominate the outcome and should take precedence.

On the technical side, two forces have been working to our favor for a long time and are now undercutting economically important thresholds: increasing available processing power and better networking technology. Compared to previous attempts of establishing a real market presence of diagnostic systems, a much better computational infrastructure at the clients' side is in place. It has become really cheap. And this process continues. Personal computers are virtually everywhere. The next wave of microprocessors is already being put on hand-held and similar devices. Future embedded systems in all kinds of everyday devices will have the computational power of former mainframe systems at their disposal. Faster, smaller, cheaper - but they should also be *more intelligent*. This opens opportunities for diagnostic applications.

The second force, better networking technology, has brought us the internet as a medium where data exchange and distribution is available at low costs practically worldwide. It can lessen the problems related to the distribution and maintenance of knowledge bases and model libraries. The network enables experts for certain de-

---

[4] Examples for diagnostic tools are found in the exhibition guide of XPS-99 [Puppe et al. 99] and on the www-pages of the GI working group 1.5.2 "diagnosis and classification": http://www.kbs.uni-hannover.de/diagnostik/

vices and technologies, for certain kinds of diseases, etc. to "publish" their work on centralized servers for use on the client side where dedicated applets interfacing to equipment and people are running. This way the costs of distribution are becoming negligible while the set of potential users increases dramatically. It will thus be easier to reach break-even for work done on the server side.

The necessary technical pre-requisites for useful diagnostic programs - after all the outcome of more than 30 years of research - are here. These enable us to do real applications with real economic value. But we also do need these *real* applications to fuel research with practically relevant questions. We do not entertain any doubts that more not less research is needed to meet future demands. Even now we are already lacking answers to relevant questions.

Taking advantage of the changing environment requires research to address practically relevant situations in which diagnosis programs might be applied. For instance, an embedded system might not necessarily be required to *localize* a fault. *Identifying* a fault's consequences is of far greater importance because it allows assessing the risk of further, probably reduced and limited operation of the device (e.g. limp home mode in cars). The need to integrate diagnosis with monitoring for embedded systems is obvious, but not much research has been done in that respect so far.

Advanced networking brings the long-term vision of co-operating diagnostic agents into focus. A necessary pre-requisite is the ability to exchange knowledge rather than data. The knowledge sharing initiative is a rather general approach, not at all specific for diagnosis, that proposes a standard ontology named KIF (knowledge interchange format; [Swartout et. al 94]) to mediate between different representations. It employs a standard protocol named KQML (Knowledge query and manipulation language [Finin et al. 94]) for exchange of data and knowledge between different agents. Multi-agent technology [Woolrigde & Jennings 95] promises to be useful to build large diagnostic systems as cooperating small and reusable agents. Each agent might be an autonomous diagnostic system with its own knowledge as well as problem solving and communication capabilities. A diagnostic agent should be able to solve problems from a well circumscribed domain, to recognize, when a problem lies outside its competence area, to suggest other agents with more competence for such problems and to communicate about known observations and proposed solutions. First examples for diagnostic multi-agent systems include ARCHON [Jennings & Cockburn 96] and Coop-D3 [Bamberger 97].

The new interest in organizational requirements is not triggered because they have changed so much. It is rather the case that diagnosis research has been ignoring them for too long. The feedback from *real* applications on a large basis has been missing. Organizational requirements are only slowly getting into focus. More overlap with other tasks is and will be identified. The question of costs is not merely a question of putting together re-usable pieces of diagnostic software components, but at its heart it is a question of how knowledge is handled in the respective organizations. Formalized knowledge used for diagnosis, but also used - or even better re-used - for other tasks is of interest to AI research. Interfacing in a larger context, however, reveals that knowledge in a more general sense represents value for companies and other organizations. The paper-based diagnostic repair manual will probably outperform the fastest diagnosis engines in the marketplace for years or even decades to come. This shifts attention to other aspects of the big picture that we need to get into focus more and more. The acquisition and smooth integration of different kinds of data and knowledge in hypermedia systems has lately attracted a great deal of interest under the label of 'knowledge management' and 'organizational memory' [Abecker & Decker 99].

Diagnosis is only a small, but important part. The user will often have to perform the most important and difficult aspects of the problem solving process. In such environments, e.g. in medicine, the user is responsible for the solution. By taking this view, critiquing systems allow one to enter preferred solutions for which potential weaknesses will be pointed out [Silverman 92, Rhein-Desel & Puppe 98]. They make use of additional knowledge about the seriousness of potential errors, about the reliability and completeness of observations, about the reliability of their own knowledge base, about user preferences, and about alternative solutions.

The organizational context implies that the potential user of a diagnosis system needs computer-based support for other related tasks as well. For example, in hotline or service support the user needs to delegate difficult cases to appropriate experts; to look up information from various kinds of documents like client contact data bases, drawings, parts lists, instructions, pictures; to ensure, that something happens and the resulting repair actions lead to success; to order spare parts; to document client contacts including accounting issues; to appease the client etc. From the organization's point of view, the data about faults should be evaluated with respect to improving design, construction, and manufacturing, thus enhancing the organizational memory.

So, do we expect a diagnostic killer application any time soon?

Certainly not ! Not in the sense that there will be one universal method that can be applied uniformly. Not in the sense that any of the presented methods has won the battle in the niche it is addressing in the marketplace either. But the external, economic conditions are becoming more and more favorable both for intelligent devices with lots of cheap sensors and chips with built-in diagnostic intelligence and for cheap interactive diagnostic advise via inter-, intra-, or extra-net.

7. References

Abecker, A. and Decker, S.: Organizational Memory: Knowledge Acquisition, Integration and Retrieval Issues, in Proc. XPS-99, Springer, this volume, 1999.

Bamberger, S.: Cooperating Diagnostic Expert Systems to Solve Complex Diagnosis Tasks, in: Proc. of German Conference on Artificial Intelligence (KI-97), Springer, LNAI 1303, 325-336, 1997.

Bartsch-Spörl, B., Lenz, M. and Hübner, A.: Case-Based Reasoning – Survey and Future Directions, in: Proc. XPS-99, Springer, this volume, 1999.

Beschta, A., Dressler, O., Freitag, H., Montag, M. and Struss P.: A Model-based Approach to Fault Localization in Power Transmission Networks. Intelligent Systems Engineering Vol.2 Nr.1 Spring 1993 .

Console, L., Torasso, P.: Integrating Models of the Correct Behavior into Abductive Diagnosis, Proceedings ECAI90, Pitman Publishing, 160-166, 1990

de Dombal, F., Leaper, D., Horrocks, J., Staniland, J., and McCann, A.: Computer-Aided Diagnosis of Acute Abdominal Pain, British Med. Journal 2, 9–13, 1972.

de Kleer ,J., Mackworth, A., Reiter, R.: Characterizing diagnoses and Systems, in [Hamscher et al. 92], 54-65, 1992.

de Kleer, J., Raiman,O., Saraswat, V.: Critical Reasoning, Proc. IJCAI93, Morgan Kaufmann Publishers, 18-23, 1993.

Dressler, O. and Struss, P.: Back to Defaults: Characterizing and Computing Diagnoses as Coherent Assumption Sets, John Wiley & Sons, Proceedings ECAI'92, 719-723, 1992.

Dressler, O. and Struss, P.: The Consistency-based Approach to Automated Diagnosis of Devices, in Brewka, G. (ed.): Principles of Knowledge Representation, 267-311, CSLI Publications, Stanford, 267-311, 1996.

Eshelman, L.: MOLE: A Knowledge-Acquisition Tool for Cover-and-Differentiate Systems, in: Marcus, S. (ed.): Automating Knowledge Acquisition for Expert Systems, Kluwer Academic Publishers, 1988.

Finin, T. et al.: KQML - A Language and Protocol for Knowledge and Information Exchange. Fuchi, K., Yokoi, T.(eds.): Knowledge Building and Knowledge Sharing. Ohmsha, Ltd. und IOS Press, 1994.

Frank, P.: Fault Diagnosis in Dynamic Systems via State Estimation - A Survey, in: Tzafestas et al (eds.): System Fault Diagnostics, Reliability & Related Knowledge-based Approaches, Vol.1 35-98, D.Reidel Press, 1987.

Gappa, U., Puppe, F. and Schewe, S.: Graphical Knowledge Acquisition for Medical Diagnostic Expert Systems, Artificial Intelligence in Medicine 5, 185-211, 1993.

Gardenfors, P. (ed.): Belief Revision, Cambridge University Press, 1992.

Guckenbiehl, T., Milde, H., Neumann, B. and Struss, P.: Meeting Re-use Requirements of Real-life Diagnosis Applications, in Proc. XPS-99, Springer, this Volume, 1999.

Hamscher, W., Console, L., de Kleer, J. (eds.): Readings in Model-based Diagnosis, Morgan Kaufmann, 1992.

Isermann, R.: Process Fault Detection Based on Modelling and Estimation Methods: A survey, Automatica, 20, 387-404,1984

Jennigs, N. and Cockburn, D.: ARCHON: A Distributed Artificial Intelligence System for Industrial Applications. In: Jennings, N.R., O'Hare G.M.P. (eds.): Foundation of Distributed Artificial Intelligence. John Wiley & Sons, Inc., 1996.

Kulikowski, C. and Weiss, S. (eds.): Computer Systems That Learn Classification and Prediction Methods from Statistics, Neural Nets, Machine Learning, and Expert Systems, Morgan Kaufman, 1991.

Masarie, F., Miller, R., and Myers, J.: INTERNIST-1 Properties: Representing Common Sense and Good Medical Practise in a Computerized Medical knowledge Base. Computer Biomed Research 18, 137-165, 1985.

Michie, D., Spiegelhalter, D., and Taylor, C. (eds.): Machine Learning, Neural and Statistical Classification, Ellis Horwood, 1994.

Mitchell, T.: Machine Learning, McGraw-Hill, 1997.

Moore, G.: Crossing the Chasm, Harper Business, New York, 1991.

Ohmann, C., Yang, Q., Franke, C.: and the Abdominal Pain Study Group: Diagnostic Scores for Acute Appendicitis, Eur. J. Surg. 161: 273-281, 1995.

Quinlan, R.: C4.5: Programs for Machine Learning, Morgan Kaufmann, 1997.

Pearl, J.: Probabilistic Reasoning in Intelligent Systems: Networks of Plausible Inference, Morgan Kaufmann, 1988.

Patton, R., Chen, J. Robustness in Model-based Fault Diagnosis, In: Atherton, D. and Borne P. (eds.): Concise Encyclopedia of Simulation and Modeling, 379-392, Pergamon Press, 1992.

Puppe, F.: Learning from Cases for Classification Problem Solving, in: Bock, H-H., Lenski, W., and Richter, M. (eds.): Information Systems and Data Analysis, Springer, 44–55, 1994.

Puppe, F.: Knowledge Reuse among Diagnostic Problem Solving Methods in the Shell-Kit D3, in: Int. Journal of Human-Computer-Studies 49, 1998.

Puppe, F., Gappa, U., Poeck, K. and Bamberger, S.: Wissensbasierte Diagnose und Informationssysteme [Knowledge-Based Diagnosis and Information Systems], Springer, 1996.

Puppe, F. et al.: Exhibition Guide of XPS-99, Internal Report, Institute of Informatics, Wuerzburg University, 1999.

Reggia, J., Nau, D., and Wang, P.: Diagnostic Expert Systems Based on a Set Covering Model, Int. J. Man-Machine-Studies 19, 437–460, 1983.

Rhein-Desel, U. and Puppe, F.: Concepts for a Diagnostic Critiquing Systems in Vague Domains, Proc. of German Conference on Artificial Intelligence (KI-98), Springer, LNAI 1504, 201-212, 1998.

Richards, D. and Compton, P.: Taking Up the Situated Cognition Challenge with Ripple Down Rules, International Journal of Human Computer Studies, Special Issue on Situated Cognition, 1998.

Russell, S. and Norvig, P.: Artificial Intelligence – A Modern Approach, Prentice Hall, 1995.

Schwartz, W.: Medicine and the Computer: The Promise and Problems of Change, New England Journal of Medicine 283, 1257-1264, 1970.

Shortliffe, E.: Computer-Based Medical Consultations: MYCIN, American Elsevier, 1976.

Silverman, B.: Survey of Expert Critiquing Systems; Practical and Theoretical Frontiers, CACM 35, No.4, 106-127, 1992.

Swartout, W., Neches, R. and Patil, R.: Knowledge Sharing: Prospects and Challenges, in Fuchi, K. and Yokoi, R. (eds.): Knowledge Building and Knowledge Sharing, IOS Press, 1994.

Van Bemmel, J. and Musen, M.: Handbook of Medical Informatics, Springer, 1997.

[VMBD 97] Vehicle Model-based Diagnosis, Brite-Euram Project, Presentation at the International Workshop on Principles of Diagnosis, Mont St. Michel, http://www.aber.ac.uk/~dcswww/vmbd/, 1997.

Wooldrigde, M. and Jennigs, N.: Intelligent agents: theory and practice, Knowledge Engineering Review 10(2), 115-152, 1995.

Knowledge-Based Configuration
– Survey and Future Directions –

Andreas Günter

Center for Computing Technology
University of Bremen
guenter@tzi.de

Christian Kühn

DaimlerChrysler AG
FT2/EK, Stuttgart
christian.kuehn@daimlerchrysler.com

Abstract
The configuration of technical systems is one of the most successful application areas of knowledge-based systems. This article overviews and evaluates the developed representation technologies and problem-solving methods, successful application fields and software-tools for configuration of the last few years. Current research themes and perspectives for the application of knowledge-based systems are presented as an outlook for the future.

1 Introduction

The configuration of technical systems is one of the most successful application areas of knowledge-based systems. Configuration and construction are used in the following as a synonym. Thus, it must be noted that most construction tasks from the areas principle-, variant- and adaptive construction can be equated with configuration. An in-depth discussion about this can be found in [Günter 93b]. Following a general analysis of configuration problems, four central aspects (with respect to knowledge types) concerned with configuration were identified. Configuration tasks have the following characteristics:

- A set of **objects** in the application domain and their properties (parameters).
- A set of **relations** between the domain objects. Taxonomical and compositional relations are of particular importance for configuration.
- A **task specification** (configuration objectives) that specifies the demands a created configuration has to accomplish.
- **Control knowledge** about the configuration process.

Firstly, a few concepts are explained in order to further present and isolate the theme. Thus the concepts of design and configuration are initially differentiated. In the United States "design" is often discussed in publications when in fact according to our viewpoint, they are actually configuration problems. In [Tong et al. 92] design is defined as follows:

"What is design? Design is the process of constructing a description of an artifact that satisfies a (possibly informal) functional specification, meets certain performance criteria and resource limitations, is realizable in a given target technology, and satisfies criteria such as simplicity, testability, manufacturability, reusability etc.; the design process itself may also be subject to certain restrictions such as time, human power, cost etc."

In addition to the general definition in [Tong et.al. 92] under *engineering design*, the project of *"physical artifacts or physical processes of various kinds"* is identified. A central aspect in this context is the creation of a structure from a functional requirement description. Design tasks are often identified as *ill-structured problems*. According to [Dörner 95] this means that no known direct mapping of functions on components exists. An additional problem often arises in the fact that this mapping is not clear, rather one component fulfils more functions or more components together provide one functionality (cp. [Ulrich et al. 92]).

Configuration is often described as routine design. This is based especially on the classification of synthesis tasks by Brown and Chandrasekaran [Brown et al. 89]. The following comments refer to this classification of synthesis tasks into three classes. Coming from the general model, the so-called routine design (design class 3) is described as a problem, where the specifications of objects, their properties and compositional structures are already given, and the discovery of a solution is based on a likewise known strategy. The task then is to assemble a configuration, which fulfils the task specification, from the known objects and according to a given strategy. An example here is the offer creation for technical systems on the basis of a complete description of components, their properties, a compositional structure and combination restrictions.

Since the named limitations are not given in the domain, then innovative design (cp. design class 2) or even further reaching creative design (cp. design class 1) can be spoken about. As a result the transitions between the different classes are smooth. In so far as a clear allocation is seldom possible, several graduations can be introduced between the routine design and the creative design. For this reason a range is assumed from routine design to creative design. An example of creative design is the artistic design of furniture.

In the following sections we discuss knowledge-based configuration methods, typical application areas, and tools for configuration. Current research themes bring this report to a close.

2 Knowledge-Based Configuration Methods

The first and for a long time most well-known knowledge-based configuration system was the R1/XCON [McDermott 82]. XCON was a rule-based system for the configuration of DEC computers. It was classed for a long time as a very successful system, however, this changed in the course of time mainly due to maintenance problems concerning the large knowledge base of XCON (see section about rule-based systems).

```
ASSIGN-POWER-SUPPLY-1

IF:
THE MOST CURRENT ACTIVE CONTEXT IS ASSIGNING A POWER SUPPLY
AND AN SBI MODULE OF ANY TYPE HAS BEEN PUT IN A CABINET
AND THE POSITION IT OCCUPIES IN THE CABINET IS KNOWN
AND THERE IS SPACE IN THE CABINET FOR A POWER SUPPLY AND
THERE IS NO AVAILABLE POWER SUPPLY
AND THE VOLTAGE AND FREQUENCY OF THE COMPONENTS IS KNOWN

THEN:
FIND A POWER SUPPLY OF THAT VOLTAGE AND FREQUENCY
AND ADD IT TO THE ORDER
```

Figure 1: A typical rule in XCON

Firstly, the most important concepts in the field of knowledge-based configuration, which are already applied, will be presented:
- Rule-based systems
- Concept hierarchies
- Structure-based approach
- Constraint-based systems
- Resource-based approach
- Case-based configuration
- Backtracking and variants of backtracking

2.1 Rule-Based Systems

The development of expert systems was occasionally strongly influenced by the rule-based paradigm. The restriction on the rule-based paradigm for expert systems was criticized on many occasions [Günter 91]. The critics referred to the following aspects: serious problems concerning knowledge acquisition, consistency checking, and in particular maintenance as well as lacking modularity and adaptability. Furthermore, it has led to the need to revise decisions concerning problems and the only unfavorable opportunities for integration of user instructions and case-based approaches.

Above deficits appeared when rules were applied as the sole formalism to represent knowledge. Those opposing our opinion concerning rules have protected their possibilities by representing and evaluating heuristic relations which is where the strengths of rules lie. The main problem is that there was an overloaded use of rules in the course of expert system research and they were utilized as uniform knowledge representation formalisms.

Consequently, rules can be used for the representation of local connections in the configuration process and also for the specification of cycles. However, the combination of both types of knowledge often leads to the mentioned problems. Diverse tools are available for rule-based systems. But configuration tasks can hardly be realized adequately with these tools alone. Using tools, only a small part of the necessary knowledge can be represented, consequently they should be used only as a method among others in a configuration framework.

2.2 Concept Hierarchies

There is a need for the representation of object knowledge in almost all configuration systems. An object-oriented concept-based representation is commonly chosen as a representation form. Such an object-centralized representation makes the bundled specification of properties and their potential value ranges possible. Thus so-called facets for the specification of application knowledge are used (for example, default values). In an experiment about methods used in configuration expert systems, Linnemann came to the conclusion that frame-like representation technologies for object presentation are used in 9 out of 10 systems [Linnemann 94].

In a predominant number of configuration systems, object descriptions are classified in *taxonomical hierarchies* (is-a-relation). Using this method of abstraction, knowledge can be structured, generic descriptions of objects can be formed (which correspond to object classes), and knowledge can be represented more efficiently and with less data redundancy using inheritance mechanisms.

With the configuration process, the compositional structure of an object according to the has-parts-relation is of great importance. It is still only this structure which is included in the solution, it links together an aggregate and its components. The idea of skeleton plans (s. [Friedland 79]) is often used in technical applications of knowledge-based systems, for example in the project ARC-TEC [Richter et al. 91]. This technique is based on compositional hierarchies which are represented here in the form of skeleton plans. The skeleton plans allow compositional relations to be represented, for example the has-parts-relations in the PLAKON-System [Cunis et al. 91] or in KONWERK [Günter 95a]. The so-called structure-based approach which is based on explicit representation of component structure is explained in one of the following sections.

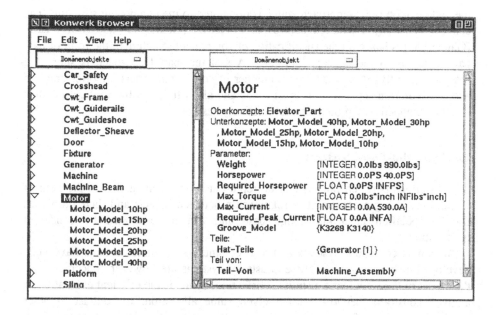

Figure 2: Example of a concept definition

2.3 Structure-Based Approach

In [Günter 91] different so-called control types are introduced. One of these is the *structure-based approach*. The compositional, hierarchical structure of an object serves thus as a guideline for the control of problem solution. Through this, a top-down-concept can be realized which orientates itself on the component structure. The control type „structure-based" can be found in many concepts and systems (also in planning systems):

- Specification of a task in the form of AND/OR-trees.
- Skeleton construction (according to [Puppe 90], derived from Friedland's skeleton plans).
- Hierarchical structured rule contexts (for example, XCON [McDermott 82]).
- Configuration tools PLAKON and KONWERK.
- Direct or indirect in a predominant number of application systems.

Therefore, structural information has two meanings (s. [Günter 91]):

- The structure of a solution is predefined by the conceptual hierarchy, it consists of hierarchically ordered components.
- Tasks can be divided into subtasks according to their structure.

The skeleton plans from Friedland [Friedland 79] are often chosen in technical domains as a starting point for the strategy (s. [Richter et al. 94; Richter et al. 91]), they allow a top-down-approach which is orientated to the component structure. The *concept hierarchy orientated control* of PLAKON [Günter 91] and KONWERK [Günter 95a] is based on the specification of component structure in the form of has-parts-relations in the concept hierarchy. A structure-based approach is supported (partly implicitly) in a predominant number of commercial tools for offer creation and configuration support. This is adequate and also often familiar to the user since it can be mapped on a product model relatively easily.

2.4 Constraint-Based Systems

Restrictions between objects can be represented and evaluated with the help of constraints. Using a constraint, a relationship between objects and their properties can be specified in a knowledge base and can be evaluated by constraint propagation.

Numerous constraint systems and also commercially available tools have been developed in the meantime. These constraint systems are however concerned with the aspect of the so-called constraint satisfaction, which is the efficient evaluation of a given constraint network with a given value allocation. In contrast to other application areas of constraint systems, the following demands arise from configuration tasks:

- Constraint networks need to be accumulated incrementally in line with the further development of partial solutions. At a given time, the complete number of the constraints to be considered is not known (except in the final solution).
- Constraints must be formulated in such a manner that they either require, forbid or limit the number of new objects.
- Symbolic, functional and numerical constraints need to be available and processed in a complete system.
- Often a complete evaluation of constraint-relations is not possible due to the magnitude of the search space. Therefore, only the upper or lower limits can be propagated but not each individual value because of complexity reasons concerning the range of parameter (property) values.

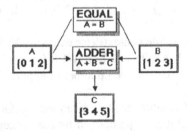

Figure 3: Example of a simple constraint net

Because of these properties, further reaching technologies are currently being developed (or have already been) for the usage of constraints in configuration systems (cf. [Cunis et al. 91; Fleischanderl et al. 98; Güsgen et al. 92]). Also the

„Dynamic CSP" approach (see also [Stumptner 97]) includes a few of the specified enhancements, in particular the dynamic structure of the constraint network. A commercial tool which fulfils these high requirements is not yet known, however in universities diverse prototypes have been successfully realized and used.

2.5 Resource-Based Approach

Resource-based configuration is based on the following elementary principle: components of a technical system are used because they offer a service which is required by the system as a whole or because other components of the system need this service (cp. [Böhm et al. 96; Emde et al. 97; Heinrich 93; Heinrich et al. 93; Jüngst et al. 98; Neumann et al. 89]). Interfaces between components are specified by the exchanged *resources*. The same is true for the relation between system and surroundings. To these resources belong technical resources such as power consumption and memory capacity in addition to mercantilistic resources such as price and maintenance effort. Components make a number of resources available and also consume resources themselves. A task specification exists in that the concrete surroundings of the chosen system are resource-based specified as components. In an interactive configuration process, the resource deficits are recognized and are thus equated by the instantiation of components (balancing methods).

2.6 Case-Based Technologies

Case-based problem-solving methods are therefore identified, that knowledge about already solved tasks is saved and is used for the solution of new tasks. The methods for selecting case knowledge from a case base can be divided into two groups, those which carry out a *preprocessing* of the case base and those which do not but work on an unstructured number of cases. Using the case knowledge which is used to support configuration, it must not always be concerned with a *complete* case. The takeover of parts is also possible. The reason being is the assumption that similar tasks lead to similar solutions. An alternative basic approach is the comparison of current tasks to already known problem solutions in the application area [Pfitzner 93].

Fundamentally two types of approaches to determine how case knowledge can be selected are:

- Retrieval and, when suitable, adaptation of the solution (transformational analogy) or
- Selection of case knowledge in individual steps. This case knowledge can also act as control knowledge (derivational analogy).

Pfitzner [Pfitzner 93] differentiates respectively between different transfer modes. Retrieval and adaptation of case knowledge however always remain separate procedures. A range of systems and applications have already been case-based realized (cp. [Bartsch-Spörl 87; Hua et al. 93; Olivier et al. 96; Paulokat et al. 93; Weß 92]).

However, case-based technologies also have a few disadvantages:
- They typically provide *conservative*, that is no – or only few – innovative solution suggestions.
- No – or only narrow – causal explanations exist for the suggested solutions.
- Case-based methods often lead to relatively *bad* solutions

2.7 Resolving of Configuration Conflicts

In general it is true that heuristical decisions are necessary for many applications due to complexity and partly due to absent knowledge (cf. [Günter 93a]). These decisions imply among other things that:
- an optimal solution is not necessarily found and
- the decisions prove to be disadvantageous during the course of further problem-solving or can even be incompatible with the rest of the solution parts.

In this situation, mechanisms for further work are necessary. Independent of the reason there are two alternative methods for conflicts:
- *Revision of decisions*
  The revision of configuration steps is also known as *backtracking*. Here one or more of the previously met decisions are taken back and are performed again with another value.
- *Repair of a partial solution*
  Instead of revising decisions, it is sometimes also possible to "repair" a partial solution using a direct modification and/or additional domain objects and thus to retransform it into a consistent state. Using such a repair method, decisions are changed likewise, however no reference to configuration history and the previous successful steps is given.

The following variations concerning the retraction of configuration decisions have been developed (see [Ginsberg 93; Günter 93a]):
- Chronological backtracking
- Backtracking over more levels
- Dependency-directed backtracking
- Knowledge-based backtracking
- Interactive backtracking
- Backtracking with data adoption

3 Applications and Transfer of Technology

Configuration with knowledge-based techniques is a successful application field for methods of the artificial intelligence area (AI). There are two application scenarios where configuration methods are principally employed (see [Brinkop et.al. 94; Haag 98; Tank 96]):
- development and construction as well as
- product configuration and feasibility analysis (offer creation and sales)

Knowledge-based configuration systems have been developed among other things for: computer systems, elevators, drive controllers, rolling mills, industrial stirring devices, passenger vehicles, image processing systems, machine parts, communication systems, pumps, trucks, switchgears, conveyor systems, SPS controls, lighting systems, manufacturing cells, aircraft vehicle cabins, liquid crystals etc.

General objectives for the development of application systems are:
- reduction costs for development and making sales offers,
- lowering of error rate,
- faster offer creation,
- successful duplication of solved applications,
- support for the quick change of products and product generations,
- general backup of the company's individual knowledge (i.e. documentation) and
- standardization of solutions.

There is no patent recipe for the transfer of research results in applications, this is valid for configuration tasks as well. The development of an integrated software system with a knowledge-based configuration system as an essential component requires the application of „classic" software engineering principles, which we will not go into here. In addition, individual process models exist for knowledge-based systems, which are mainly based on the two fundamentally different statements of prototype-based and model-based methods. A multitude of process models for the development of expert systems try to combine both approaches.

The following steps are not necessary in every application area, need not be arranged in a strict sequence, and may include feedback. Nevertheless this appears to us as a meaningful structuring method (see [Günter et al. 98]):
- Analysis of the application problem
- Definition of a pilot study or example
- Knowledge acquisition
- Feasibility investigation
- Economical analysis
- Tool selection
- Demonstration prototype
- Specification and realization
- Step-by-step implementation
- Integration

Due to our experiences we would like to comment as follows on the above points:

- *Quick analysis*
  Already in the first discussion an initial classification of the problem must be made and statements to the solution possibilities must be given. At this point it is clear to both sides that nothing obligatory has to be said, the first impression and reaction to it is important. This requires experience in the solution of configuration problems and of the analysis of applications. Computer scientists have frequently the task of solving „other people's" problems. This demands communication abilities and a service awareness. Both hardly play a role in the university education of computer scientists.

- *Technical possibilities*
  Not everything which is technically possible should necessarily be realized. What is realized should orientate itself around economic considerations, the business environment and the integration strategies.

- *Tools vs. individual software*
  Individual software is cost-intensive, both in development and maintenance. If possible, software tools should be used. This is not even a new discovery but it is hardly ever considered.

- *Meaning of (university) prototypes*
  We have realized same applications with KONWERK [Günter 95b], while it was clear that this would find no entrance in the application system. Nevertheless such a prototype represents a „convincing" help in supporting arguments. This is also valid for our opinion when the prototype is based on a university tool. Software tools are a decision aid for the transfer of technology (cp. [Neumann 95]).

- *Early inclusion of the user*
  What do users expect in the future? A question which is often asked too late. An early discussion with the user improves the system and in particular the acceptance of it.

- *Software-ergonomical considerations*
  The usability instead of the functionality is in the foreground of ergonomics. Also through the inclusion of the user in the early phases of system development, the requirements can be in principle better fulfilled.

- *Integration*
  Configuration systems are used in a context. A link to data bases, CAS systems or internet/intranet is often necessary and must be already included in the run up to system development.

4 Software Tools

Computer support using knowledge-based configuration can be identified for various tasks, especially for product development, offer creation and technical feasibility analysis.

There are several available tools on the market for supporting the configuration of variety-rich products for offer creation (e.g. CAS, Cosmos, et-epos, SalesPlus, SCE, Secon, Sellor, SC-Config). On the other hand only university tools have been developed for complex tasks, which lie in the field of supporting engineering tasks.

The tasks which can be carried out using available CAS tools range from price calculations (including the evaluation of rules for discounts and mark-ups), consistency checking, generating bills of materials, and the creation of written offers on the basis of predefined text modules. Here the following technologies are used: object-oriented representation of configuration objects with properties and relations (partly in connection with a database), rules, and user-driven configuration. The application of technologies such as constraints, heuristics, resource-based methods, case-based methods, modeling of complex requirements, and functional modeling, however is only now realized in individual applications, or rather supported through prototype software tools.

A university tool system for configuration is KONWERK. A fundamental assumption connected with the development of KONWERK was that the efficient, economic employment of knowledge-based methods can only be successful if a domain independent tool can be made available and can support this problem-specific aspects of configuration problems. KONWERK (cp. [Günter 95b]) was founded as a problem class specific framework system in which configuration methods were integrated and made available.

A central requirement for tool systems is that suitable concepts for different domains must be given and that also no unnecessary complex mechanisms are made available (i.e. all necessary mechanisms, but only these). Our solution provides here a sub-section in problem-solving modules which are built on each other. KONWERK was realized as a domain-independent module-based construction set which makes modules available for the following aspects:

- Representation of domain objects and their properties,
- Representation and processing of relations and restrictions,
- Formulization of objectives specifications (task formulation) and
- Control of the configuration process.

Therefore both standard mechanisms (basic modules) as well as conceptual further-reaching methods in the form of enhancement modules are available in a complete framework system.

Structuring in the problem-solving modules of KONWERK lies on a technical level, that is, not on a level of human solving. The structuring as a module-based construction set allows a flexible combination of modules for the applications. The user-necessary functionality is made available through the "configuration" of the modules to an application system.

KONWERK allows several applications from different domains to be realized:
- Selection and arrangement of friction bearings
- Configuration and dimensioning of jointed shafts
- Design of liquid crystals
- Configuration of passenger cabins in vehicle aircrafts
- Configuration of hydro-geological models
- Configuration of elevators (VT-domain)
- Modeling of bills of materials in automobile production
- Arrangement and dimensioning of drive control systems

Due to the modeling of real domains, it has been shown that the concepts are also suitable under application-based aspects. There the requirements were based both on KONWERK and on the known deficits of preceding prototype production with help of PLAKON [Cunis et.al. 91]. The heterogeneity of the considered applications, which among other things include several of the specified aspects, ensure the usability of KONWERK for a wide range of application problems. With the university tool KONWERK applications can be adequately realized for the prototyp (cp. [Neumann 95; Richter 96]).

5 Current Research Themes

In the presentation of current research themes, the following methods and application problems will be considered:
- Model-based configuration and simulation
- Truth maintenance systems (TMS) and assumption-based TMS
- Description logics
- Extensions of constraint techniques
- Functional requirements and specification through sketching
- Explorative configuration
- Integration in a product model and workflow
- Configuration of software and embedded systems

5.1 Model-Based Approaches

The concept "model-based" is used here in analogy to model-based diagnosis. Such methods are based on a qualitative representation of technical laws, general principles, and knowledge about functions of technical devices and processes (cp. [Früchtenicht 88; Günter et.al. 97; Stein 95; Stein et al 96]). The aim is, on the basis of this general knowledge, to design (new) technical systems. This includes also tasks from creative design. An important argument for model-based methods is that technical systems are often so complex that they offer the possibility to work with a simplified (qualitative) model.

5.2 Truth Maintenance Systems (TMS) and Assumption-Based TMS

The employment of *Truth Maintenance Systems* (cp. [Doyle 79]) represents a promising possibility in improving construction systems. There are several systems in which the employment of TMS has been discussed and partly implemented (cp. [Cunis et al. 91; Paulokat 92; Schädler 95]). The motivations for application TMS are to support knowledge-based backtracking (possibilities to data adoption) and to improve explanations concerning design decisions. The most important functionality of TMS is that in the case of revised decisions, all the dependent consequent decisions are identified and are revised where appropriate.

One possibility of configuration strategy can be developing and managing all partial solutions during problem-solving. Several concepts exist here for configuration which are based on the application of ATMS (*Assumption-Based Truth Maintenance Systems*, introduced by [DeKleer 86]) (see [Bräuer 91; Haag 95; Hein 91; Paulokat 92; Schirp 96]). Inconsistent part solutions are thus accordingly marked and are no longer considered later on. This method manages a breadth-first search. For configuration it has to be stated that none of these systems have so far left the prototype stage. Indeed relatively simple configuration tasks can be solved using this method.

5.3 Description Logics

Taxonomical hierarchies in the AI have already been investigated in-depth and have culminated in the conception of terminological systems as an application of description logics. Description logics are based on formal semantics which allow certain consistence predictions on a knowledge base and include also interesting inference procedures (e.g. classification). Description logics are expressive, include fundamentally investigated inferences, are formally funded, and form a quasi-standard in the theoretical AI; these arguments highlight that they are to be included also in configuration systems. Up to now this has not been possible without problems especially because configuration-specific requirements have only been partially considered (see [Baader et.al. 96; Baader et.al. 98, McGuiness et.al. 98; Wright et.al. 93]).

5.4 Extension of Constraint Techniques

In order to enhance the constraint techniques research work is being done at this time on different problems. Lots of the work deal with the enhancement of the Constraint Satisfaction Problems (CSPs) to allow the possibility to dynamically enlarge these amounts, not only for fixed, enumerated sets of variables.

An extension of the CSPs are the dynamic CSPs (DCSPs), which differentiate between meta-level constraints and compatibility constraints. While compatibility constraints have no influence on the activities of the variables, variable activation can be directly achieved or rather prevented by the meta-level constraints. An introduction to DCSP is given in [Stumptner 97], for example.

A further topic that raises a lot of questions is the constraint relaxation, i.e. the fading out of constraints in over-constrained conflict situations. For this, domain-dependent knowledge about the relaxability of the constraints is necessary. The revision of constraints often results in too many constraints (in the worst case all) having to be withdrawn. An idea exists that the same restriction of one domain is modeled through several constraints of different relaxability (as constraint bundles), so that the conflict can be solved locally through the successive cancelling of individual constraints from the bundle (cp. [Cunis et al. 91]).

A further statement which also exists in connection with constraint relaxation is the introduction of fuzzy constraints, in that the value combinations, which are permitted by a constraint, understand the parameters as a quantity, to which a membership measurement can be defined. In [Schumann et.al. 95] an evaluation of fuzzy constraint relations exists through a projection on fixed constraints.

Further research work deals with the efficient evaluation of constraints. This is for example possible through the definition of domain-specific evaluation strategies, when for instance, there is a given sequence of constraints or of variable mapping (cp. [Buchheit et.al. 94; Stumptner 97]). An efficiency improvement of the constraint propagation can be achieved by the parallelization and distribution over several workstations. The difficulty here lies in the high degree of dependencies in constraint networks and therefore finding the most independent sub-network (see [Hotz 96]). A further unsolved problem are relation with temporal restrictions, which for example are necessary for the configuration of reactive systems like control systems.

5.5 Functional Requirements and Sketches

Up to now the specification of a task formulation has taken place in configuration systems, mostly using the direct selection of the solution features. An important and interesting addition are the opportunities of giving functional requirements to configuration using optimization objectives. This means that the necessary functionalities are formulated as part of the task formulation and a configuration system maps this on the objects and parameters which are necessary for it. So-called sketch functions are a further addition. Using a sketch function a user should be in the position to produce a task formulation as a sketch. The sketch is therefore based on application-specific by which graphically describe a task formulation. An example is the application-specific user-interface of the system art deco [Stein 95]. Both requirements are particularly valid for the employment of configuration technologies in internet-based applications. An internet configuration system must be in the position to make expert knowledge transparent to the user and represent it graphically. The users will give here only under-specified requirements and therefore focus very strongly on pure functional and price aspects. It is necessary to map functional requirements on the concrete solution level.

5.6 Explorative Configuration

An explorative strategy is necessary in many complex application domains. Here the following two points are of particular importance (see [Navinchandra 91]):

- the *redesign* of partial solutions and
- exploration into "new" areas.

In simple design tasks, the changing of partial solutions is avoided where possible using skilful strategies. In opposition to this, the alteration of a partial solution within design tasks is a natural procedure also for the constructor. A central requirement for design and construction tasks is consequently the opportunity of (interactively) changing the partial solutions. A possible procedure is the application of so-called repair knowledge (see [Günter 93a; Kühn 95; Marcus et.al. 88]). This was implemented, for example, into the system VT for configuration of elevators. One important feature is the direct modification (redesign) of partial solutions without reference to "development history" (which is always considered using backtracking).

5.7 From Configuration to Design

Whereas for the routine configuration field, a multitude of successful technologies have already been developed and partly implemented, there is a need for research work on the automation of designs in ill-structured domains[1]. For such domains, which hardly allow used structures to be recognized for configuration, the methods of routine configuration are no longer sufficient [Dörner 95]. Instead new technologies are required, which belong to areas of innovative and creative design (cp. design classes 2 and 1 in [Brown et.al. 89]). Special mechanisms are required, which can handle incomplete, uncertain, and fuzzy knowledge.

We are, however, of the opinion, that also a complex design process can be partly supported by the integration of configuration methods, so that the human designer is relieved of routine application work. Such an approach is followed for example by [Faltings et.al. 93] for the design of mechanical systems. For design support, Faltings and Sun have used technologies from qualitative physics.

The previously mentioned approaches – model-based techniques, functional modeling, and explorative configuration – principally also belong to the field of knowledge-based design. These techniques should not be considered as competitive techniques, but rather as methods that give the ability to supplement one another.

---

[1] Strictly speaking ill-structured domains are thought of as domains, for which only ill-structured models are known [Dörner 95].

5.8 Integration in a Product Model and Workflow

The integration of different methods is especially important for the successful transfer of technology. Although great success has been achieved in the research field of knowledge-based systems, the transfer of such success depends heavily on the practical integration of combined management with other technologies. A constructive cooperation is especially necessary with technologies from the areas of databases, graphical engineering systems (CAD), software ergonomics, distributed system architectures, optimization, simulation of systems, as well as validation and verification. A further level of integration is found in the application field, where different disciplines like electrical engineering, mechanical engineering, and economics in addition to information technology often take part.

Furthermore, integration plays an important role in management cycles. Due to the fact that it does not always suffice to deal with the configuration tasks individually, it is often necessary to view the complete product process chain because certain processes and strategies have effects on other parts of the process chain. The advantages of a continuous configuration concept which is embedded in the workflow of a company begin with improved documentation and end with clear improvements of compatibility and tuning between individual steps in the process chain.

Consequently, continuity is required also for the creation and maintenance of a knowledge base. This should be integrated together with component libraries in a complete product data model.

A further, more important aspect is the operative introduction of knowledge-based configuration technologies. Here the strategies are to be worked out and the acceptance of introduced systems is to be considered (cp. [Günter et.al. 98]). In a VDI-guideline, the three "dimensions" of integration are considered: technical, organizational, and social integration [VDI 93].

5.9 Configuration of Software and Embedded Systems

The configuration of software or rather of embedded systems can prove to be a very complex task, in that it concerns realizing functional and dynamic concept aims in a software-based system. Thus requirements of the produced system include efficiency, correctnes and reliability. These requirements are particularly important in safety-critical applications where embedded systems are frequently used. The employment of software can lead to the ability to set parameters to a higher grade as well as more frequent modification and adjustment. Software in an embedded system has to interact directly with electronic components (sensors and actuators) and – in case of mechatronic systems – indirectly with mechanical components. Thus embedded systems often require the production of software for hardware platforms which do not yet exist.

The knowledge-based configuration of software does not deal in this context with the free, creative development of software systems or rather products, but rather deals with choosing and assembling software components, parameter setting and allocate suitable hardware. Thus a complete method is to be developed which takes into account the following sub-problems:

- How can software suitable be modeled for configuration. That is, which structure criterions exist, how can software components be adequately modeled with their interfaces and what are the most important concept properties for configuration? How can the dependency between software and hardware structures be modeled?
- In which way can requirements on system behavior be formally specified (safety requirements, functional and dynamic requirements)?
- How can heuristical, domain-dependent knowledge for drawing conclusions from specification features to solution features be adequately modeled, especially on software structures and properties?
- Integration of validation and verification mechanisms in the configuration process: Which technologies are suitable for guaranteeing safety requirements, how can a suitable cooperation between synthesis steps and analytical validation and verification methods take place?

A possible application example is the configuration of vehicle electronic systems consisting of control units which are networked with each other using a CAN-Bus system as well as with sensors and actuators. The tendency to realize even more functionality through software leads to higher requirements in the development of electronic systems. Thus special control units employed for various different functions (for example, like control units for engine, gears, break etc.) could be replaced in the future by universal control units which are independently programmable, can carry out more sub-functionalities at the same time and later allow themselves to be modified (redesign).

6. Summary

Knowledge-based configuration and construction methods have been developed in the last few years "for the market", included in applications, and implemented into software tools. Their main advantages are improved maintainability, shorter development time, and problem functionality.

Although several software-tools (computer-aided selling) are available on the market for the production of offers, procedures for the technical configuration of complex products (both in development as well as for technical feasibility analysis and product adjustment) are not yet a component of marketable tools. Concerned tools have been provided up to now almost exclusively by university tools.

References

Baader, F., Sattler, U. *Description Logics with Symbolic Number Restrictions*. in: Proc. 12th European Conf. on Artificial Intelligence, Budapest 1996, p. 283-287

Baader, F., Sattler, U. *Description Logics with Concrete Domains and Aggregation*. in: Proc. 13th European Conf. on Artificial Intelligence, Brighton, UK, 1998, S 336-340

Bäckström, C., Jonsson, P. *Planning with Abstraction Hierarchies can be Exponentially Less Efficient*. in: Proc. 14th Int. Joint Conf. on Artificial Intelligence, Montréal, 1995, p.1599-1605

Bartsch-Spörl, B. *Ansätze zur Behandlung von fallorientiertem Erfahrungswissen in Expertensystemen*. in: KI 4/87, Oldenbourg-Verlag, p.32-36, 1987

Böhm, A., Uellner, S. *Kundenspezifische Konfiguration von Telekommunikationssystemen*. in: J. Sauer, A. Günter, J. Hertzberg (Hrsg) 10. Workshop Planen und Konfigurieren, infix Verlag, p. 149-159, 1996

Brinkop, A., Laudwein, N., Maassen, R. *Routine Design for Mechanical Engineering*. in: 6th Innovative Application of AI Conference (IAAI), p. 3-13, Seattle, 1994

Brown, D.C., Chandrasekaran,B. *Design Problem Solving* Pitman, Research Notes in AI, 1989

Buchheit, M., Klein, R., Nutt,W. *Configuration as Model Construction: The Constructive Problem Solving Approach*. in: J. Gero & F. Sudweeks (Hrsg.), Artificial Intelligence in Design, Kluwer Academic Press, 1994

Cunis, R., Günter, A., Strecker, H. (Hrsg.) *Das PLAKON Buch - Ein Expertensystemkern für Planungs- und Konfigurierungsaufgaben in technischen Domänen*. Springer, 1991

DeKleer, J. *An Assumption-Based TMS*. in: Artificial Intelligence Journal, Vol. 32, p. 231-272, 1986

Dörner, H. *Konfigurieren in schwach strukturierten Domänen*. in: [Günter 95b], p. 33-38

Doyle, J.A. *A Truth Maintenance System*. in: Artificial Intelligence Journal, Vol. 12, p. 231-272, 1979

Emde, W. et al. *Interactive Configuration in KIKon*. in: P. Mertens, H. Voss (Hrsg.) Wissensbasierte Systeme '97, infix Verlag, p. 79-92, 1997

Faltings, B., Sun, K. *Computer-Aided Creative Mechanism Design*. in: Proc. IJCAI-93, p. 1451-1457, 1993

Fleichanderl, G. et al. *Configuring Large Systems using Generative Constraint Satisfaction*. in: IEEE Intelligent Systems Jul/Aug 98, p. 59-68, 1998

Friedland, P.E. *Knowledge-Based Experiment Design in Molecular Genetics*. Report STAN-CS-79-771, Stanford University, 1979

Früchtenicht, H.-W. (Hrsg.) *Technische Expertensysteme: Wissensrepräsentation und Schlußfolgerungsverfahren*. Oldenbourg, 1988

Ginsberg, M.L. *Dynamic Backtracking*. in: Journal of Artificial Intelligence Research, Vol. 1, p. 25-46, 1993

Güsgen, H.-W., Hertzberg, J. *A Perspective of Constraint-Based Reasoning*. Springer, 1992

Günter, A. Flexible *Kontrolle in Expertensystemen für Planungs- und Konfigurierungsaufgaben in technischen*. Domänen Dissertation, Universität Hamburg, 1991

Günter, A. *Verfahren zur Auflösung von Konfigurationskonflikten in Expertensystemen*. in: KI 1/93, p. 16-22, 1993a

Günter, A. *Modelle beim Konfigurieren*. in: O. Herzog et al. (Hrsg.) KI-93, Springer Verlag, p. 169-176, 1993b

Günter, A. *KONWERK - ein modulares Konfigurierungswerkzeug*. in: F. Maurer & M. M. Richter (Hrsg.) Expertensysteme 95, Kaiserslautern, infix Verlag, p. 1-18, 1995a

Günter, A. (Hrsg.) *Wissensbasiertes Konfigurieren – Ergebnisse aus dem Projekt PROKON.* infix Verlag, St. Augustin, 1995b

Günter, A., Kühn, C. *Einsatz der Simulation zur Unterstützung der Konfigurierung von technischen Systemen.* in: Mertens, Voss (Hrsg.) Expertensysteme '97, infix Verlag, p. 93-106, 1997

Günter, A., Kühn,C. *Erfahrungen beim Transfer von Konfigurierungsmethoden.* in: J. Sauer & B. Stein (Hrsg.) 12. Workshop Planen und Konfigurieren, Paderborn, Bericht Universität-GH Paderborn, p. 59-64, 1998

Haag, A. *The ATMS* – An Assumption Based Problem Solving Architecture Utilizing Specialization Relations.* Dissertation, Universität Kaiserslautern, 1995

Haag, A. *Sales Configuration in Business Processes.* in : IEEE Intelligent Systems Jul/Aug 98, p. 78-85, 1998

Hein, M. *Effizientes Lösen von Konfigurierungsaufgaben.* Dissertation, TU Berlin, 1991.

Heinrich, M. *Ressourcenorientiertes Konfigurieren.* Künstliche Intelligenz, 7 (1), p.11-15, 1993

Heinrich, M., Jüngst, E.-W. *Konfigurieren technischer Einrichtungen ausgehend von den Komponenten des technischen Prozesses: Prinzip und erste Erfahrungen.* in: F. Puppe, A. Günter (Hrsg.), Expertensysteme 93, p. 98-111, Springer Verlag, 1993.

Hotz, L. *Überlegungen zur parallelen Verarbeitung in Konfigurierungssystemen.* in: J. Sauer, A. Günter, J. Hertzberg (Hrsg.) Beiträge zum 10. Workshop „Planen und Konfigurieren, Bonn, Infix, p. 172-178, 1996

Hua, K., Smith, I., Faltings, B. *Integrated Case-Based Building Design.* in: Proc. EWCBR '93, Springer, p. 436 - 445,1993

Jüngst, W.E., Heinrich, M. *Using Resource Balacing to Configure Modular Systems.* in: IEEE Intelligent Systems Jul/Aug 98, p. 50-58, 1998

Kühn, C. *Konfigurierung von Fahrstühlen mit VT/KONWERK.* in: [Günter 95b], p. 327 - 336

Kühn, C. *Konzeption und Implementation von Modulen zur Integration funktionaler Modelle und Simulationsunterstützung in ein Konfigurierungssystem.* Diplomarbeit Fachbereich Informatik, Universität Hamburg, 1997

Linnemann, B. *Technologietransfer von KI-Methoden in Konfigurierungs-Expertensysteme.* Diplomarbeit, Hamburg, 1994

Marcus, S., Stout, J., McDermott, J. *VT: An Expert Elevator Designer That Uses Knowledge-Based Backtracking.* in: AI Magazine, Vol. Spring 88, p. 95-112, 1988

McDermott, J. *R1: A Rule-Based Configurer of Computer Systems.* in: Artificial Intelligence, Vol. 19, (1), p. 39 - 88, 1982

McGuiness, D.L., Wright, J.R. *An Industrial-Strength Description Logic-Based Configurator Platform.* in: IEEE Intelligent Systems Jul/Aug 98, p. 69-77, 1998

Navinchandra, D. *Exploration and Innovation in Design* Springer Verlag, 1991.

Neumann, B., Weiner, J. *Anlagenkonzept und Bilanzverarbeitung.* in: 3. Workshop Planen und Konfigurieren, Berlin, 1989 Arbeitspapiere GMD

Neumann, B. *KONWERK – Technologietransfer mit einem Werkzeug.* in: [Günter 95b]

Olivier, P., Nakata, K., Landon, M., McManus, A. *Analogical Representations for Mechanism Synthesis.* in: Proc. 12ᵗʰ European Conf. on Artificial Intelligence, Budapest 1996, p. 506-510

Paulokat, J., Weß, S. *Fallauswahl und fallbasierte Steuerung bei der nichtlinearen hierarchischen Planung.* in: Beiträge zum 7. Workshop Planen und Konfigurieren, Hamburg, GMD-Arbeitspapier Nr. 723, p. 109 - 120, 1993

Paulokat, J. (Hrsg.) *(A)TMS in Expert Systems.* SEKI-Report Universtät Kaiserslautern, 1992

Pfitzner, K. *Fallbasierte Konfigurierung technischer Systeme.* in: Künstliche Intelligenz (1), p. 24-30, 1993

Puppe, F. *Problemlösungsmethoden in Expertensystemen.* Springer Verlag, 1990

Richter, M.M., B. Bachmann, A. Bernardi *ARC-TEC - ein Beitrag zur wissensbasierten Unterstützung der industriellen Praxis.* in: Künstliche Intelligenz, 8 (2), p. 52-56, 1994.

Richter, M.M., A. Bernardi, C. Klauck, R. Legleitner *Akquisition und Repräsentation von technischem Wissen für Planungsaufgaben im Bereich der Fertigungstechnik.* Research Report, RR-91-23, DFKI, 1991

Richter, M.M. *Neue Aufgaben beim Planen und Konfigurieren.* in: J. Sauer, A. Günter, J. Hertzberg (Hrsg) 10. Workshop Planen und Konfigurieren, infix Verlag, p. 3-15, 1996

Schädler, K. *Ansätze zur Abhängigkeitsverwaltung in KONWERK.* in: [Günter 95b], p. 217-228, 1995

Schirp, W. *Einsatz expliziter Begründungen in einem Assistenzsystem für Konfigurierungsaufgaben.* in: J. Sauer, A. Günter, J. Hertzberg (Hrsg) 10. Workshop Planen und Konfigurieren, infix Verlag, p. 75-86, 1996

Schumann, O. Schumann, S. *Modellierung von Unschärfe in KONWERK.* in: [Günter 95b], p. 97-117

Stein, B. *Functional Models in Configuration Systems.* Dissertation, GH-Universität Paderborn, 1995

Stein, B., Curatolo, D. *Model Formulation and Configuration of Technical Systems.* in: J. Sauer, A. Günter, J. Hertzberg (Hrsg) 10. Workshop Planen und Konfigurieren, infix Verlag, p. 56-70, 1996

Stumptner, M. *An overview of knowledge-based configuration.* in: AI Com 10 (2), p. 111-126, 1997

Tank, W. *Ein produktorientierter Technologietransfer für wissensbasiertes Konfigurieren.* in: J. Sauer, A. Günter, J. Hertzberg (Hrsg) 10. Workshop Planen und Konfigurieren, infix Verlag, p. 46-54, 1996

Tong, C., Sriram, D. (Hrsg.) *Design Representation and Models of Routine Design.* Academic Press, 1992

Ulrich, K.T., Seering, W.P. *Function Sharing in Mechanical Design.* in: C. Tang & D. Sriram (Hrsg.) Artificial Intelligence in Engineering Design, Vol. II, p. 185-214, Academic Press, 1992

VDI *Methodik zum Entwickeln und Konstruieren technischer Systeme und Produkte.* VDI-Handbuch Konstruktion, Beuth Verlag, Berlin, 1993

Weß, S. *Fallbasiertes Schließen in Deutschland – Eine Übersicht.* in: KI 4/92, FBO-Verlag Baden-Baden, p.46-51, 1992

Wrigth, J.R. et al. *A Knowledge-based Configurator that Supports Sales, Engineering and Manufactiring at AT&T Network Systems.* in: AI Magazine Vol. 14, No. 3, p. 67-88, 1993

Case-Based Reasoning - Survey and Future Directions

Brigitte Bartsch-Spörl[1], Mario Lenz[2], and André Hübner[3]

[1] BSR Consulting GmbH, Wirtstrasse 38, D-81539 München Email:
brigitte@bsr-consulting.de
[2] Humboldt University, Dept. of Computer Science, Unter den Linden 6, D-10099
Berlin Email: lenz@informatik.hu-berlin.de
[3] tecInno GmbH, Sauerwiesen 2, D-67661 Kaiserslautern Email:
huebner@tecInno.com

Abstract. This paper surveys the field of case-based reasoning (CBR)
- both in science and in industrial applications. It starts with a short introduction to the essential ideas and concepts CBR is built upon. Then
follows a bit of history that is interesting for understanding the development and the current state of the field. Its main part introduces and
reviews the most important sub-fields of CBR: theoretical foundations,
CBR for document retrieval, product selection, help-desk support, diagnosis, configuration, planning, and design. In the last part, we discuss
why the field has developed rather well and will have a promising future,
particularly in new areas like self-service and e-commerce applications in
the world wide web.

1 What is Case-Based Reasoning?

Case-Based Reasoning (CBR) is an approach to develop knowledge-based systems that are able to retrieve and reuse solutions that have worked for similar
situations in the past.

This sounds - and is - simple but deserves some explanations of what are
the prerequisites, the essential steps, and the differences compared to other approaches for building knowledge-based systems. The first and most important
prerequisite is a collection of experiences, embodied in so-called cases, and stored
in a case base. Every single *case* consists at least of a problem description part,
called the problem, and a solution description part, called the solution. These
two basic ingredients are usually enriched by an administrative part including,
e.g., a case number, an explanation or justification part that provides more information about the step from the problem to the solution, a context description
part, and an evaluation part that contains information about the quality and
reusability of the case. Moreover, there may be attachments in any format that
multi-media computer equipment is able to record, view, and play.

In addition to the case base, there may be some *general knowledge* in the
form of models or rules or constraints available and used. The case base and
the general knowledge constitute a partial domain model - with the consequence

that in general for CBR the closed world assumption does not hold. Problem solving with CBR now proceeds as follows: A new problem comes into existence and is described as the problem part of a new case, sometimes also called the query. Then, old cases containing problems that are similar to the new problem are retrieved and the most suitable one of their solutions is suggested to become the solution of the new problem. This solution is then tested in reality which may lead to a revised solution worth to be stored as a new case. This last step is a form of incremental learning that enables CBR systems to adapt to changing environments rather smoothly.

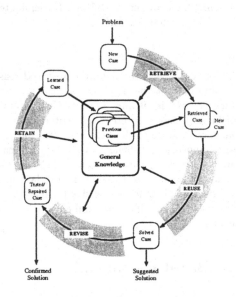

Fig. 1. The case-based reasoning process model after Aamodt and Plaza (1994)

Integrated in this CBR cycle, there are three processing steps that deserve special attention:

- The *retrieval* of cases that have a similar problem description part is something where neither relational data bases nor common information retrieval tools are good at. Therefore, the field of building case representations that are good for similarity assessment and efficient retrieval of the most similar cases in a ranked order is one of the most active areas in CBR research and due to these activities one of the best investigated areas as well.
- The *adaptation* of retrieved solutions is necessary in application domains where the solution is more than just a class name, maybe accompanied by a fixed remedy. Adaptation may range from adjusting a few parameter values according to some formulae or rules and go such far that the full range of knowledge-based problem solving is necessary. This explains why adaptation

in CBR is a topic of active research but, in spite of all insights gained, the average industrial CBR application has no sophisticated adaptation mechanisms yet.

- The *retainment* of learned cases – and the reorganisation of the case base as well – becomes important with the growth of industrial CBR applications and their case bases. There is active research in this area and there are also industrial solutions that show manual, partialy or fully automatic procedures to decide what to do with a new case and the case base as well.

The way cases are represented, the way similarity is determined, the way adaptation can be carried out and the way to decide how many cases have to be stored in order to get a good coverage of an application domain all depend on one another and influence each other deeply [37]. For example, the better the adaptation capabilities the less cases have to be stored. The more comprehensive the models of adaptation the easier similarity can be substituted by adaptability [43]. The higher the requirements for precision in case retrieval the more knowledge and modelling and specific similarity measures are needed etc.

The knowledge about these interdependencies and especially what has to be done in order to build CBR systems that meet given requirements or what has to be done in order to improve a CBR system along given lines constitutes the expertise of a rather small group of case-based reasoning specialists. In order to make the field grow and provide easier access to the necessary expertise, methodologies for how to build CBR systems have been developed and applied in practice. Thus, CBR as a simple and convincing idea has meanwhile been complemented by a technology that is similarly easy to apply.

2 A Bit of History

2.1 The Pioneers

First we have to point out that the roots of the idea to write computer programs that try to use old cases to support problem solving in similar situations go back to Roger Schank [40] and Janet Kolodner [22] who developed models and built research prototypes inspired from cognitive science research that, e.g., reuse scripts from former cases for behaving adequately in new situations. Also, the term case-based reasoning was coined there.

All this was completely unknown to Brigitte Bartsch-Spörl when she started a technical expert system project for Volkswagen in Wolfsburg in early 1987. This project would have become a clear failure unless she would not have watched the experts there solving new problems by reusing their experience from similar problems in the past and would not have tried to support this approach to problem solving by a software system that was built by means of a knowledge engineering environment embedded in Lisp. Thus, a first industrial case-based decision support system was developed and became well accepted by its users without a long history in research or many generations of throw-away prototypes.

The result of this project had only one drawback: it had to be kept secret – at least as long as the system had been in operation.

In order to communicate the idea and its clear benefits compared to other knowledge engineering approaches, the approach was moved to another domain and a first short article about the essential ideas and insights appeared in the German AI magazine in autumn 1987 [8]. The article was part of the practitioner's corner and published without the usual scientific reviews – otherwise it would have never been printed. These few pages found an unusual amount of readers and active interest – both from practitioners who made very similar experiences and also from some scientists who were attracted by the plausibility of the approach.

Among those scientists were Stefan Wess and Klaus-Dieter Althoff at the University of Kaiserslautern. In late 1987, they started their research work in CBR and gained first practical experiences with case-based approaches to the diagnosis of CNC machines [47, 4]. Within a few years, the group around Michael M. Richter at the University in Kaiserslautern became one of the most renowned centres of CBR expertise world wide. They were and are involved in nearly all important European joint research projects that focus on CBR, such as INRECA I, INRECA II, WebSell and many others. Characteristic for their activities is the combination of sound theoretical concepts with the ambition to get these concepts running by means of solid software engineering approaches. This way of doing research produces both scientific progress and practical experience in a rather short time.

Another important centre for CBR evolved at the German research centre for computer science GMD in Sankt Augustin. In Thomas Christaller's group, Angi Voss, Barbara Becker and a long list of other GMD researchers did pioneering research work and were the driving forces behind the rather big joint research project FABEL that was partially sponsored from 1992 till 1996 by the German ministry for research and technology. FABEL dealt with integrating CBR with other knowledge engineering approaches in an architectural design domain [15].

Since about 1992, Hans-Dieter Burkhard and Mario Lenz from Humboldt University in Berlin have worked on CBR and meanwhile they have become a major player in the CBR community. Mario Lenz' first CBR system was Ca-BaTA, a travel arrangement advisor that was very easy to understand for non-CBR-experts and that provided a case base that is still in use for demonstration purposes in several CBR tools. CaBaTA had follow-up systems in other application domains and since about 1995 the Berlin group is renowned for their case retrieval nets (CRNs), their textual CBR approaches [30] and internet applications e.g. for the selection of last minute travels [24].

2.2 How the CBR Approach Grew Up

During the pioneer days, the enthusiasm of the case-based reasoners was contrasted by a certain disregard from researchers that followed more classical AI approaches and had lots of good reasons why case-based reasoning is somewhat questionable from a scientific point of view. The certainty that CBR really works in practice prevented us from giving up too early – but during the first years it did not help us very much in getting CBR papers accepted at the established AI conferences. So we had little other choice than to found our own community. In Germany, this happened immediately after a first workshop on CBR that attracted more participants than we ever dreamed of. From this day in September 1991 there has been a group of persons feeling responsible for the development of the field and enabling its growth in various ways. For example, since then there have been national workshops every year. In November 1993, the first European CBR workshop took place and since 1995 there is an international conference held every two years and a European workshop in the year in between. A good example for being meanwhile accepted within the AI community was the IJCAI best paper award for two CBR researchers from Ireland [44]. For the intra community communication between these workshops and conferences there are two electronic newsletters and CBR homepages in the web, the first one is made in Kaiserslautern and the second one in Salford, UK.

But the scientific progress is only one side of the CBR coin. On the other side, there are companies like Inference in the US that since the early nineties develop CBR tools for mainly help-desk applications and have turned this into a profitable business and world-wide market leadership. In Europe, the European Commission partially sponsored two projects called INRECA I and II that enabled AcknoSoft in Paris and tecInno in Kaiserslautern to improve and apply their CBR tools in a way that they are now able to face the competition with Inference and even able to win. AcknoSoft's KATE tools are used mainly in technical diagnosis applications whereas tecInno's CBR Works family of products is heavily used in E-Commerce applications in the web.

A very important characteristic of the CBR field are the close personal relationships between CBR research institutions and CBR tool providers and consulting companies. The applications made, e.g., in the INRECA project were good sources for delivering feedback and new challenges to the researchers and the tool development companies involved could profit from the results of research in a very short time. In principle, there is no better way of transferring knowledge than by offering the developer of an innovative CBR research component his/her first job after leaving the university. Thus knowledge transfer happens at certain places preferably through people who bring their scientific work to a point where it runs in practice and helps users to solve problems quicker and better than without the tool.

3 State of the Art in Case-Based Reasoning

This chapter tries to give a short but comprehensive overview of what can be regarded as the current state of the art in case-based reasoning. We will have a certain bias in presenting mostly European achievements, systems, and applications not only because we are closer to these developments but also because we are convinced that they are representative for the state of the art on an international level. The sequence of sub chapters starts with theoretical foundations and then goes along the most important problem classes where CBR is appropriate for supporting the reuse of experience. These problem classes are somewhat ordered by increasing complexity of underlying models which means on the other hand increasing effort for building applications and decreasing numbers applications really built and fielded. We start the parade with CBR for text document retrieval, then follows CBR for product selection tasks, help-desk problem solving support, diagnosis tasks, configuration tasks and end with planning and design.

3.1 Some Theoretical Foundations of CBR

Similarity of Cases: Similarity in CBR is an attempt to model how useful a previous case is for solving the actual problem at hand. In fact, one has to struggle with a kind of paradox: a case should be considered as similar to the current problem, if the solution of that case can (easily) be reused for the problem. But, in general, this can only be determined *after* one has tried to reuse that solution! The paradox is resolved by assuming that the more similar a previous case is to the current problem at hand, the more useful the solution of that case will be. So, in fact, not similarity of cases is of interest but the similarity of the problem description of a former case to the problem description of an actual problem. Depending on the knowledge representation used, a number of standard measures exist which can be used when implementing a CBR system [48, 11].

The Knowledge Container View on CBR: Each of the four phases retrieve, reuse, revise, and retain of the so-called R4 model (see figure 1) is a kind of *container* for a number of refined techniques that might be used to implement it. Retrieve, for example, includes the identification of the relevant features, the search through the case memory, the calculation of the similarity values, and the selection of the most similar cases. The search itself can again be implemented by a number of alternative techniques, such as indexing, linear search, special search structures and so on. This is known as the *task-method decomposition model* [1].

The so-called knowledge container model has been introduced by [37]. It is particularly useful for describing what kind of knowledge can be incorporated in a CBR system and how these components interact (see also [38]). A knowledge container is used to take knowledge of a certain structure. For example, in traditional rule-based systems there are three containers, namely facts, rules, and an inference engine.

In Case-Based Reasoning, four major containers can be identified:

- the *vocabulary* used to describe cases;
- the *similarity measure* used to compare cases;
- the *case base*, or case memory, containing all the stored cases;
- the *adaptation knowledge* required for transferring solutions.

There is no strict separation between these four containers with respect to the overall problem solving task. That is, each container can, in principle, carry any piece of knowledge and provide this for solving the problem at hand. For example, when having a complete case base (i.e. a case base in which each potential case is stored), one would need neither a similarity measure (this could be reduced to identity) nor adaptation knowledge. In fact, the entire system could be implemented as a traditional database.

Methods for Case Retrieval: In recent years, a number of techniques have been developed that can be used to implement the retrieval task, i.e. the search for cases similar to a query, including:

- *kd-trees* combine CBR and induction and, thus, allow for a similarity-based retrieval based on decision trees [48]. A major advantage of that approach is that CBR methods can seamlessly be integrated with inductive learning techniques [5]. This appears to be particularly useful for diagnostic tasks [32, 28].
- The *Fish-and-Shrink* model developed within the FABEL project [39], [15] appears to be particularly useful for domains in which highly structured cases have to be dealt with, such as in design [12].
- The model of *Case Retrieval Nets*, on the other hand, is best suited for domains with simpler case representations but can efficiently deal with huge case bases [29] which is essential in E-Commerce applications [50]. Also, the flexibility of the CRN model allows it to be used for highly unstructured cases such as in textual CBR (see below).

Each of these techniques has its specific properties, advantages, and shortcomings. When designing a particular CBR system, the domain has to be carefully analysed in order to figure out which retrieval method is best suited.

Adaptation of Cases: When having retrieved cases similar to a given query, these cases will hardly ever be directly applicable as there will be differences between the cases' problem descriptions and that of the actual query. Hence, the solutions that had been applied to the cases have to be adjusted accordingly which is referred to as adaptation. In the general case, adaptation falls into the same problem class as knowledge-based problem solving. But in practice, there are situations where adaptation is a lot easier to achieve and can be seen as and solved by e.g. parameter adjustment according to rules and formulae or configuration methods according to rules and constraints [10].

3.2 CBR for Document Retrieval

Traditionally, CBR has been applied mainly to structured data where cases can be represented by means of feature vectors, graphs etc. But, given that people prefer to use natural language for storing their experiences or querying an information system, and that CBR is concerned with reusing prior experiences for problem solving, the question arises how CBR can deal this knowledge.

Know How Documents: A particular promising area is knowledge management based on so-called know how documents, i.e. documents that contain knowledge about a specific application, such as collections of frequently asked questions (FAQs), news group files, or manuals [30, 26]. The information contained in these documents cannot be handled by traditional information retrieval methods. This is true because simple keyword matching or statistics about word frequencies do not provide sufficient insight into the meanings associated to terms, such as product names and error codes. Also, knowledge about the structure of the domain cannot be taken into account. Likewise, it would be unrealistic to attempt to build a highly complex model, such as an ontology based on which a natural language processing tool could work. Even if one could provide this, users would still query the system using natural language expressions without really keeping to some rigid grammar.

Textual CBR: A more promising approach is to consider the existing documents as cases, the requests by users as queries, and then to apply CBR for finding the most relevant documents for a given query. A number of alternative techniques for this have been developed in recent years [27]. We will describe here in some detail the CBR-Answers system developed in co-operation between tecInno and the Humboldt University.

CBR-Answers is a tool that is particularly suitable for hotline support and help-desk applications. The idea is to analyse existing know how documents, such as FAQs, in such a way that for a user's query the most relevant documents can be identified. For this, a number of knowledge layers will be used each of which contains a specific type of knowledge about the particular application domain [25]. In particular, no case-authoring process is required as the existing documents are directly utilised and analysed by a parser which converts the textual documents to the internal case representation. However, CBR-Answers is not a stand-alone system in the sense that it is directly applicable to a new domain. Rather, it requires customisation with respect to interfaces, data structures, and the knowledge layers. An example of this will be given in the following description of the Simatic Knowledge Manager.

The Simatic Knowledge Manager: Siemens is selling a wide range of automation systems within its SIMATIC program world-wide. Subsidiaries of Siemens as well as other companies are engaged in repairing and maintaining this equipment. To support technicians when trying to solve problems at the customer's side, Siemens has a hotline for customer support which answers telephone calls. Also, web pages are used increasingly for providing information to customers and technicians, such as updates of drivers or news about the latest products.

To further improve this service, Siemens decided to implement an *automatic hotline* in the sense that external technicians are referred to a set of FAQs and related documents before they consider calling the telephone hotline. In order to efficiently find related information in the huge amount of documents available, the CBR-Answers system has been selected for implementing an intelligent search engine working on textual documents provided by the hotline. A major objective of the automatic hotline on behalf of Siemens is to achieve call avoidance, i.e. to avoid that hotline staff is bothered again and again with problems that have been solved before. Instead, the hotline should only be contacted in case of truly difficult, previously unsolved problems.

An analysis of the domain revealed that there are six different types of documents that should be used in the Simatic Knowledge Manager. Each of these document types is being used for a specific context, such as FAQs, information about downloadable software, or about updates of components. Also, the contents of the knowledge layers have been specified, for example to represent the product structure and the relationships among the various products [13].

The first version of the Simatic Knowledge Manager, available to internal users only, had been installed at Siemens in March 1998. The Internet version went online in June 1998. At that time, the system handled approximately 7,500 German documents. A first CD-ROM had been shipped in April 1998 at the Industrial Fair in Hanover. In August 1998 an English version was published.

Related Applications: Besides the Simatic Knowledge Manager there are similar applications in use, e.g. the FAllQ system at LHS for retrieving technical documents in a help-desk environment and the ExperienceBook system for the computer system administrators of the Humboldt University.

In general, we see a good application potential for this kind of CBR approach in situations where relevant trouble shooting knowledge in a technical domain has been documented in thousands of text documents and where it would be too expensive to convert these text documents to more structured cases. Moreover these textual CBR applications can have a very simple and intuitive user interface which is very quickly and well accepted by naive computer users.

3.3   CBR for Product Selection Tasks in E-Commerce Environments

Due to the wide-spread availability of the world wide web, electronic commerce applications are becoming more and more important [50]. Generally speaking, three sub-areas of E-Commerce can be distinguished:

Pre-Sales: providing the customer with information about a product or service
Sales: negotiation about products and services as well as the actual selling process
After-Sales: customer support when problems in using the products are encountered

The Need for Intelligent Support: CBR can play a key role in all three phases. In particular during pre-sales, CBR methods can be used for implementing a more intelligent interface that can cope with the customers' needs. What does this mean in practice? As long as there is only a fairly limited number of products in an E-Commerce application, it is sufficient to list all these on a web page and possibly to include some kind of structuring according to product groups etc. If, however, there is a large number of products then some kind of query interface is required by means of which a customer can enter his/her requirements and search the product database for an appropriate offer. Given this, three principle situations might occur:

- The customer might know precisely what s/he is looking for and how this specific product is referred to in the product database. Also, this product is available. Then, the customer will be lucky as s/he has found directly what s/he was looking for.
- The customer might still have a precise desire but either s/he does not know what the name of the product is in the database or the product may be currently out of stock.
- Often situations occur in which customers do not know precisely what they are looking for. Rather, they have some kind of need they want to fulfil and a more or less vague idea of what the solution might look like.

Standard database technology has in particular problems in dealing with the last two situations. Either the customer is overwhelmed with hundreds of offers or s/he is left alone with no solution at all [51].

Obviously, neither of these situations is satisfying. Rather, some kind of *knowledge* is required in order to suggest alternative products and to infer from the customers' needs which products might be appropriate. This knowledge has to be represented and dealt with in addition to the product database.

The Virtual Travel Agency: A major problem in the daily business of travel agents is the handling of *last minute offers*, i.e. tour packages that become available only some days prior to the departure date and that can be purchased for a reduced price. Every day, up to 6,000 of such offers are released just by one of the major German tour providers; during peak season there are sometimes 250,000 tour packages available. Hence, it should be clear that appropriate tools are required for dealing with these. Furthermore, a simple database of all tour packages would not suffice as it is unlikely that the desires of a customer can be fulfilled all at once. Rather, appropriate alternatives have to be suggested in the sense of alternative departure dates, neighbouring airports, or even other destinations. As this knowledge can be represented in a straightforward manner by means of similarity relationships, CBR is a promising approach for the implementation of a system that will rank the available offers with respect to how well they fit the users' needs.

As a consequence, a system that can be considered as a direct successor of the CaBaTA system [24] has been built. Based on the data provided by the tour operators, a case base is constructed in which each case can be represented as a simple feature vector. Similarity of cases can be determined based on the similarity of destinations, departure airports, departure dates, comfort classes and the like. Based on a common-sense understanding of the domain, building an initial similarity model had been straightforward. This model had then been refined by the travel agents who actually run the system. To be able to efficiently deal with the huge number of offers, the model of case retrieval nets has been used internally to implement the search for the most appropriate offers.

The Virtual Travel Agency went online [1] in March 1997. It offers most of the services provided by travel agents over the WWW, including flights, car rentals, and information about destinations and the climate. In the very heart of the system, however, is the last minute server. From March 1997 to July 1998 about 500,000 search requests were processed and approximately 1,400 tour packages had been booked.

Related Applications: Meanwhile there are lots of similar applications available on the WWW, some of these applications have "real CBR inside" like e.g. Analog Devices system for finding the most appropriate operational amplifiers or travel advisors for various travel agencies. Other applications are rather "CBR look-alikes" working inside of credit card or car or computer equipment selection applications in the web.

We think that smart support for product selection tasks in the web is an area where CBR and CBR look-alikes are of use in very many applications. Therefore, we expect that functionality of this kind will become a natural part of those E-Commerce systems that can deal with a bit more complicated products to buy or to sell over the web. For the really complex products, CBR should preferably be used in combination and co-operation with a full product configuration system.

3.4 CBR for Help-Desk Applications

Essentially, CBR help-desk applications are diagnosis applications for technical equipment usually manufactured in large numbers and used by people whose area of expertise is not the maintenance of their equipment. The large numbers of the same or very similar pieces of equipment raise the probability that occurring problems are in fact re-occurring problems and that solutions found and documented once can be reused again and again. This reuse factor is very important for all return on investment calculations in this area.

Additional requirements come from the fact that the equipment users are no experts and can often give only incomplete and not always correct information about the state of their equipment and that human help-desk agents are to appear as experienced and competent partners even if they are rather new in their job. The main focus in this situation lies on decision support – what is to be done in the current situation – and not so much on finding precise causes and explanations for the problem.

There are CBR tools available that are exactly tailored to this kind of situation. With these tools, a case is usually described by a first observed symptom and a question and answer dialogue about additional findings and facts. The solution consists normally of a short piece of text that can be easily communicated

---

[1] http://www.reiseboerse.com

via telephone but it might also come with a drawing, a picture or even a video. The CBR help-desk tools provide a user interface that gives even rather new help-desk agents the feeling that the system gives guidance and is knowledgeable and supportive especially in situations where they have no own experience at hand.

Some Application Examples: As there are many articles around about successful CBR help-desk applications for, e.g., Compaq, IBM, HP, 3Com and a lot of other high tech companies, we will not go further into one of these widely known success story here. In Germany, there is also an impressive list of customers using mainly the CBR tools from Inference or tecInno for telecommunication and computer hardware, software and network problems.

Why is there no Exponential Growth in this Area? For many years, help-desk applications were the area where the largest number of CBR system users could be found. These applications are still around and growing – but with less speed than all the other WWW applications. These differences in system building time and effort have to do with the fact that the knowledge for giving good travel package selection advice can be acquired much more quickly and easily than the knowledge for giving advice for Windows NT problems in different software and hardware environments. In spite of the existence of CBR tools that are especially tailored for such help-desk situations, the case acquisition is still a mostly manual process requiring experienced project team members on both sides, CBR case engineers as well as equipment trouble shooting experts. In the US, there are firms that offer collections of trouble shooting cases for the most commonly used PC software and local network packages. But as these case bases are rather expensive and their quality is hard to judge before having bought and used it, this essentially good idea for reducing the case acquisition effort didn't really take off, at least not till now.

Self-Service over the WWW is a Better Solution: We think that help-desk applications will continue to be build during the next few years especially by mayor telecom and PC software and hardware firms. But there is a trend visible towards using the WWW for offering self-service applications instead because this is much cheaper for the firm and more comfortable for the user who becomes independent from service hours, occupied telephone lines and endless waiting music. A good example for this trend was set by Broderbound with after-sales service solutions for their computer games. Only through such WWW self-service offerings they are able to master the inevitable peaks of demand for help-desk support at Christmas time or when new games are released. Other firms offering e.g. free PC help-desk support are working towards similar solutions and we hope that the good experiences from these cases will be reused by others many times in the future.

3.5 CBR for Diagnosis Tasks

The help-desk applications described in the last section constitute an important part of the topic CBR for diagnosis tasks. But there are also other diagnostic application domains, e.g. in medicine [16] and in troubleshooting of more complex machines than PCs [28]. Therefore, we will give a short overview of these other diagnostic tasks and applications here.

CBR Applications in Medicine: Lothar Gierl and his group recognised very early that case-based reasoning is especially adequate for medical diagnosis because

— it is cognitively adequate which means that medical doctors just work that way
— the experience embodied in cases is explicit and therefore easy to understand and to control
— it allows to use both subjective and objective knowledge in combination and
— cases in the form of patient records are widely available in modern clinical information systems.

But besides these good reasons to use CBR in medicine, there are also some serious obstacles:

— multiple disorders deserve special attention and treatment because they occur very often in medical cases
— doctors and nurses do not have much time to sit down and interact with a system before they have to decide about a patient's treatment and
— a diagnostic system has to be integrated into the existing information systems in a hospital and get from there all relevant data for the patient, available resources for the treatment etc.

To overcome these obstacles means to develop special variants of CBR, to find efficient ways of interacting with such a system and to avoid stand-alone CBR systems in favour of CBR components integrated into clinical information and administration systems.

The group around Lothar Gierl, formerly in Munich and now in Rostock, has built a couple of systems that have found their way to daily use in the hospital. Among these systems is GS.52 [17] for the diagnosis of dysmorphic syndromes, a rather rare disease with many varying symptoms that initiated the development of a prototype-based reasoning approach. Another application, called COSYL, gives case-based advice for the treatment of liver-transplanted patients and the ICONS system acts as an antibiotics therapy advisor for intensive care patients.

CBR Applications in Machine Diagnosis: Michel Manago and his colleagues at AcknoSoft in Paris have built CBR systems that are good examples for how to diagnose complex technical equipment. One of the best documented systems in the CBR literature is the CASSIOPEE system for troubleshooting a type of engines that is widely used for Boeing and Airbus planes [20]. Another example is the LADI system for troubleshooting robots that unload plastic injection machines. Both applications are built on top of the KATE tools and use a hybrid approach that combines induction of decision trees with case-based reasoning in rather flexible ways. Also common to both applications is that they were started during a project partially sponsored by the European community and, therefore, the information about these projects is publicly available, at least to a certain degree. Besides these two applications, there is a long list of similar projects fully paid by the manufacturers of complex equipments like diesel engines, trains or aircrafts where the information is less freely available.

But in summary, there is no doubt that CBR is doing a good job in these technical diagnosis domains and that this topic has left the research area and changed to a normal software business area.

3.6   CBR for Configuration

Up to this point we have discussed different sorts of analytic CBR application domains. For all these analytic problems, the solution usually consists of something rather simple like a defect together with its remedy, an entry in a product catalogue, or a disease with an adequate treatment. In contrast to these analytic tasks, there are the so-called synthetic tasks. The term synthetic stands for the need to build up a solution from parts – mostly obeying to a set of domain specific construction rules. Particularly characteristic features for CBR approaches in synthetic domains are the following ones:

- It is very unlikely that a former solution can be taken over without changes. From this arises the necessity to provide at least a certain level of adaptation capabilities.
- Due to different aspects involved and the overall complexity of the cases, it is less easy to rank solutions of similar problems according to their utility for the problem at hand. Therefore, additional criteria like "minimal adaptation effort" or "minimal risk of adaptation failures" become more interesting than pure similarity.
- General knowledge usually plays an important role because it is an necessary prerequisite for the adaptation of former solutions and for assessing the quality of several candidate solutions.

The synthetic tasks are usually subdivided into configuration (this section), planning and design (next section).

Characteristic for configuration problems is that

- all parts are known in advance
- the rules and constraints of how the parts can be combined are also known in advance
- it can be determined whether an intermediate solution fulfils the actual requirements and

– it is possible to solve these problems with algorithms that systematically search through the solution space.

This means that for configuration problems it is possible to construct a full model and to apply other knowledge-based problem solving methods as well - with the consequence that CBR for configuration tasks stands in competition with complete configuration systems that are available and used in growing numbers.

The benefit of using CBR for configuration lies in the fact that CBR can deliver very quickly a former solution that contains about 90% of what is needed. The remaining 10% have to be achieved by an adaptation component that can range from something rather simple to a full configuration from scratch system. The "simplistic approach" allows to build CBR configuration systems with rather little effort – but for the price that not always the optimal solution is constructed. The "perfectionistic approach" makes only sense if the shortcuts obtained by using CBR save more effort than the additional CBR part requires for being built and being used.

Some Examples for CBR Configuration Systems Built: This last sentence may be the reason why there are not very many applications available that use CBR for configuration problems. One of the first industrial CBR systems was CLAVIER [7], a CBR system for designing loads for an autoclave. Its developers reported about some acceptance problems by the experts that give reason to believe that the CLAVIER domain is an open world problem and belongs – according to our classification criteria – to innovative design and not to configuration. COMPOSER [36] can be either regarded as a CBR system that uses a full constraint system for adaptation or as a constraint system that uses former cases a starting point. The system has been used for sequencing electric motor assemblies. Our last example for CBR configuration systems develops recipes for the production of mash in brewing [3] without any user assistance. From the structure of its outcome, it can also be regarded as a closed planning system.

In summary, CBR for configuration tasks is a good idea for the efficient automation of problem solving in synthetic closed world domains. It is a pity that only very few people seem to make use of it.

3.7 CBR for Planning and Design

The last and most complex class of problems CBR approaches can be applied to are planning and design. In planning, there is an established distinction between

– closed planning problems that can be modelled completely and solved by algorithms with predictable behaviour and
– open planning problems where only some modelling is feasible and as a consequence of this partial modelling neither the solvability of the problem nor the effort necessary to find acceptable solutions are clear in advance.

In analogy to this distinction, design problems are classified as

- routine design problems that correspond to closed planning problems and are essentially the same as configuration problems (see Section 3.6)
- innovative design problems that correspond to open planning problems and contain at least certain non-routine elements that defy proper modelling and
- creative design problems where no systematic approach can be made and solutions are usually not based on former experience but on creativity and good luck.

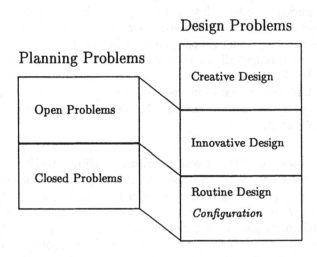

Fig. 2. The ordering of design tasks and the equivalence to planning problems

As presented in detail in [52], CBR is not able to support creative design tasks because the approach is not able to invent new kinds of artefacts. What remains to be supported are closed planning and routine design tasks where CBR approaches have to compete with algorithms that solve the problem from scratch and open planning or innovative design tasks where CBR approaches offer a good chance to receive at least a certain degree of problem solving and assessment of solutions support. The benefit of trying CBR approaches for planning and design problems at all lies in the fact that with CBR, shortcuts from the problem to the solution are possible and that these shortcuts can save a remarkable amount of time and effort. In open world application domains, CBR components typically act as a planning or design assistant and leave the full responsibility about what to (re-)use from former solutions to the user.

Some Examples for CBR Systems Built in Planning and Design: As planning and design problems are not easy to solve resp. to support adequately, there is still a lot of research in this area and only very few prototypes are or have been in practical use.

Worth to mention are some domain-independent case-based planning systems from research institutions like PRODIGY/ANALOGY [45], CAPlan/CbC [34] and PARIS [9]. PRODIGY/ANALOGY combines generative and case-based planning in a way that considerably enhances the overall efficiency of the system. This system has been successfully applied to a transportation logistics domain. CAPlan/CbC enhances a first-principles-planner by a CBR component and thus achieves significant reductions in time and effort for solving tool selection problems in a manufacturing scenario. PARIS investigates the use of abstract cases on several levels of abstraction. This system has also been applied to the tool selection domain and the empirical studies show not only a significant reduction of the effort needed for problem solving but also an interesting increase in the flexibility to reuse one case for many new problems.

Numerous case-based design aids have been built till now, many of these systems deal with architectural design, such as ARCHIE [14], CADRE [21] or FABEL [46]. ARCHIE has been a first try that mainly showed how complex the domain really is and that CBR alone will be of little help. CADRE studied case-based adaptation in a CAD environment but the solutions were a bit hard to explain and showed some lack of profound background knowledge. FABEL combined a set of tools for retrieval, construction, and adaptation for users that like to experiment and are able to judge the outcome of the tools. Today we can say that it is state of the art that in complex design domains CBR has to be used in integration with model-based approaches like this has been done e.g. in KRITIK [18], DOM-ARCADE [6] and EADOCS [35]. KRITIK was the first system that combined case-based with model-based reasoning in order to design physical devices. DOM-ARCADE uses a domain ontology derived from a methodology of how to build technical installations for heating, ventilating etc. as a basis for case-based assessment, adaptation and construction aids. EADOCS is a hybrid system for aircraft panel design that combines a case-based approach with existing numerical techniques for assessing the quality of a solution.

We can conclude that the more complex an application domain is the more it is necessary to combine CBR approaches with other proven methods of problem solving in order give comprehensive support to the users. There are no questions left about the feasibility of such combinations and that CBR can significantly shorten the path to an adequate solution. Still missing in this area are ambitious industrial projects with partners that are aware that the way will be long and steep but worthwhile to go.

4 Some Reasons Why the Field is Still Alive and Moving Forward

Compared to other groups in the AI community, the CBR field had relatively little ups and downs and till today no real crisis. For this robustness against promises that do not come true, conceptions that turn out to be misconceptions, failures that inevitably happen etc. we think there is a bundle of reasons we will discuss in the following sections.

4.1 Acceptance of the "Defects" of the Real World

Unlike most other sub fields of AI, CBR does *not* assume that the world - and accordingly all models we are making of the world - is ideal in a sense that it is reliably stable, complete, and consistent. Many AI scientists are both rationally convinced and believe from the bottom of their heart that you cannot do anything serious without relying on these assumptions. From a theoretical point of view, they may be right – it just does not help to solve practical problems in application domains that cannot be modelled with logic-based knowledge representation formalisms. Our – practically proven – truth is that you can do something – you only have to be aware that you cannot guarantee that the results of your reasoning process are always correct. And from the moment you have grasped this essential difference you can start to deal with application domains where other – more formal – approaches have failed and build applications that are as imperfect as the models they are based upon – but nevertheless they are useful and save their users time and money. Therefore one of the main reasons for the field being successful is that CBR has a real market niche in applications that are reluctant to logically sound modelling efforts.

4.2 A Sense of Community

It is a well known phenomenon that enemies from the outside world strengthen the coherence of a group. This effect was recognisable in the very early days of AI when all the world laughed at these crazy guys who started out to build intelligent machines. For the CBR community this phenomenon could also be recognised during the early years but it was less strong and disappeared while the field became more and more accepted. Since about 1993 there exists the idea of forming a European CBR network. This idea is – in spite of several trials – till today not supported by the European Community but in spite of this lack of official organisation an informal network has evolved that is constituted by people who got to know each other during workshops, then wrote joint proposals for European projects and finally are or have been working together in such projects. We think that especially in Germany we have managed to give priority to co-operation and to a sort of competition that is healthy for the progress of the field. In Germany even the small CBR firms co-operate – which is not always easy and natural but in the end more beneficial for all sides than resource consuming competition.

4.3 Some Real Champions

Seen from another perspective, the CBR community is also held together by a group of people that are real champions in their field. Around such champions evolve CBR groups and projects and applications and even at rather "poor" universities after a few years the outcome of results has an international visibility. A similar or even bigger amount of championship is necessary and invested by the people who are building up the CBR firms from rather small amounts of money to invest and just a few employees to a size where complex CBR projects can be carried out and important customers have been won. Success in our field is – from our personal experience – not so much a matter of good luck but rather a matter of the right mixture of talents, a strong belief in the reachability of goals and a lot of hard work.

4.4 Applying CBR to Itself: Learning from Experience

We think there is another element that also contributes to the progress of the field: CBR people can gain efficiency from using the principles of the CBR approach for their own work. Of course, very many people outside the field use similar approaches in a way that they systematically collect and exchange experience but most of them do this without a clear strategic view, with less stress on documenting the solutions in a way that they are reusable for others and without adequate software support. Just one recent example is a web site[2] where everybody can retrieve CBR systems that have solved a problem that is similar to his problem at hand. The systems are both described by their main characteristic features and accompanied by written experiences from their development and usage.

5 Perspectives for the Future

It is never easy to make good predictions of what will happen in the future. But based on a few trends have been around for some time already [42] we will use this last section to point out what we expect that will happen in and with case-based reasoning in the future.

5.1 Self-Service Applications in the Web

An important current and future trend is offering more service without having to increase the service personnel accordingly. As the ways and means to get service people more productive are limited, the best idea around is to build self-service applications and let the customer solve his/her PC problem or select the right sort of birthday present on his/her own. There are quite a number of these applications already in use. Good examples for self-service problem solving are the CBR application of Lucas Arts for computer game users or Siemens Automation and Drives for plant maintenance technicians. In E-Commerce scenarios, there are both real CBR applications e.g. for selling travels or computer equipment or electronic parts and some CBR look-alikes e.g. for selling cars or credit cards. The user interfaces of these web applications become animated sometimes more quickly than the necessary data transport capacities grow. This enables the CBR system developers to model and present solutions in many other forms than plain text, e.g. illustrated with pictures, sound, video or even with a virtual 3D service technician or salesman.

---

[2] http://www.iese.fhg.de/Competences/QPE/QE/CBR-PEB.html

5.2 Solutions Become Active (Repair) Agents

Another important trend is the wish to deliver as a solution not only information what the customer should do in order to solve his service problem but to send an active repair agent in order to assist the customer through problem solving and in the extreme case – e.g. when the repair action consists of activating a program or installing a piece of new software – to let the agent just fix the problem. There are projects underway where such solutions are aimed for. As this is a rather innovative field, the firms don't like to have to too much information distributed yet.

5.3 CBR will Become More and More Invisible

In summary, we see good perspectives for all typical CBR problems around to get solved – but we are much less optimistic about the survival of the term case-based reasoning or the technology as a clearly identifiable part of a system. This has to do with the fact that case-based reasoning is much more useful in the role of a component in an integrated system than as a stand-alone application. Such components often get new and different names from marketing people and in case of success they become "cloned" by competitors and in the end it will be difficult to see from the outside whether a system has the original "CBR inside". We think that this fate is inevitable for technologies that have proven to be useful and capable of being integrated into more comprehensive application environments. It is a sign for having reached the main stream of the software industry where most small rivers do not really disappear but become invisible in the end.

Acknowledgements

This survey paper profits by work that has been carried out in the course of making the book "Case-Based Reasoning Technology" [31]. Therefore, we would like to thank all our CBR friends and companions that contributed to this book and indirectly to this survey paper as well.

References

1. A. Aamodt and E. Plaza. Case-based reasoning: foundational issues, methodological variations, and system approaches. *AI Communications*, 7(1):39–59, 1994.
2. A. Aamodt and M. Veloso, editors. *Case-Based Reasoning Research and Development, Proceedings ICCBR-95*, Lecture Notes in Artificial Intelligence, 1010. Springer Verlag, 1995.
3. R. J. Aarts and J. J. Rousu. Towards CBR for bioprocess planning. In Smith and Faltings [41], pages 16–27.
4. K.-D. Althoff. *Eine fallbasierte Lernkomponente als integrierter Bestandteil der* MOLTKE-*Werkbank zur Diagnose technischer Systeme*. PhD thesis, Dept. of Computer Science, University of Kaiserslautern, Germany, 1992.

5. E. Auriol, S. Wess, M. Manago, K.-D. Althoff, and R. Traphöner. INRECA: A seamlessly integrated system based on inductive inference and case-based reasoning. In Aamodt and Veloso [2], pages 371–380.

6. S. Bakhtari, B. Bartsch-Spörl, and W. Oertel. DOM-ARCADE: assistance services for construction, evaluation, and adaptation of design layouts. In J. S. Gero and F. Sudweeks, editors, *Artificial Intelligence in Design'96*, pages 681–699, Standford, 1996. Kluwer Academic Publishers, Dordrecht.

7. R. Barletta and D. Hennessy. Case adaptation in autoclave layout design. In K. J. Hammond, editor, *Proceedings CBR89*, pages 203 – 207. Morgan Kaufmann Publishers, 1989.

8. B. Bartsch-Spörl. Ansätze zur Behandlung von fallorientiertem Erfahrungswissen in Expertensystemen. *KI – Künstliche Intelligenz*, 1(4):32–36, 1987.

9. R. Bergmann. *Effizientes Problemlösen durch flexible Wiederverwendung von Fällen auf verschiedenen Abstraktionsebenen*. PhD thesis, Universität Kaiserslautern, 1996. Available as DISKI 138, infix Verlag.

10. R. Bergmann, H. Muñoz-Avila, M. Veloso, and E. Melis. CBR Applied to Planning. In *Case-Based Reasoning Technology – From Foundations to Applications* [31], chapter 7, pages 169–200.

11. R. Bergmann and A. Stahl. Similarity Measures for Object-Oriented Case Representations. In Smyth and Cunningham [42], pages 25–36.

12. K. Börner. CBR for Design. In *Case-Based Reasoning Technology – From Foundations to Applications* [31], chapter 8, pages 201–234.

13. K.-H. Busch. Customer Support for Siemens Products on the Internet and CD-ROM. Talk at EWCBR-98 Industry Day, 1998.

14. E. A. Domeshek and J. L. Kolodner. A case-based design aid for architecture. In J. S. Gero, editor, *Artificial Intelligence in Design '92*, pages 497–516, Pittsburgh, 1992. AID, Kluwer Academic Publishers, Dordrecht.

15. F. Gebhardt, A. Voß, W. Gräther, and B. Schmidt-Belz. *Reasoning with Complex Cases*, volume 393 of *International Series in Engineering and Computer Science*. Kluwer Academic Publishers, Boston, 1997.

16. L. Gierl, M. Bull, and R. Schmidt. CBR in Medicine. In *Case-Based Reasoning Technology – From Foundations to Applications* [31], chapter 11, pages 273–298.

17. L. Gierl and S. Stengel-Rutkowski. Integrating consultation and semi-automatic knowledge acquisition in a prototype-based architecture: Experiences with dysmorphic syndromes. *Artifical Intelligence in Medicine*, 6:29–49, 1994.

18. A. K. Goel. *Integration of Case-Based Reasoning and Model-Based Reasoning for Adaptive Design Problem Solving*. PhD thesis, Department of Computer and Information Sciences, The Ohio State University, 1989.

19. G. Görz and S. Hölldobler, editors. *KI-96: Advances in Artificial Intelligence*, Lecture Notes in Artificial Intelligence, 1137. Springer Verlag, 1996.

20. R. Heider. Troubleshooting CFM 56-3 Engines for Boeing 737 Using CBR and Data Mining. In Smith and Faltings [41], pages 512–518.

21. K. Hua, I. Smith, and B. Faltings. Exploring case-based design: CADRE. *Artificial Intelligence for Engineering Design, Analysis and Manufacturing (AI EDAM)*, 7(2):135–144, 1993.

22. J. L. Kolodner. *Retrieval and Organizational Strategies in Conceptual Memory*. Lawrence Erlbaum, Hillsdale, New Jersey, 1984.

23. D. B. Leake and E. Plaza, editors. *Case-Based Reasoning Research and Development, Proceedings ICCBR-97*, Lecture Notes in Artificial Intelligence, 1266. Springer Verlag, 1997.

24. M. Lenz. Case-based reasoning for holiday planning. In W. Schertler, B. Schmid, A. M. Tjoa, and H. Werthner, editors, *Information and Communications Technologies in Tourism*, pages 126–132. Springer Verlag, 1994.

25. M. Lenz. Defining Knowledge Layers for Textual Case-Based Reasoning. In Smyth and Cunningham [42], pages 298–309.

26. M. Lenz. Managing the Knowledge Contained in Technical Documents. In U. Reimer, editor, *Proc. Practical Aspects of Knowledge Management (PAKM-98)*, 1998.

27. M. Lenz and K. D. Ashley, editors. *Proceedings of the AAAI Workshop on Textual CBR*. AAAI, AAAI Press, 1998.

28. M. Lenz, E. Auriol, and M. Manago. Diagnosis and Decision Support. In *Case-Based Reasoning Technology – From Foundations to Applications* [31], chapter 3, pages 51–90.

29. M. Lenz and H.-D. Burkhard. Case Retrieval Nets: Basic ideas and extensions. In Görz and Hölldobler [19], pages 227–239.

30. M. Lenz and H.-D. Burkhard. CBR for Document Retrieval - The FALLQ Project. In Leake and Plaza [23], pages 84–93.

31. M. Lenz, H.-D. Burkhard, B. Bartsch-Spörl, and S. Wess. *Case-Based Reasoning Technology – From Foundations to Applications*. Lecture Notes in Artificial Intelligence 1400. Springer Verlag, 1998.

32. M. Lenz, H.-D. Burkhard, P. Pirk, E. Auriol, and M. Manago. CBR for Diagnosis and Decision Support. *AI Communications*, 9(3):138–146, 1996.

33. C. S. Mellish, editor. *Proceedings of the 14th International Conference on Artificial Intelligence IJCAI-95*, 1995.

34. H. Muñoz-Avila and F. Weberskirch. Complete eager replay. In J. Sauer, A. Günter, and J. Hertzberg, editors, *Beiträge zum 10. Workshop 'Planen und Konfigurieren' (PuK-96)*, 1996.

35. B. D. Netten. *Knowledge-based conceptual design: An application to reinforced composite sandwich panels*. PhD thesis, Faculty of Technical Mathematics and Informatics, Delft University of Technology, 1997.

36. L. Purvis and P. Pu. Adaptation using constraint satisfaction techniques. In Aamodt and Veloso [2], pages 289–300.

37. M. M. Richter. The knowledge contained in similarity measures. Invited Talk at ICCBR-95, 1995. http://wwwagr.informatik.uni-kl.de/˜lsa/CBR/Richtericcbr95remarks.html.

38. M. M. Richter. Introduction. In *Case-Based Reasoning Technology – From Foundations to Applications* [31], chapter 1, pages 1–16.

39. J. Schaaf. *Über die Suche nach situationsgerechten Fällen im fallbasierten Schließen*. DISKI 179, Universität Kaiserslautern, 1998.

40. R. C. Schank. *Dynamic Memory: A Theory of Learning in Computers and People*. Cambridge University Press, New York, 1982.

41. I. Smith and B. Faltings, editors. *Advances in Case-Based Reasoning*, Lecture Notes in Artificial Intelligence, 1186. Springer Verlag, 1996.

42. B. Smyth and P. Cunningham, editors. *Advances in Case-Based Reasoning*, Lecture Notes in Artificial Intelligence, 1488. Springer Verlag, 1998.

43. B. Smyth and M. T. Keane. Retrieving adaptable cases: The role of adaptation knowledge in case retrieval. In Wess et al. [49], pages 209–220.

44. B. Smyth and M. T. Keane. Remembering to forget. In Mellish [33], pages 377–382.

45. M. M. Veloso. *Planning and Learning by Analogical Reasoning*. Number 886 in Lecture Notes in Computer Science. Springer, Berlin, 1994.

46. A. Voß. Case reusing systems – survey, framework and guidelines. *The Knowledge Engineering Review*, 12(1):in print, 1997.

47. S. Wess. PATDEX/2: ein System zum adaptiven, fallfokussierenden Lernen in technischen Diagnosesituationen. Diploma thesis, University of Kaiserslautern, 1990.

48. S. Wess. *Fallbasiertes Problemlösen in wissensbasierten Systemen zur Entscheidungsunterstützung und Diagnostik.* PhD thesis, Universität Kaiserslautern, 1995. Available as DISKI 126, infix Verlag.

49. S. Wess, K.-D. Althoff, and M. M. Richter, editors. *Topics in Case-Based Reasoning. Proceedings of the First European Workshop on Case-Based Reasoning (EWCBR-93)*, Lecture Notes in Artificial Intelligence, 837. Springer Verlag, 1993.

50. W. Wilke. Case-based reasoning and electronic commerce. Invited Talk at ICCBR-97, 1997.

51. W. Wilke, M. Lenz, and S. Wess. Intelligent Sales Support with CBR. In *Case-Based Reasoning Technology – From Foundations to Applications* [31], chapter 4, pages 91–114.

52. W. Wilke, B. Smyth, and P. Cunningham. Using Configurations Techniques for Adaptation. In *Case-Based Reasoning Technology – From Foundations to Applications* [31], chapter 6, pages 139–168.

Meeting Re-use Requirements of Real-Life Diagnosis Applications

Thomas Guckenbiehl[1], Heiko Milde[2], Bernd Neumann[2], and Peter Struss[3]

[1] Fraunhofer-Institut IITB, Fraunhoferstr. 1, 76131 Karlsruhe, Germany
guc@iitb.fhg.de
[2] Laboratory for Artificial Intelligence, University of Hamburg,
Vogt-Koelln-Str. 30, 22527 Hamburg, Germany
milde@kogs.informatik.uni-hamburg.de
neumann@informatik.uni-hamburg.de
[3] Technische Universität München, Department of Computer Science,
Orleansstr. 34, 81667 Munich, Germany
struss@in.tum.de

Abstract. This report addresses re-use issues in computer-based diagnosis. It is shown that in order to obtain re-usable components it is useful to categorize the knowledge and software for a diagnosis system along two dimensions, generality and genericity. Several new contributions to diagnosis technology are presented which illustrate different re-use categories and show the benefits of improved re-usability. The contributions pertain to different tasks related to the diagnosis of real-life systems of diverse domains: FMEA, workshop diagnosis, generating diagnosis manuals, generating fault trees and operator assistance in post mortem diagnosis. The work has been performed by three research groups involved in the joint research project INDIA (Intelligent Diagnosis in Industrial Application).

1 Introduction

Efficient development of diagnosis equipment, use of available resources, and re-usability of software components are the main advantages which industry expects from innovative diagnosis technology. This has been the experience of the authors in several diagnosis projects with industrial partners, in particular in the joint research project INDIA (Intelligent Diagnosis in Industrial Applications). In this project, three teams, each consisting of a research institute, a software supplier, and an industrial production company, have joined to apply model-based diagnosis technology to real-life diagnosis problems and pave the way for successful applications elsewhere. The particular diagnosis problems provided by the industrial partners represented an interesting subset of industrial diagnosis applications. One application area is on-line diagnosis of automotive equipment, another one is off-line diagnosis support for transport vehicles, the third one deals with operator assistance in post mortem diagnosis of machinery.

It is well-known that model-based methods promise applications with attractive problem-solving capabilities and significant economical advantages. Reviewing the attractive features of model-based diagnosis, the main benefits are connected with the compositionality and transparency of the model, from which diagnosis knowledge can be generated. Compositionality bears the potential for re-using components, building component libraries and inheritance hierarchies, alleviating version control and easing modifications. The transparency of component-based behavior descriptions may add further benefits, including complexity management, exploitation of information from the design phase, and a large degree of compatibility with other life-cycle product data including documentation. Hence, important benefits can be gained from model-based diagnosis technology.

All this can be stated without reference to a particular diagnosis procedure. In fact, one of the insights which this report wants to convey is about possible (re-)uses of model-based techniques beyond the diagnosis procedures which are traditionally associated with model-based diagnosis.

We believe that real-life engineering applications and re-use of model-based techniques may become possible at a large scale provided the characteristics of today's diagnosis practise are taken into consideration:

- First of all, many producers of technical systems provide only limited diagnosis support of their products to begin with. There are only few large market segments where producers develop sophisticated diagnosis support (e.g. the automotive and aircraft industry). This is changing, however, as the cost of maintenance personnel becomes more important and improved service is required to remain competitive. But in many cases, the initial demand for diagnosis support will be quite modest.
- A second point to observe is the industrial tradition of employing decision trees or fault trees. These techniques have been developed from a maintenance rather than from a design perspective. Since traditionally, diagnosis matters are a concern mainly to the service division of a company, not to the design division. However, as technical systems become larger and more complicated, the design of decision trees becomes more demanding and problems arise. Furthermore, frequent product changes cause excessive costs for the maintenance of such diagnosis equipment. Hence there is growing awareness of the need for re-usability of diagnostic information.
- A third problem to cope with is the natural desire of industry to perform changes in small steps. The introduction of model-based reasoning for complete automation of diagnosis is often perceived as too different from the traditional ways of doing diagnosis. Existing know-how would become worthless and new know-how would have to be acquired. As noted above, the organizational structure would be affected, with diagnosis tasks shifting from the service to the design division.

This led us to focus our diagnosis research on ways to exploit the advantages of model-based diagnosis techniques compatible (to some degree) with existing industrial traditions and requirements.

In Section 2 we identify several different kinds of re-use and propose a classification scheme which can be generally applied to re-use phenomena in complex industrial environments. Section 3 presents new diagnosis methods for three application domains, illustrating different ways to improve re-usability. It is shown that computer-based behavior models can be used for various real-life diagnosis tasks and thus play a key part for improving re-usability of diagnosis components.

2 A Categorization for Re-use of Knowledge and Software

2.1 Different Tasks - Shared Knowledge and Skills

During the life cycle of a product, a broad range of different tasks are performed, from conceptual design via production planning to maintenance. This includes various forms of fault analysis and diagnosis, such as failure-modes-and-effects analysis (FMEA), design for diagnosability, test generation and testing, creation of on-board diagnostics, production of diagnosis guidelines, workshop diagnosis, repair and reconfiguration. Despite their different goals and conditions, many of these tasks are based on similar knowledge, information and skills which are (or ought to be) exchanged between the people and departments performing these tasks. Identifying and analyzing these shared elements is a starting point for designing computational tools in a manner that exploits re-use of these elements in an optimal way. In a knowledge-based approach, such elements are both collections of represented knowledge fragments and software components.

Obviously, information and knowledge about the subject, the technical system itself, is central to all tasks, and model-based systems reflect this explicitly. It comprises the *device structure* (the blue print) and knowledge about the *behavior of its components*, both under *normal operation* and in the presence of some *malfunction*. Furthermore, there is knowledge about the *function*, i.e. the *purpose* of a system or a particular *role* to be fulfilled by a component or subsystem. For planning and performing tests and repairs, information about the *assembly* of parts, *accessibility* of probing points, *equipment* required and the *cost* associated with the actions are important.

A fundamental reasoning skill required to exploit this knowledge (and, hence, a candidate for software procedures) is the capability to *infer global system behavior* from the structure of the device and the behavior of its components. The various diagnostic tasks require procedures for *relating observations* ("symptoms") *to hypotheses of faults*, whilst testing is based on *determining actions* that are likely to *lead to observable distinctions between different behaviors*.

Already this incomplete list of elements of knowledge and software gives some hints on their potential re-use, but it is still too coarse-grained. Applying a classification scheme which is part of a methodology for developing models and model-based systems (see [7]), we take a closer look at this list.

2.2 Classification

The first distinction is made according to the generality of the respective entities of knowledge, information, or methods:

- *physical principles*, which are fundamental and valid for all systems (devices) in a particular domain and regardless of the special task (sometimes called domain theory) e.g. Ohm's Law,
- *device-specific* (or device-type-specific) entities, i.e. knowledge and information characterizing a particular system, for instance the value of the parameter resistance of a part of the device,
- *task-specific* entities: knowledge, information, and algorithms for solving a certain type of problem, for example an algorithm for computing a decision tree based on a set of behavior models and possible measurement points.

Obviously, reflecting this distinction in the design and implementation of systems helps to re-use the physical principles for several devices and in different tasks. Of course, exploiting device information in different tasks and applying a problem solver to various devices is also a desire. This requires a systematic separation of "How" and "What" (the problem solver and its subject, that is), a principle which is central to knowledge-based systems and to model-based systems, in particular.

Our experience shows that a structuring of knowledge and information and design of software components cannot be optimal w.r.t. re-use unless at least one more, orthogonal, distinction is made. We need to separate

* *generic* knowledge and methods from
* a representation and treatment of *pragmatic* elements.

In our context, the former are related to representation of and reasoning about the abstract behavior of a system according to the "laws" of physics, while the latter reflect the particular physical implementation of a system and the preconditions imposed on a special task by the real environment. To illustrate this in the context of our work, the circuits in a car subsystem in two vehicles may have the same structure in the sense of the blueprint and include components of the same type, nevertheless differ fundamentally in how they are laid out and installed in the vehicles. This means, their behavior models are the same and will, for instance, lead to the same diagnostic candidates. However, the respective test sequences to be generated have to be different, because the accessibility of probing points varies significantly. While this is determined by the device, the actual costs of a test sequence may, furthermore, depend on the pragmatic context the task has to be performed in, for instance the equipment available in a certain type of workshop.

With respect to the scope of our work in model-based systems, we obtain the classification displayed in Table 1. It is the simplest one, in fact it is somewhat oversimplified, as already indicated by overlap between device- and task-specific pragmatic elements: the actual actions that have to be performed to carry out a test may be determined by both the physical device and the contextual constraints on a task. More caveats are discussed below. Nevertheless, an analysis along these lines already provides useful criteria for the design of knowledge representation schemes, data base structures, and modularization of software under the aspect of re-use.

2.3 Discussion

Although the distinctions made in the above analysis are fairly obvious, they are not necessarily present in current practice of product documentation, actual work processes, and traditional software systems. In fact, the scheme provides a way for analyzing the inherent limitations of different approaches to software tools for the kind of tasks considered here. Many tools for engineering tasks do not provide a clear distinction along the horizontal axis at all turning them into unique solutions, and even if they are model-based, they do not provide a method for composing the device model by re-using physical principles. Fault-tree-based diagnosis offers a general inference mechanism for processing the trees, but the trees inseparably merge component knowledge, device structure, and task knowledge including the pragmatic aspects. This is why this technology is obsolete, unless a way is provided to generate the trees from first principles as described in Section 3. But limitations become evident also for several AI techniques. Case-based systems, for instance, do not represent the principled layer and do not separate device-specific from task-specific knowledge, which also holds for neural-network-based solutions.

Table 1. Classifying knowledge and software elements

	generic	pragmatics
physical principles	behavior model fragments (component library)	
devices	structure parameters behavior (intended and faulty) state	function criticality tolerance assembly / replaceable units measurement points
		actions • measurements
tasks	model-based inference mechanisms • model composition • behavior prediction • model-based diagnosis • model-based test generation	• disassembly equipment cost
		inference mechanism reflecting pragmatics • cost-oriented test proposal / test plan generation

We would like to emphasize that the discussion clearly shows that the problem of re-use cannot be solved by means of general software engineering techniques, but requires an analysis of the problem domain at the knowledge level and then, of course, appropriate software architectures and knowledge representation facilities. This is why knowledge-based systems, Artificial Intelligence, and, in our application domain, model-based reasoning techniques promise significant progress and superiority to traditional approaches.

As a side remark should be stated that much of what we discussed does not only apply to re-use of knowledge through computer systems, but also to re-use of knowledge by humans. If knowledge is not structured and indexed appropriately, for example by mixing device and task knowledge, it is likely to be useless to a human expert who is working in a different context. This is why the solutions advocated here are also a contribution to the area of knowledge management which receives more and more attention.

Despite the fact that we will not easily find the necessary distinctions present in current practice, the analysis is not an academic one. Rather, it has a significant, if not decisive, impact on the competence and flexibility of software systems and on the cost of producing and maintaining them. Taking the classification into consideration when designing knowledge bases and software solutions will already have a tremendous effect. In our case studies, not only sharing of the component library and the device model across the three tasks could be demonstrated, also software components, such as model composition and behavior prediction, are re-used for the prototypes.

However, we have to mention that the schema presented above needs extensions, refinements, and even further research. In particular, although we may be able to identify the general principles and generate a device model from them, the result may not be appropriate in a particular context:

- The *task* may influence the granularity of the *behavior* model. While a qualitative model may do for the early phase of design and also for diagnosis, the final design needs a numerical model.
- *Pragmatic aspects*, for instance the replaceable units, can have an impact on the appropriate granularity of the *structural and behavioral model*. Another example is the interaction between the function (purpose) of a device and its behavior model: component models, say of pipes and valves, have to include transportation of oxygen, carbon oxide, etc. in the intake and exhaust in order to analyze problems with emissions in vehicles, whereas for other pneumatic or hydraulic subsystems (for instance, those controlling valves), only pressure matters.

As an answer to such issues, the transformation of generic, compositional models under task-dependent and pragmatic criteria is part of our work (see e.g. [1]).

3 Towards Re-use in Practical Applications

In this section we describe work in three application areas which illustrates re-use of diagnostic components. Note that this work has been driven by real industrial requirements and not by academical interests to demonstrate re-use. Hence also other aspects besides re-use will be touched.

3.1 Three Automotive Applications

In collaboration with Robert Bosch GmbH as a major supplier of mechatronic car subsystems, the Model-based Systems and Qualitative Modeling Group (MQM) at the Technical University of Munich works on three prototypes that support different tasks related to fault analysis during the life cycle of a product:

Failure-Mode-and-Effects Analysis (FMEA). This task is performed during the design phase of a device. Its goal is to analyze the effects of component failures in a system implemented according to the respective design. The focus is on assessment of the criticality of such effects, i.e. how severe or dangerous the resulting disturbance of the functionality is in objective or subjective terms (e.g. inconvenience for the driver, environmental impact, risk of hazards). In addition, the probability of the fault and its detectability is considered. Based on this analysis, revisions of the design may be suggested. Because of the safety and environmental aspects, it has to be as "complete" as possible, not only w.r.t. the faults considered, but also in the sense that all possible effects under all relevant circumstances (driving conditions of a vehicle, states of interacting subsystems, etc.) have to be detected.

Workshop Diagnosis. The diagnostic task in the repair workshop starts from a set of initial symptoms which are either customer complaints or trouble codes generated and stored on-board by one of the Electronic Control Units (ECU) responsible for various subsystems of the vehicle. Except for the obvious cases, some investigations, tests, and measurements have to be carried out in order to localize and remove the fault, usually by replacement of components.

Generation of Diagnosis Manuals. The mechanic in the repair workshop is educated or guided by diagnosis manuals produced and distributed by the corporate service department (on paper, CD-ROM, or via a network). Here, engineers compile various kinds of information (tables, figures, text) which is required or useful for carrying out the diagnosis. Such documents have to be produced for each variant of the various subsystems and specific to a particular make, type, and special equipment of a vehicle, a broad set of issues for a supplier. The core of each document is a set of test plans that guide fault localization starting from classified customer complaints or trouble codes of the ECU.

In practice, these tasks are usually not extremely difficult to perform by an expert. However, they can be time-consuming since they have to be carried out for each specific instance of a general device type which includes collection of all the information specific to this instance. This situation of routine work applied to a large set of variants justifies computer support to be developed. And because knowledge about physical devices is the key to solving the tasks, model-based systems offer a perspective.

With the background discussed in Section 2, a major goal in our work was to demonstrate the possibility of re-use of knowledge and software modules and, particularly, of grounding the tools on the same model libraries. As depicted in Figure 1, the software basis of the three tools can share several software components (exploiting the modeling and diagnosis environment RAZ'R [6]):

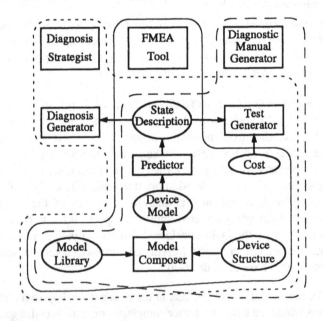

Fig. 1. Tools for workshop diagnosis, FMEA and diagnosis manual generation

- The *FMEA-Tool* is based on model composition and behavior prediction from which the task specific part has to extract the information that is critical to the function (see [8]).
- *Workshop diagnosis* additionally needs the generation of diagnostic candidates and could exploit a test generation (or measurement proposal) module. The latter is not included in our prototype which is intended to only demonstrate the possibility of interactive diagnosis based on customer complaints and trouble codes (see [9]).
- The tool for the *generation of diagnosis manuals* adds an explicit representation of car subsystems and automatic test generation to the classical functionality of an authoring system.

3.2 Model-based Fault Tree Generation

Computer-based systems for off-line diagnosis constitute the main diagnostic equipment for more than 100.000 forklifts made by the german company STILL GmbH. The diagnostic knowledge provided by these systems is contained in fault trees consisting of fault sets as nodes and tests along the edges. To support the diagnosis task of service engineers, the system guides through the fault tree by asking for tests until the possible faults have been narrowed down to a single one.

Due to the complexity of the electrical circuits employed in forklifts, fault trees may consist of more than 5000 nodes. When forklift model ranges are modified or new model ranges are released, fault trees are manually generated or adapted by service engineers who apply detailed expert knowledge concerning faults and their effects. Obviously, this practice is costly and quality management is difficult. Hence, there is a need for computer methods to systematically support modifications and re-use of components of diagnosis systems.

Model-based fault-tree generation has been developed to improve this situation. The idea is to generate diagnostic knowledge by model-based computer simulation and then use this knowledge to automatically generate the fault-tree structure for the diagnosis system. Figure 2 shows the main steps.

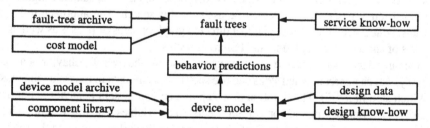

Fig. 2. Basic concepts of model-based fault-tree generation

The first step is to model a device using design data and expert knowledge concerning intended device behavior, expected faults, available measurements etc. Modeling is supported by a component library and a device model archive. As a second step, correct and faulty behavior is computed based on this model, resulting in a potentially large table of behavior predictions. The third step is to build a fault tree by grouping faults into fault sets and selecting tests. This step is supported by a fault-tree archive and a cost model for the tests.

Behavior prediction and fault-tree formation involve several innovative procedures which can only be briefly sketched in the following. The procedures have been implemented in the prototypical system MAD (Modeling, Analyzing and Diagnosing).

For behavior prediction - which is restricted to steady-state behavior - aggregates are modeled by idealized voltage sources, consumers, conductors and barriers, or their equivalents for domains other than the electrical. Also integrated circuits and software-in-the-loop may be included based on steady-state models. A qualitative calculus is employed - similar in scope to the CIRQ system of [3] - where currents and voltages are described by qualitative values and deviations from reference values. To improve the accuracy of qualitative prediction, a propagation technique has been developed which prevents spurious solutions.

Fault trees may be generated automatically from fault-symptom tables and a cost model, using the A* algorithm to optimize average diagnosis cost. In order to permit re-use and manual adaptation, MAD offers editing operations, such as moving a certain fault from one fault set to another and recomputing the corresponding tests. Due to model-based prediction, fault trees are correct and complete with respect to the underlying device model and the faults (or fault combinations) considered in the fault-symptom table.

We have evaluated model-based fault-tree generation in the STILL application scenario and found that using the modeling techniques of MAD, more than 90% of the faults of the current handcrafted diagnosis system can be handled successfully.

3.3 Searching for Failing Steps of a Technical Process

The approaches to model-based diagnosis discussed in this paper, so far, are adopting the view of "searching for faults of components". However, for many technical systems an alternative approach seems preferable, which searches for failures in steps or phases of a technical process rather than components, at least in the initial phases of diagnosis. The work of Fraunhofer IITB in INDIA has demonstrated that the standard algorithms for consistency based diagnosis may be used for this search. The approach relies on models, which structure a process into a directed graph of steps or phases as well as on models of successful completion and failure of such steps.

Our approach is preferable if domain experts describe the overall behavior of a technical system as interconnected steps and use such mental models in focussing diagnosis ("Which step failed?"). The duration of a step in a certain system behavior is not necessarily fixed but may depend on certain events, like variables reaching certain values, time-outs or operator commands. Such systems are particularly common in the process and manufacturing industries.

Re-use of temporally structured models is crucial in process industries, since the essential know-how of many companies is condensed into a library of procedures. New procedures are usually developed by modifying successful procedures from the library. Re-use of step models in process technology is supported by a strong tendency to describe and classify steps on an abstract level (cf. [2]).

Our approach employs standard consistency-based diagnosis by justifying every inference from a structured model with correctness of the structure, every inference from a model of a successful step with success of the step and every inference from a model of a failed step with the proposition that the step failed in the corresponding way. A diagnosis then states that one or more steps have failed. Such diagnoses may be refined by analyzing structured models for the suspected steps. Standard correctness and completeness results of consistency-based diagnosis are still valid for temporally structured models, and the quality of diagnosis still depends on the precision of the models.

Our guiding example in INDIA is the chemical distributor (CHD) from THEN GmbH, a system to distribute liquids in a dye house. Domain experts describe a typical task processed by the CHD as measuring out certain amounts of certain chemicals, transporting the mixture to the requesting dying machine and finally rinsing the pipes involved with water. These steps can be used to construct a temporally structured model of the overall behavior of the CHD (Figure 3).

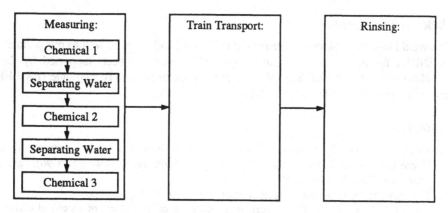

Fig. 3. Composing a train of chemicals and sending it to a certain dyeing machine

In developing models for our approach one can employ the same techniques for information re-use which were described in Section 2 with respect to component models. For instance, analysis of the control flow diagram of the control program of the CHD shows that measuring out some chemical or the separating water, transport of the mixture and rinsing may be viewed as instances of a general step type depicted in Figure 4, and hence the same set of models may be used to describe these steps.

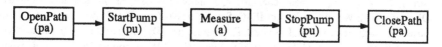

Fig. 4. Transporting amount a with pump pu along path pa

4. Conclusions

We have addressed re-usability in connection with several diagnosis tasks in an industrial environment. From our experience, re-usability is one of the prominent features model-based techniques have to offer in this domain.We have shown that in order to improve re-usability it is useful to categorize the knowledge and software for a diagnosis system along two dimensions, generality and genericity.

This has been illustrated by presenting innovative diagnosis approaches for different tasks in diverse domains. In the automotive domain, several components could be identified which are re-usable across different tasks. The work on model-based fault-tree generation demonstrates improved re-usability by separating device-specific from task-related knowledge and generic from pragmatic aspects. It is interesting that this approach combines advantages of model-based diagnosis systems with the familiarity of traditional fault-tree systems.

Finally, we have demonstrated that the re-usable building blocks for modeling the behavior of devices need not represent components. Consistency-based diagnosis techniques remain applicable if a technical process is described as a series of steps constrained by certain propositions for correct or faulty behavior.

Acknowledgments

We would like to thank our colleagues at IITB, LKI and TUM as well as our partners in INDIA for their valuable contributions. This work has been supported by the Bundesministerium für Bildung, Wissenschaft, Forschung und Technologie (BMBF) under the grant 01 IN 509 D 0, INDIA.

References

1. Heller, U., Struss, P.: Transformation of Qualitative Dynamic Models - Application in Hydro-Ecology, in: 10th International Workshop on Qualitative Reasoning (QR-96), Fallen Leaf Lake, Ca (AAAI Press), 1996.
2. Hemming, W.: Verfahrenstechnik. Würzburg. 7. Auflage 1993. (in german)
3. Lee, M. H., Ormsby, A. R. T.: Qualitative Modeling of the Effects of Electrical Circuit Faults, Artificial Intelligence in Engineering, vol. 8, pp. 293-300, 1993.
4. Mauss, J.: Analyse kompositionaler Modelle durch Serien-Parallel-Stern Aggregation, DISKI 183, Dissertationen zur Künstlichen Intelligenz, 1998. (in german)
5. Milde, H., Hotz, L., Möller, R., Neumann, B.: Resistive Networks Revisited: Exploitation of Network Structures and Qualitative Reasoning about Deviations is the Key, in: Proc. DX-97, 8th International Workshop on Principles of Diagnosis, 1997.
6. http://www.occm.de/
7. Struss, P.: Contributions to a Methodology of Model-based Systems for Diagnostic Tasks. In preparation, 1999.
8. Struss, P., Malik, A., Sachenbacher, M.: Qualitative Modeling is the Key to Automated Diagnosis. 13th World Congress of IFAC, San Francisco, CA, USA, Pergamon, 1996.
9. Struss, P., Sachenbacher, M., Dummert, F.: Diagnosing a Dynamic System with (almost) no Observations. Workshop Notes of the 11th International Workshop on Qualitative Reasoning, (QR-97) Cortona, Italy, June 3-6, pp. 193-201, 1997.

Towards Reusable Intelligent Scheduling Software

Jürgen Dorn

Institut für Informationssysteme
Technische Universität Wien
Paniglgasse 16, A-1040 Wien
Email: dorn@dbai.tuwien.ac.at

Abstract. Production scheduling plays a key enabling technique in improving the efficiency of modern production enterprises facing the international competition. Although the trend in software development for business application demands standard software, there exist no applicable standard scheduling software package. In this paper a special architecture based on object-oriented application frameworks and AI-reasoning methods is proposed as a mean to narrow this gap.

1 Motivation

Modern production management has to face considerable organizational problems due to the shifting from mass production to more specialized small lot-size production. The production of smaller lot sizes and the requirements for fast reactions to market demands poses a manifold of constraints on the usage of available resources on the shop-floor level. To be competitive in the global market, companies must especially solve the efficient coordination in their production to avoid as much as possible of the so called hidden costs.

The coordination of all activities that have to be performed to fulfill a customer's order are a key process to eliminate these costs. Due to the diversity of products as well as the diversity of required resources such as human resources, machines, energy, material, tools, and others, it becomes impossible to realize scheduling systems with standard software. Each production unit is unique and requires dedicated solutions and moreover, it will change due to new production technologies available and changing market demands. Further, typically scheduling problems are NP-hard problems that cannot be solved easily. Thus different applications require application-dependent heuristics.

Knowledge-based scheduling systems were proposed to solve these knowledge-intensive problems (Fox 1987). However, such systems were commercially not as successful as expected. Although some systems were successful fielded (e.g. Dorn and Shams 1996), the effort to build them is high and moreover, they inhibit some drawbacks in system maintenance. A promising new software engineering technique are so called object-oriented application frameworks that offer reusable semi-complete applications that can be specialized to produce custom applications. An application framework is based on a domain analysis that states the basic assumptions on a number of related applications. The main inputs to a domain analysis are general theories of the domain and existing applications.

In the following different techniques to support reuse of software are discussed. Two of these approaches rely on a domain analysis. The scheduling domain is then analyzed and a reusable framework able to incorporate theories of knowledge-based systems is presented.

2 Reuse Techniques

There are several techniques available that support the reusability of software. Three approaches namely high-level languages, application generators, and object-oriented application frameworks are presented in more detail here. Further approaches that seem to be not so important for scheduling are discussed in (Krueger 1992).

2.1 Reuse by High-level Languages

High-level languages provide certain features that facilitate the description of scheduling problems on a high level of abstraction. By using such a language a developer must not consider certain implementation details and the "cognitive distance" between the problem and the formalization is smaller (Krueger 1992). Parts of the problem solving process may already be available by the system that interprets the high-level language. Three approaches for scheduling problems:

Integer or mixed-integer programming (Garfinkel and Nemhauser 1972) is a high-level language in which optimization problems can be expressed by mathematical equations and inequations. This approach developed in the field of Operations Research is very general. There is a sizable body of literature which suggests solving scheduling problems by recasting them as integer programs. These recast problems may be solved by standard algorithms, which have been developed for solving general mathematical programs. A huge body of research has resulted in many improvements and very efficient algorithms for the integer programs over the last decades. Hence, translating a scheduling problem into an integer program, solving this program and translating the solution back, we obtain optimal schedules. Stated simply, this sounds a very promising approach; in practice it is not, because the standard mathematical programming algorithms are practically applicable only to small problems (French 1982). Furthermore, to translate a problem profound mathematical background is necessary. Although existing standard programs apply general heuristics, it is always a considerable problem to apply domain heuristics in this approach.

The second approach is *constraint satisfaction*. Starting with the research of Fox (1987) many systems were developed based on this approach. The constraint satisfaction model allows a very natural description of scheduling problems especially the declarative description of legal schedules. Many improvements were made over the years so that today problems with thousands of variables can be solved in an acceptable time frame. Although constraints are a very natural concept for scheduling problems, one type of knowledge is not so easy to be represented by crisp constraints. In most scheduling problems there are one or more optimization functions. Several researchers have shown how constraint satisfaction techniques can be applied to single criteria optimization problems. However, the optimization function is not anymore declarative represented and the representation of multiple criteria is not addressed in these investigations.

Another approach is *constraint optimization* in which constraint satisfaction plays a subordinate role. For example in our approach (Dorn and Slany 1994) hard temporal constraints are handled implicitly by a specialized reasoning technique. They are considered as so fundamental for scheduling problems so that they are not a base of variation between different applications. Soft constraints are represented explicitly and they are a matter of optimization. This approach has lead to very good problem solving behavior (Dorn et al. 1996).

The drawback of all high-level languages is that they are designed only to solve the combinatorial scheduling problem. There are other aspects that must be handled by scheduling systems. Most important is the interaction with the user of the scheduling system. In most complex industrial applications the problem formalization can only be an abstraction because the reality is so complex and many aspects are unknown during the development of a system. Thus the user must always be able to overrule the system and change solutions proposed by the system. On one side this means that the system has to visualize its solutions in an appropriate fashion and on the other side the solution must be easy manipulatable by the user. Since the software is able to check for constraint violations more reliable than the human user, it should visualize also constraint violations to the user. Other aspects not addressed by the high-level languages is the interface to the environment and that of reacting to disturbances in the actual production process (i.e. reactive scheduling).

2. 2 Application Generators

Application generators operate like programming language compilers – input specifications are automatically translated into executable programs (Cleaveland 1988). Application generators differ from traditional compilers in that the input specifications are typically very high-level, special purpose abstractions from a very narrow domain. By focusing on a narrow domain, the code expansion in application generators can be one or more orders of magnitude greater than code expansion in programming language compilers.

In application generators, algorithms and data structures are automatically selected so that the software developer can concentrate on *what* the system should do rather than *how* it is done. That is, application generators clearly separate the system specification from its application. At this level of abstraction, it is possible for even non-programmers familiar with concepts in an application domain to create software systems (Horowitz et al. 1985). Application generators are appropriate in application domains where

- many similar software systems are developed
- a software system is modified many times during its lifetime or

- many prototypes of a system are necessary to converge on a usable product.

In all of these cases, significant duplication and overlap results if the software systems are built from scratch. Application generators generalize and embody the commonalties, so they are implemented once when the application generator is built and then reused each time a software system is built using the generator.

Application generators were developed very successful for high-level report generation, data processing, database management and data display techniques. Also the SAP R/3 standard software uses the concept of application generators.

Krueger (1982) also classifies expert system shells as a kind of application generator. Instead of reusing algorithms, expert system development with such shells focuses on reusing common expert problem-solving methods. Thus diagnosing methods are applied for medical problems as well as for car maintenance.

Several researchers have tried to identify such problem solving methods also for scheduling applications. However, it seems that there are no standard "expert" problem solving methods in scheduling. The main problem in scheduling is the inherent combinatorial complexity and problem solving methods must mainly address this complexity.

In scheduling research a so called tool box approach were investigated by several researchers (e.g., Sauer et al. 1997). These systems try to provide all necessary data structures, algorithms and heuristics to the developer in a library from which the developer may select the appropriate ones. Although theoretically promising, the problem with this approach is that the developers of the tool-box must foresee which data structures and heuristics will become necessary eventually.

2.3 Object-oriented Application Frameworks

Object-oriented application frameworks are a technology for reifying proven software designs and implementations in order to reduce the cost and improve the quality of software. A framework is a reusable, "semi-complete" application that can be specialized to produce custom applications (Fayad and Schmidt 1997), (Fayad et al. 1998). In contrast to earlier object-oriented reuse techniques based on class libraries, frameworks are targeted for particular application domains.

The primary benefits of object-oriented application frameworks stem from the modularity, reusability, extensibility, and inversion of control they provide to developers. Frameworks enhance modularity by encapsulating volatile implementation details behind stable interfaces. Framework modularity helps improve software quality by localizing the impact of design and implementation changes, which reduces the effort required to understand and maintain existing software.

The stable interfaces provided by frameworks enhance reusability by defining generic components that can be reapplied to create new applications. Framework reusability leverages the domain knowledge and prior effort of experienced users in order to avoid re-creating and revalidating common solutions to recurring application requirements and software design challenges. Reuse of framework components can yield substantial improvements in programmer productivity, as well as enhancing the quality, performance, reliability, and interoperability of software.

A framework enhances extensibility by providing explicit hook methods (Pree 1994) that allow applications to extend its stable interfaces. Hook methods systematically decouple the stable interfaces and behaviors of an application domain from the variations required by instantiations of an application in a particular context. Framework extensibility is essential to ensure timely customization of new application services and features.

The run-time architecture of a framework is characterized by an inversion of control. This architecture enables canonical application processing steps to be customized by event handler objects that are invoked via the framework's reactive dispatching mechanism. When events occur, the framework's dispatcher reacts by invoking hook methods on pre-registered handler objects, which perform application-specific processing of events. Inversion of control allows the framework (rather than each application) to determine which set of application-specific methods to invoke in response to external events.

2.4 Domain Analysis

Both approaches, application generators as well as application frameworks rely on a thorough analysis of the application domain. A domain analysis is the process of identifying, collecting, organizing, and representing the relevant information in a domain to support reuse of software artifacts for systems to be built in this domain (Neighbors 1989). Domain analysis is based on the study of existing systems and their developing histories, knowledge captured from domain experts, and existing domain theory.

Common objects and operations are likely to occur in multiple applications within a domain and thus are candidates for reusable components or classes. A domain is analyzed by studying several of its representative systems and by developing an initial view of the structure and functionality of these systems. During software development, information of several kinds is generated. One of the objectives of domain analysis is to make all this information readily available. When familiarity with the domain has been achieved and the representative systems are understood, information used in developing these systems as well as their common and variable parts are identified, captured and organized for later reuse in developing new systems in that domain.

Domain analysis stresses the reusability of analysis and design, not code. This is done by deriving common architectures, generic models or specialized languages that substantially increase the power of the software development process in the specific problem area of the domain. Domain analysis can be seen as a continuing process of creating and maintaining the reuse infrastructure in a certain domain.

A vertical domain is a specific class of systems such as the domain of scheduling systems. A horizontal domain contains general software parts being used across multiple vertical domains. Examples of horizontal reuse are operating system interfaces or string handling functions.

Domain specific reuse is usually accomplished by separating domain engineering and application engineering. The goal of domain engineering is to identify objects and operations of a class of similar systems in a particular domain. Typical activities in domain engineering are domain analysis, architecture development, reusable component creation, component recovery, and component management. Application engineering means software engineering taking the results of the domain engineering process into consideration, i.e., identifying reuse opportunities and providing feedback to the domain engineering process.

3 Analysis of the Scheduling Domain

In the following the scheduling domain is analyzed briefly and some of the core objects of any scheduling system are introduced. These objects can be realized in a framework as abstract classes as was done in DÉJÀ VU (Dorn et al. 1998). This analysis model is used later to show the application and reusability of intelligent reasoning techniques. We do not consider here the user interface or the interface to other applications which are of course also very important.

3.1 Order, Product, and Process Plan

If we consider a typical scheduling process, the first object to be handled is an *order*. An order describes what shall be produced. Thus it must reference one or more *products* to be produced and some information how this product may be produced – i.e. a *process plan*. Products often are aggregated from different parts that must be handled differently during the production. Thus in the general case, we model a product as an object composed of different parts where a part may be itself a composite object. The composite design pattern (Gamma et al. 1995) can be used to model such products. Furthermore, an order may contain itself a group of products.

Orders must be distinguished in *client orders* and *production orders*. A client order describes an order of one client that may contain several products that may not be produced together because some technological or efficiency constraints will prohibit this. A production order may also contain different products but these must be compatible (i.e. they must be producable together). Orders may also be grouped to reflect that they should be produced together because they are all compatible. Again, the composite design pattern is used here.

The process plan describes a number of operations that must be performed on certain resources. It contains temporal information on the duration as well as knowledge about allowed sequences. These sequences are technological constraints. Furthermore, allowed intermediate time periods when the product must wait or is stored in intermediate storages are described in process plans.

3.2 Resources

One of the main concepts in scheduling is that of a *resource*. Resources are required to perform certain operations that are applied in order to produce some product. From the view of an application many resources must be distinguished such as machines, tools, energy, personnel, and many more. Sometimes these resource types must be differentiated still more to model certain characteristics of the resources. However, from the scheduling point of view the differences are not so great. To elicitate these differences we must investigate how a scheduling algorithm uses a resource.

A scheduling algorithm as well as a human scheduler will place operations on the resource giving them either a fixed starting point or some allowed time frame, when this operation is to be performed. Often the availability of the resource is restricted because the plant where the resource is located operates in a two-shift mode, holidays must be considered, or some break-down or a maintenance period is to be considered. Such temporal availability should not lead to different resources but to configurable resources. Thus, resources have a calendar to describe their availability.

From the scheduling point we can distinguish resources that allow only one operation at a time to be allocated and resources that can be used for more than one operation. For example available storage can be used for different products leading to different allocations with overlapping time intervals. In principle, resources that can handle only one operation at a time and the others can be managed with the same methods. However, the reasoning will be much more efficient if we define different allocation methods for both types. Thus, we identify *non-sharable resources* and *sharable resources*.

Another type or resource that plays an important role are groups of resources. If we define such groups as an own type of resource we can easily define hierarchies where groups contain again groups. A *resource group* is necessary if a number of similar resources exist in an application. Then it will be a subproblem of the scheduling problem to find the best resource in the group for a given order (i.e. a routing problem).

3.3 Job and Allocation

A job describes the performance of operations to fulfill a given order. Each operation is mapped to a so called allocation representing the association between an operation, a resource, and a time interval when the operation shall be performed. Jobs can also be grouped like orders. A job has a starting and a finishing time. Further attributes that may be present are a due date, release date, and more. Both objects are abstract objects that are used in every scheduling application. For example, a job is scheduled or two jobs may be exchanged in a schedule. Consequently, there is an abstract job defined that can be refined for a certain application to reflect specialized characteristics of jobs in this application. Three specializations that reflect differences made in the scheduling theory are a *simple job* (having only one operation to be scheduled), a *charge* (operations are scheduled in a fixed sequence), and a *complex job* whose operations can be constrained by explicit temporal sequence constraints. The allocations of a job are scheduled on resources and may be shifted, swapped or moved on a resource or in some cases also moved to another resource.

3.4 Schedule and Soft Constraints

A schedule can now be seen as a number of resources to be filled with operations (allocations). Different schedule types should be distinguished to reflect different problem types. In scheduling theory (e.g. French 1982) job-shop and flow-shop scheduling are differentiated. In a flow-shop the resources are used for all orders in the same sequence. This reduces the combinatorial complexity and if we are to build a new application it is wise to apply specialized algorithms for a *flow shop schedule* if appropriate. The jobs in a flow shop are modeled by a charge. In contrast, the *job shop schedule* allows some modifications that are not supported in a flow shop. We further define a *resource schedule* which contains only one resource.

If schedules (i.e. solutions to a scheduling problem) shall be evaluated, different aspects must be "measured". This can be done by *soft constraints* that are evaluated individually. The evaluation of all constraints associated with a schedule can then be aggregated in order to have a measure for the quality of the schedule. Although all constraints shall be aggregated into one measure, it makes sense to distinguish further some abstract types according to their appearance. So we distinguish between *job constraints*, *allocation constraints*, *resource constraints* and *schedule constraints*. The associated objects such as job and resource are now responsible for the creation, modification, and deletion of constraints whereas the scheduling object is responsible for computing the overall evaluation.

A typical application dependent constraint is for example a tardiness constraint that evaluates how well a due date of a job is satisfied in a schedule. The creation is initiated by a job that has a due date and if the job's finishing time is changed, it must also adjust the evaluation of the constraint. A schedule is, however, responsible to consider this value in the aggregated evaluation.

3.5 Scheduling Task and Schedule Improvement

A scheduling task models potential modifications in a schedule. Some scheduling tasks describe methods how a job can be inserted into a schedule. Other tasks are used to model such modifications as moving allocations or jobs in the schedule. In principle, all actions a user ise able to do with a schedule should be modeled by such tasks. A scheduling task follows the command design pattern (Gamma et al. 1995) thus supporting a common behavior of undoing and redoing actions. This design supports also the iterative improvement methods (Dorn 1995). These methods are based on the definition of a neighborhood of a schedule. A neighborhood can be generated by a method that decides which scheduling tasks are applicable on a given schedule. These methods are dependent on the type of the schedule.

4 Incorporation of Knowledge and Knowledge-based Techniques

In the most easiest case, one can reuse software as it is. Otherwise, the key aspect of the reuse process is how difficult it is to apply the required changes. The proposed architecture can be seen as a two-level architectur. The basic level is reusable to almost any scheduling problem and applies techniques that come from model-based expert systems. For example, temporal consistency algorithms are applied to secure that schedules that are produced are always legal schedules. Also consistency of capacitive constraints are handled on this level. This level also provides generic methods to construct schedules such as explicit enumeration and branch-and-bound search techniques. The drawback of such exhaustive model-based techniques is that they are usually very complex, because most scheduling related algorithms are intractable in theory. For example, a branch-and-bound algorithm with a domain-independent lower bound function can only solve scheduling problems of a very restricted size.

Thus, if we know certain simplifications or a heuristic appropriate for an application, we refine in derived classes the model-based behavior to enable acceptable response times of the scheduling system. Although such heuristics are applied we can still use some consistency mechanisms to enforce that produced solutions are legal. In the following discussion we differentiate the applied knowledge according to the KADS ontology (Schreiber et al. 1993).

4.1 Domain Knowledge

Some objects identified in the domain analysis will have very specialized attributes that cannot be foreseen in a domain analysis. Thus, if a new application is to be built this knowledge must be modeled in derived classes. One object for such a derivation is the order class. For almost every application a new order class has to be defined. One method that must be realized always is a read-method that knows how the order is to be read from a certain media. The objective is now that as few other classes of the framework as possible are dependent on such a derivation. The abstract factory design pattern (Gamma et al. 1995) helps to locate such changes to a single class. This means the derived order class acts as the concrete factory that has to construct appropriate objects required somewhere in the framework.

Of course, object-oriented techniques are also an important mean to localize such changes. For example, compatibility of orders plays an important role in the sub-domain of steel scheduling. Thus an abstract steel order is derived that provides an interface containing a method that determines the compatibility of orders. This method cannot be realized for abstract steel orders, but by declaring the method as pure virtual in a C++ realization, the developer of a new application will be forced to define this method if s/he wishes to derive an order from the steel order class.

4.2 Inference Knowledge

Since scheduling is usually an intractable problem heuristics are necessary in scheduling to find good schedules. We can identify different places where heuristics can be applied. The first kind of heuristic is used to select an order from the list of given orders to schedule it then. This heuristic can be based on the characteristic of the given orders or on the situation of the already scheduled orders. We may select first orders that are urgent or those that are difficult to be scheduled. This strategy is often called ordered-centered heuristic. A resource-oriented heuristic would select first these orders that are to be scheduled on resources that are identified as bottleneck resources.

In the "MakeHeuristicSchedule"-method of the general scheduler class we define a general skeleton how a schedule can be constructed heuristically. This method calls methods to select the most important order or to detect a bottleneck. In the derived scheduler class, we may either overwrite the called methods to reflect appropriate heuristics of an application or if necessary we may overwrite the calling method.

4.3 Task Knowledge

We have defined several iterative improvement techniques such as tabu search or simulated annealing that can optimize given schedules. These techniques rely on the definition of scheduling tasks. Thus, for a new application we must define which tasks are appropriate. For certain types of schedules default tasks are defined. However, there is a great number of possible tasks and the efficiency of the improvement techniques rely on the size of the neighborhood.

In the abstract core classes large neighborhoods are generated, because all defined scheduling tasks are tried in order to find a good neighbor. For tabu search where the whole neighborhood is investigated this means a great effort to find the best neighbor. For simulated annealing where only single neighbors are evaluated this large neighborhood means that the acceptance of bad schedules is relative high. These drawbacks can be improved by applying application dependent heuristics. Thus, we define a general "ApplicableTasks"-method in a flow-shop schedule and refine this method in an application schedule.

5 Discussion

We have argued that for the requirements in modern production processes, application frameworks are more suitable than high-level languages such as an explicit constraint satisfaction model because overhead to field such systems in actual applications is still to immense. Furthermore, it seems that for a domain such as scheduling where a great variation between applications exist, an application generator will be insufficient because not all required features can be foreseen during the development of the generator. If such an approach shall be taken, the domain must be restricted more than in an approach such as application frameworks. Application frameworks are an *open* develoment approach.

The generator approach as well as the framework approach rely on a thorough analysis of the domain at hand. We have presented a first reduced domain analysis. A complete analysis is in preparation, but this analysis still needs some input from other applications. We have a good overview on the scheduling theory, but it was detected in our application for the steel industry that in an application much more details have to be considered than in theory is treated. Furthermore, our investigations were focused by our special architecture.

Another important issue that was not addressed here is the process-oriented analysis of the application of scheduling systems. Business Process Engineering (Hammer and Champy 1993) advises us to look at business processes in order to close the gap between such functional tasks as scheduling with its environment in an enterprise.

Due to these reasons this paper should be understood as a discussion base to widen our focus on other scheduling applications.

6 References

Cleaveland, J. C. (1988) Building application generators, *IEEE Software* **5** (4) pp. 25-33.

Dorn, J. and Slany, W. (1994) A Flow Shop with Compatibility Constraints in a Steel making Plant in Zweben and Fox(eds) *Intelligent Scheduling*, Morgan Kaufmann, pp. 629–654.

Dorn, J. and Girsch, M. (1994) Genetic Operators Based on Constraint Repair, *ECAI'94 Workshop on Applied Genetic and other Evolutionary Algorithms*, Amsterdam, August 9.

Dorn, J. (1995) "Iterative Improvement Methods for Knowledge-based Scheduling", *AICOM* Journal, pp. 20–34 . March 1995.

Dorn, J. , Girsch, M., Skele, G., and Slany, W. (1996) Comparison of Iterative Improvement Techniques for Schedule Optimization, *European Journal of Operational Research*, pp. 349-361.

Dorn, J. and Shams, R. (1996) Scheduling High-grade Steel Making *IEEE Expert* February, pp. 28-35.

Dorn, J., Girsch, M. and Vidakis, N. (1998) DÉJÀ VU – A Reusable Framework for the Construction of Intelligent Interactive Schedulers, *Advances in Production Management Systems - Perspectives and Future Challenges -*, Okino et al. (eds.) Chapman & Hall, pp. 467-478.

Fayad, M.E. and Schmidt, D.C. (1997) Object-Oriented Application Frameworks, *Communications of the ACM* **40** No. 10, pp. 32-38.

Fayad, M.E., Schmidt, D.C., and Johnson, R.E. (1998) Object-Oriented Application Frameworks: Implementation and Experience, Wiley N.Y.

Fox, M. S. (1987) *Constraint-Directed Search: A Case Study of Job-Shop Scheduling*, London: Pitman.

French, S. (1982) *Sequencing and Scheduling – An Introduction to the Mathematics of the Job-Shop*, Chichester: Ellis Horwood.

Gamma, E., Helm, R, Johnson, R., and Vlissides, J. (1995) Design Patterns: Elements of Reusable Software Architecture, Addison Wesley, Reading, Mass.

Garfinkel, R. S. and Nemhauser, G. L. (1972) *Integer Programming*, John Wiley.

Hammer, M. and Champy, J. (1993) Reengineering the Corporation, Harper Business.

Horowitz, E, Kemper, A. and Narasimhan, B. (1985) A survey of application generators, *IEEE Software* 2 (1) pp. 40-54.

Krueger, C.W. (1992) Software Reuse, *ACM Computing Surveys* 24 (2), pp. 131–183.

Neighbors, J.M. (1989) DRACO: A Method for Engineering Reusable Software Systems, in *Software reusability Part 1: Concepts and Models*, Ted J. Biggerstaff and Alan J. Perlis (eds), pp. 295–319.

Pree, W. (1994) *Design Patterns for Object-Oriented Software Development*, Addison Wesley, Reading, Mass.

Sauer, J., H.-J. Appelrath, Bruns, R. and Henseler, H. (1997) Design-Unterstützung für Ablaufsysteme, KI 2, pp. 37-42.

Schreiber, G., Wielinga, B. and Breuker, J. (1993) KADS: A Principled Approach to Knowledge-based System Development, Academic Press, London.

Organizational Memory: Knowledge Acquisition, Integration, and Retrieval Issues

Andreas Abecker[1] and Stefan Decker[2]

[1] German Research Center for Artificial Intelligence (DFKI) GmbH,
Postfach 2080, D-67608 Kaiserslautern, Germany
e-mail: Andreas.Abecker@dfki.de
[2] Universität Karlsruhe, Institut AIFB,
D-76128 Karlsruhe
e-mail: Stefan.Decker@aifb.uni-karlsruhe.de

Abstract. The demand on Knowledge Management in the management and business sciences has lead to a growing community of IT people who have adopted the idea of building organizational memories or organizational memory information systems (OMIS). However, the range of ideas associated with these terms is enormous, and the community is far from being homogeneous or aligned to a common goal or technological approach. In this paper, we try to contribute to a coherent view on organizational memory. We sketch some important technical requirements, describe some work contributing to these goals and try to envision some beneficial future work.

1 Approaches to Organizational Memory

Enterprise Knowledge Management (KM) has been a constantly evolving term during the last few years in the business and management sciences. Managers have recognized that, due to a number of reasons, effective development and management of an enterprise's organizational knowledge base will be a crucial success factor in the knowledge-intensive markets of the next century. Identification, acquisition, development, dissemination, utilization, and preservation of knowledge in the enterprise have been identified as basic KM activities [14, 29].

A number of recent events and publications addressed the topic of IT support for KM [11, 22, 40]. However, all such comprehensive volumes are characterized by an enormous heterogeneity of goals and techniques which makes it almost impossible to identify a common technical core and philosophy. Even worse, in many articles it is not possible to see why the achievements described should be called "Knowledge Management" although exactly the same research topics were categorized as information systems, expert systems, CBR technology, CSCW systems, workflow engines, data warehouses, data mining, document management, etc., a short time ago. In [21] we proposed to distinguish two basic categories of IT contributions according to their main focus and approach:

1. The *process-centered view* mainly understands KM as a social communication process which can be improved though IT-means by various aspects of *groupware systems*. It is based on the observation that the most important knowledge source in an enterprise are the employees. Furthermore, solving really *wicked problems* [13] is merely a process of achieving social commitment than one of problem solving. Basic techniques for this approach come from Computer-Supported Cooperative Work (CSCW) and from Workflow Management [28, 34].

2. The *product-centered view* focuses on knowledge documents, their creation, storage, and reuse in computer-based *corporate memories*. It is based on the explication, documentation, and formalization of knowledge to have it as a tangible resource. The user's individual knowledge development and usage shall be supported by presenting the right knowledge sources at the appropriate time. Basic techniques come from Document Management, Knowledge-Based Systems, and Information Systems [21, 37].

In the following section, we will try to give an idea where this diversity of technical approaches comes from. This results in the observation that there is no single goal and approach of Organizational Memory, but merely a bundle of motivations and technical aims. We identify some requirements which should nevertheless (in the ideal case) be fulfilled by a system which claims to be an OMIS (section 3). We review a part of the state-of-the-art in the information-system inspired OMIS community pointing out our ideal view, current research approaches, and open questions (sections 4, 5, and 6). This review is mainly based on the approach and results of several research and application projects running at the authors' groups in Karlsruhe and Kaiserslautern, respectively. Both authors' groups have a strong history in the field of expert systems. These, however, exhibit serious deficiencies in industrial practice. Analysing the problems of expert systems has lead to the development of OMIS approaches: instead of *fully* automating *specific* tasks in an enterprise (like diagnosis or configuration) by *completely new* IT approaches (problem-solving methods and formal knowledge-bases), the goals are now more focused on *supporting* the user in performing *arbitrary* processes leveraging and exploiting the knowledge *already contained* in manifold representations in the enterprise. However, to realize such support the given representations are enhanced incrementally for further applications. And here, it turned out that manifold well-known AI techniques (ontologies, inference systems, CBR, etc.) are very well applicable. Finally, we conclude with the proposal to see the integration of product-centered and process-centered view as the abstract goal to be addressed by OMIS research and development (section 7). This paper is an extension of [4].

2 KM Starting Points

In this section we discuss the KM phenomenon from a bird's eye view. In later sections, however, we focus on IT support for KM. In our opinion, the current hype in KM in the business world cannot be explained by a single reason, but is promoted by a number of trends coming together in these days. To mention but a few:

Under the label of *lean management*, the last wave of enterprise reengineering efforts cut off the middle management from many organizational structures. But for decades, just this level of employees had been an important stakeholder of know-how and experience about projects, customers, and products, and used to perform the important task of knowledge gathering, filtering, interpretation, and routing as a preprocessing step preparing the decisions of the upper management.

KM tries to compensate (i) the loss of stable procedural knowledge by explication and formalization using, e.g., organization handbooks or workflow management systems, (ii) the loss of project, customer, or project related experiences and know-how by establishing best practice or lessons learned databases [37], and, (iii) the loss of the middle management information analysis and routing services through new IT solutions like, e.g., intranets, data mining, or data warehouses [25].

Together with the *globalization of businesses*, an enormous market pressure enforces ever shorter product-life-cycles. On the other hand, modern information technology allows world-wide geographically dispersed development teams, virtual enterprises [32], and close cooperation with suppliers, customer companies, and outsourced service providers. All these factors make necessary complex communication and coordination flows, complex both in technical and in conceptual terms. The role of IT is to optimize the information and document through-put, to enable world-wide communication and synchronization. CSCW and groupware tools are often used in such scenarios.

Further, new customer-oriented management and quality principles like *Total Quality Management* (TQM) promote new styles of communication and decision-making in company departments. Following the *concurrent engineering* paradigm, expertise, information, and feedback from customers as well as many, previously separated and timely sequential development steps are thrown together at very early stages in order to have earlier a comprehensive and holistic view on requirements and design. This requires complex communication and collaboration of many people with completely different educational backgrounds and personal goals and perspectives. It requires also a combination of the documents, information flows, and decision processes coming from previously separated groups of people. Here, IT can support cooperative work and store decision processes to enable subsequent decision tracing under changed conditions; it can also support the preparation of well-structured documentation required for quality certification.

All these business phenomena produce a whole bunch of KM related activities comprising (i) better exploitation of already available but unsufficiently used documents, (ii) formalization of business rules in workflows, (iii) better usage of human skills and knowledge through CSCW techniques or enterprise yellow pages and competency databases, (iv) explication of experiences and know-how in best practice databases, and much more. Most of these activities can also be supported by information technoloy, and are in fact already partly supported by conventional computer systems [14]. However, what is still missing, is a comprehensive view on OMIS which characterizes its specific properties.

3 Crucial Points for Realizing OMIS

Since we adopt the IT point of view here, we concentrate our considerations on technical aspects of OM, i.e. the OMIS. Of course, for building and deployment of operational systems in practice, especially the non-technical aspects are of crucial importance. In [41, 21] we elaborate a bit on these issues.

For a thorough system-theoretic analysis of functions and properties of an OMIS, please refer to [35], and to [30] for a recent review of definitions found in the contemporary IT literature. As a working definition, we propose the following:

> An Organizational Memory Information System (OMIS) integrates basic techniques (see section 1) into a computer system which—within the enterprises' business activities—continuously gathers, actualizes, and structures knowledge and information and provides it in different operative tasks in a context-sensitive, purposeful and active manner in order to improve cooperative, knowledge-intensive work processes.

If we have a closer look at the definition and regard some practical aspects which can be extracted from industrial studies [21, 36], we can identify some requirements on each of the three levels of any information or knowledge system (capture, storage, and usage). These conditions help to establish specific requirements for designing and building an OMIS.

All three levels must be able to cope with a huge *variety* of possible knowledge sources and formats, ranging from databases, over text or multimedia documents, to some formal knowledge representation. Especially for the knowledge repository at the core of the OMIS, coping with technical as well as conceptual heterogeneity is a demanding task.

Figure 1 gives an impression what existing enabling technologies can be used for tackling these issues. Now, we will discuss the three levels in some more detail.

4 Knowledge Acquisition and Maintenance

Knowledge acquisition and maintenance are crucial for successful deployment of an OMIS as for any knowledge-based system [21, 14]. In the ideal case, an OMIS would be self-adaptive and self-organizing, gathering within the usual business operations the information and data useful for later reuse without disturbing the normal flow of work of the employees. This would minimize knowledge acquisition costs. This, however, is of course not always possible: manual knowledge

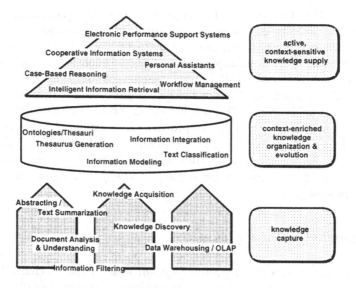

Fig. 1. Some Basic Technologies for Building an OMIS [1]

acquisition performed by a knowledge engineer still remains often necessary, e.g., for establishing ontologies or adding meta data.

In many best-practice projects in consulting companies [27] as well as in the area of "Experience Factories" for learning software organizations [8, 9], the role of a Knowledge- or Experience Manager has been proposed who acts as kind of a knowledge clearinghouse and is responsible for preparing knowledge for reuse, bringing it into a useful form and adding appropriate meta data to ease later reuse.

Though this makes sense for rather complex and worthful pieces of enterprise knowledge (like best practices are), it is quite an expensive strategy, especially in large and diverse organizations. Furthermore, it is not appropriate for many less complex, less important, and less ambitious knowledge acquisition and mainte-nance tasks. It is also not appropriate being confronted with huge amounts of data and information to be scanned and analyzed for useful knowledge.

In such cases, acquisition tools and automated approaches would be help-ful. Consequently, the knowledge capture level in Figure 1 shows several input streams which feed the OMIS with knowledge extracted from texts and from databases. As a first approximation, we propose to have specialized analysis tools and knowledge discovery agents constantly searching the enterprise internal and external web and knowledge sources in order to feed interesting input into the OMIS; see [25] for some examples implemented at Price Waterhouse. Another part are user-friendly system interfaces which collect user feedback, comments, and memos in a context-sensitive and inobtrusive manner.

Although there have been interesting results in document analysis and understanding (DAU) since more than one decade (see, e.g., [17]), the application scenarios for methods like document structure analysis, information extraction, and automated summarization are still quite limited. The Price Waterhouse systems show that already simple text analysis technology can produce useful results. The DAU community should tackle more such comprehensive application scenarios. First steps toward analysis of Web pages have already been done (see, e.g., [12]), topics like Web OCR are still in their infancy and currently known as "Wrapper generation" (cf. [39]). We propose usage scenarios where DAU facilities are deeply integrated with the overall business information infrastructure: in the DFKI VirtualOffice project [10], knowlegde about open workflows is used for improving DAU results by generating some expectations which guide the analysis process.

5 Knowledge Integration

The core of an OMIS is a repository system which must—technically seen—grow out of the integration of several legacy systems (which usually cannot be replaced) enriched by some new information and meta data that allows retrieval of useful knowledge and documents in a given application situation. This repository is characterized by heterogeneity wrt. several dimensions:

Concerning *meaning and content* of knowledge, categories such as product and process related knowledge, reasons for decisions, individual competencies and skills, etc., can be found in an enterprise. Contemporary systems usually manage just one kind of such knowledge. However, the power of KM comes exactly from the playing-together and synergetic view on multiple kinds of knowledge in their usage and creation context. Concerning *representation*, text and hypertext documents, e-mails, graphics etc. are often already there and are much more comfortable and expressive for the human user than any formal knowledge representation. On the other hand, only formalized notions allow for sophisticated inferences and precise retrieval. So we have to aim at a meaningful combination of formal and informal knowledge items.

A good example for the beneficial synergy between several kinds of knowledge are *Issue-based Information Systems*. The QuestMap tool [33] allows to embed design artifacts (like graphics, minutes of meetings, or requirements texts) into a graphical notation of the discussion and decision process of the design group which led to these artifacts. So, one can retrieve all pros and cons encountered in a discussion, or can trace all decisions influenced by some preconditions in the case that the preconditions change.

Also in the design area, we tested how additional, complementary views for business process modeling (BPM) could be used for analyzing and controlling document and knowledge creation, utilization, and flow in a design project [23, 16]. To us, extending BPM toward representing knowledge, documents, and expertise seems to be a promising approach. Moreover, it must be possible that several kinds of knowledge and documents interact, thus generalizing the quite specific IBIS idea.

Concerning technical integration of multimedia information types, the KA-RAT system [3, 36] developed at DFKI provides a simple, yet robust and useful solution. Assuming that all information items to be managed are available in the intranet and can be displayed by a WWW browser, we simply generated an HTML page for each information unit containing a link to the original source, some textual descriptions and additional textual information for each information unit (annotations), plus an arbitrary set of classification links. These links either establish predefined relationships (e.g., part-of, or causal relationships) between information units or associate an information unit with classes chosen from freely definable organization models which allow for a flexible multi-criteria classification of information. The tool can also generate suggestions for associating information units to model categories on the basis of IR text categorization models. However, since all freely defined organization models are internally handled just as flat lists of categories the semantics of which is not known to the system, KARAT is not able to draw sophisticated inferences over organization models for finding information units.

Just this goal was tackled by the Karlsruhe Ontobroker project [15]. Here, (informal) text in web pages is annotated wrt. a domain ontology using new HTML (or, XML, resp.) attributes such that a formal representation can be automatically extracted. Now, the formal representation can be processed with the help of the ontology and additional domain background knowledge for query answering and retrieval across the borders of single HTML pages. So there is a formal-informal combination which enables powerful inferences, but is still easy to maintain. The knowledge (ontology) and inference part of the Ontobroker system is based on Frame-Logic [20].

In the DFKI KnowMore project [1] the idea of an independent, knowledge-rich information modeling level is elaborated. It encapsulates access to the several knowledge sources and holds all relevant meta data (see Figure 2). Similar to the Ontobroker approach, the information modeling level is based on a formal knowledge representation thus providing the inferences services missing in KARAT.

The whole area of information modeling and meta modeling for precise-content retrieval is an active and demanding field since it is the playground for knowledge retrieval and exploitation agents (section 6). Interesting subproblems are efficient inference mechanisms scalable for large OMIS knowledge bases, as well as the appropriate processing of uncertainty naturally occurring in Information Retrieval. [38] pointed out semantical problems when melting together deep formal models of background knowledge and parts of the application ontology with rough, pragmatic classification systems usually employed for describing content of legacy document bases and libraries.

6 Knowledge Retrieval

From the point of view of knowledge utilization, we see two important features which should distinguish an OMIS from conventional information and knowledge

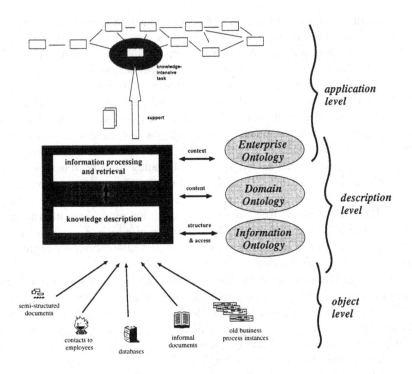

Fig. 2. OMIS Levels in The KnowMore Project [1]

systems: (i) the *active, context dependent* supply of knowledge and information useful for the user in a given situation, and (ii) the *application independence* of the OMIS knowledge base which should be useful for manifold task specific assistant systems. To this end, task specific OMIS exploitation and retrieval services can act as intelligent assistants to the user that

- accompany the execution of tasks, and
- present relevant information which helps the employees to do their work better and more effectively.

Consequently, such an intelligent assistant must have some notion of the work process it supports and must be able to perform a precise-content retrieval from the OMIS archive. A first step in this direction are user, group, or task specific knowledge push mechanisms constantly filtering and actively delivering interesting OMIS contents to their subscribers.

Of course, activeness and task independence are somewhat conflicting goals. Really "intelligent" approaches to active support require so much domain and task knowledge that they can hardly be built in an application-independent manner. [21] describe an early OMIS prototype, the KONUS system for conservation of crankshaft design rules. KONUS already actively suggests design decisions or generates a warning if the user violates stored rules. However, these services are paid for by a completely task and domain specific architecture. Moreover, they are based on a fairly expensive knowledge acquisition and modeling process.

In [31], the EULE/2 prototype is presented which supports employees at Swiss Life Corporation on the basis of a declarative, knowledge-rich formalization of business processes, business rules, and relevant laws and regulations. These formal models are employed for controlling open workflows, for automated data gathering for open cases, and for semi-automatic consistency-checks for user decisions with relevant business rules and laws. In the case of violations, the system can actively warn the user and offer the relevant pieces of rules and legal texts. Though it is a specific business solution for Swiss Life Corporation, we see an important contribution made by the EULE/2 system: it introduces some notion of business process model for controlling the KM process.

The DFKI KnowMore project [1] goes a step further and proposes conventional business process models (BPMs) as a first step to KM solutions. The process of building and analyzing BPMs is used as a vehicle to organize enterprise KM in the same stream of work. Knowledge-intensive tasks are identified as integral parts of "tame" business processes. Standard BPMs are extended by variables which carry decisions from previous business activities thus defining kind of context and input for subsequent knowledge-intensive tasks. Workflow enactment controls the overall business process and thus gives us a chance to activate specific task assistants as a hook on the conventional workflow engine. If some knowledge item is created within such a business process, the actual workflow context already defines its creation context which might be assessed for its later reuse in other business processes.

Cased Based Reasoning (CBR) can provide robust and effective techniques for retrieval. Meta data is added to knowledge resources. Queries are processed employing an appropriate measure which estimates the similarity between query situation and stored experiences. An experience factory like approach along these ideas is described in [6]. The advantage is the possibility of incremental formalization: at first, cases can be described very roughly; more sophisticated meta data can be added if required by the application. Similar to the approaches in section 5, sophisticated retrieval is based on an ontology for formulation of resource meta data.

The above mentioned workflow-embedded activation model for knowledge retrieval agents is still in its very first stage. It has to be clarified how far already existing *knowledge broker* approaches can be used and tailored inside an enterprise [7, 18, 42]. Agent-based approaches for exploiting the OMIS content seem definitely appropriate in order to tackle the manifold integration problems in a scalable manner. Such approaches are typically based on wrapper/mediator architectures as proposed by Wiederhold and others in the database area [39]. Moreover, up to now, we have only investigated quite structured business processes with knowledge-intensive tasks embedded as black boxes. It is an open question whether there can also some aspects of knowledge-intensive tasks be modeled to ease knowledge supply.

7 Conclusions

In this paper, we sketched some necessary conditions for an OMIS to be a real evolution from conventional information systems. We see active knowledge supply, heterogeneity of knowledge sources with a predominance of informal representations, and task-independence of the architecture as the main challenges in this area. We also reviewed some contemporary work and proposed possible future developments. In our projects, we will primarily address the above challenges in the areas of (i) intelligent assistants exploiting the OMIS repository, (ii) knowledge-centered enterprise modeling for identifying knowledge needs, defining knowledge context, controlling support processes and controlling information flow, (iii) knowledge-intensive, contextually enriched information modeling at the core of the repository system, and (iv) learning and self-adaptive knowledge discovery agents for capturing knowledge and filling the archive. Innovative approaches often grow out from the integration of known technolgies at the borders of different technologies and dimensions. Consider, e.g., the DFKI VirtualOffice project at the intersection of workflow and document analysis, or the AIFB Ontobroker at the interface between formal and informal representations. Coming back to the introductory chapters, we consider it an excellent point made by Borghoff & Pareschi [11]: most approaches to KM concentrate either on storage and retrieval of documents (this is what we call the product view on KM), or on collaboration support for people (the process view). Next generation systems will come from the integration of both views via some *knowledge flow* mechanism on the basis of some *knowledge cartography*. This view is consistent with Nonaka & Takeuchi's [24] analysis of kinds of enterprise knowledge and knowledge transformation processes; it is also reflected by O'Leary's recent analysis who argued that KM essentially amounts to *making connections* [26]: connecting people and people, connecting knowledge and people, and so on. Although such considerations are still quite abstract, we hopefully gave some concrete hints for possible technical contributions in the future. One other still open point arises when building an enterprise-wide OMIS from several previously independent archives. Since it is not realistic to expect an enterprise-wide, consistent organization schema and terminology, the questions of ontology mapping and ontology merging for organizing the overall system seem crucial to us.

Acknowledgment. The final version of this paper profited very much from the numerous and valuable reviewer comments and suggestions.

References

1. A.Abecker, A. Bernardi, K. Hinkelmann, O. Kühn, and M. Sintek. Toward a technology for organizational memories. *IEEE Intelligent Systems*, May/June 1998.
2. A.Abecker, S.Decker, K. Hinkelmann, and U. Reimer. Workshop on Knowledge-Based Systems for Knowledge Management in Enterprises, Freiburg, Germany. Document D–97–03, DFKI GmbH, September 1997.

3. A. Abecker, S. Aitken, F. Schmalhofer, and B. Tschaitschian. KARATEKIT: Tools for the knowledge-creating company. In *[19]*, 1998.

4. A. Abecker, S. Decker, and O. Kühn. Organizational memory. *Informatik Spektrum*, 21(4):213–214, 1998. In German.

5. A. Abecker, S.Decker, N. Matta, F. Maurer, and U. Reimer. *ECAI-98 Workshop on Building, Maintaining, and Using Organizational Memories*. August 1998.

6. K.-D. Althoff, F. Bomarius, and C. Tautz. Using case-based reasoning technology to build learning software organizations. In *[5]*, 1998.

7. J.-M. Andreoli, Ch. Fernstrom, N. Glance, and A. Grasso. The Coordination Technology Area at XRCE Grenoble: Research in Support of Distributed Cooperative Work. Xerox Research Centre Europe.

8. V. R. Basili and H. D. Rombach. The TAME Project: Towards improvement-oriented software environments. *IEEE Trans. on Software Engineering*, 14(6), 1988.

9. V.R. Basili, G. Caldiera, and H.-D. Rombach. Experience factory. In J. Marciniak, editor, *Encyclopedia of Software Engineering*, volume 1. John Wiley & Sons, 1994.

10. S. Baumann, M. Malburg, H.d Meyer auf'm Hofe, and C. Wenzel. From paper to a corporate memory—a first step. In *[2]*, 1997.

11. U. M. Borghoff and R. Pareschi. *Information Technology for Knowledge Management*. Springer, Berlin, Heidelberg, New York, 1998.

12. T. Catarci, L. Iocchi, D. Nardi, and G. Santucci. Accessing the Web: exploiting the DB paradigm. In *[5]*, 1998.

13. E.J. Conklin and W. Weil. Wicked problems: Naming the pain in organizations. URL http://www.gdss.com/wicked.htm, 1997.

14. T.H. Davenport, S.L. Jarvenpaa, and M.C. Beers. Improving knowledge work processes. *Sloan Management Review*, 37(4):53–65, 1997.

15. S. Decker, M. Erdmann, D. Fensel, and R. Studer. Ontobroker: Ontology based access to distributed and semi-structured information. In R. Meersman et al., editor, *DS-8: Semantic Issues in Multimedia Systems*. Kluwer Academic Publisher, 1999.

16. S. Decker and R. Studer. Towards an enterprise reference scheme for building knowledge management systems. In *Proc. "Modellierung 98", Münster*, 1998.

17. A. Dengel and K. Hinkelmann. The specialist board—a technology workbench for document analysis and understanding. In *Integrated Design & Process Technology, Proc. of the Second World Congress*. Society for Design and Process Science, 1996.

18. R. Fikes, A. Farquhar, and W. Pratt. Information brokers: Gathering information from heterogeneous information sources. Stanford University.

19. B. R. Gaines and M. A. Musen, editors. *11th Workshop on Knowledge Acquisition, Modeling and Management (KAW'98)*. University of Calgary, April 1998.

20. M. Kifer, G. Lausen, and J. Wu. Logical foundations of object-oriented and frame-based languages. *Journal of the ACM*, 42:741–843, 1995.

21. O. Kühn and A. Abecker. Corporate memories for knowledge management in industrial practice: Prospects and challenges. In *[11]*, 1998.

22. J. Liebowitz and L.C. Wilcox, editors. *Knowledge Management and Its Integrative Elements*. CRC Press, Boca Raton, New York, 1997.

23. M. Daniel, S. Decker *et al.* ERBUS—towards a knowledge management system for designers. In *[2]*, 1997.

24. I. Nonaka and H. Takeuchi. *The Knowledge-Creating Company*. Oxford University Press, 1995.

25. D. O'Leary. Enterprise knowledge management. *IEEE Computer*, March 1998.

26. D. O'Leary. Knowledge management systems: Converting and connecting. *IEEE Intelligent Systems*, May/June 1998.

27. D. O'Leary. Using AI in knowledge management: Knowledge bases and ontologies. *IEEE Intelligent Systems*, May/June 1998.

28. W. Prinz and A. Syri. An environment for cooperative knowledge processing. In *[11]*, 1998.

29. G. Probst, S. Raub, and K. Romhardt. *Wissen managen: Wie Unternehmen ihre wertvollste Ressource optimal nutzen.* Gabler, Wiesbaden, 1997.

30. R.Dieng, O. Corby, A. Giboin, and M. Ribière. Methods and tools for corporate knowledge management. In *[19]*, 1998.

31. U. Reimer. Knowledge integration for building organisational memories. In *[2]*, 1997.

32. M. Ribière and N. Matta. Virtual enterprise and corporate memory. In *[5]*, 1998.

33. S. Buckingham Shum. Negotiating the construction of organisational memories. In *[11]*, 1998.

34. C. Simone and M. Divitini. Ariadne: Supporting coordination through a flexible use of knowledge processes. In *[11]*, 1998.

35. E.W. Stein and V. Zwass. Actualizing organizational memory with information technology. *Information Systems Research*, 6(2), 1995.

36. B. Tschaitschian, A. Abecker, and F. Schmalhofer. Information Tuning with KARAT: Capitalizing on existing documents. In *EKAW-97*, Sant Feliu de Guixols, Catalonia, Spain, October 1997. Springer Verlag, LNAI 1319.

37. G. van Heijst, R. van der Spek, and E. Kruizinga. The lessons learned cycle. In *[11]*, 1998.

38. C. Welty. The ontological nature of subject taxonomies. 1998. Int'l Conference on Formal Ontology in Information Systems (FOIS'98).

39. G. Wiederhold and M. Genesereth. The conceptual basis for mediation services. *IEEE Intelligent Systems*, pages 38–47, September/October 1997.

40. M. Wolf and U. Reimer, editors. *PAKM'96, First Int. Conference on Practical Aspects of Knowledge Management, Basel, Switzerland.* October 1996.

41. T. Wolf, S. Decker, and A. Abecker. Unterstützung des Wissensmanagements durch Informations- und Kommunikationstechnologie. In *WI'99 - 4. Int. Tagung Wirtschaftsinformatik, Saarbrücken*, 1999. In German. To appear.

42. B.C.M. Wondergem, P. van Bommel, T.W.C. Huibers, and Th.P. van der Weide. Agents in cyberspace: Towards a framework for multi-agent systems in information discovery. University of Nijmegen, The Netherlands, September 1997.

A Competence Knowledge Base System as Part of the Organizational Memory

Minghong Liao, Knut Hinkelmann, Andreas Abecker, and Michael Sintek

German Research Center for Artificial Intelligence (DFKI) GmbH
P.O.Box 2080, D-67608 Kaiserslautern, Germany
Phone:+49 631 205 3474, Fax:+49 631 205 3210
{liao,hinkelma,aabecker,sintek}@dfki.uni-kl.de

Abstract. Personal competences of experienced employees are the most important knowledge assets of knowledge-work oriented enterprises. Thus, it makes perfect sense to start IT support for enterprise knowledge management with a system that facilitates finding of appropriate contact persons for business tasks which require specific knowledge, experiences, or skills. We propose such a competence knowledge base system (CKBS) which builds upon an ontology-based model of competence fields, the use of which allows (i) comprehensive multi-criteria organization and queries for personal competences, (ii) complex heuristic inferences for finding knowledgeable persons in spite of vaguely specified information needs, and (iii) easy integration of the CKBS into an overall organizational memory information system.

1 Introduction

Enterprises are realizing how important it is to "know what they know" and be able to make maximum use of their knowledge. Especially in industrialized countries with highly educated but expensive employees, products and services must be outstanding in terms of innovation, flexibility, and creativity. A prerequisite for being able to face current and future challenges is the systematic management of the knowledge assets of the enterprise (see, e.g., [20]).

Despite the use of knowledge-based systems for decision support and expert task assistance, of groupware and workflow tools for improving communication and collaboration, and of advanced document management and artifact repositories for better reuse and experience documentation, the tacit knowledge, personal competences, and skills of experienced employees are still the most important resources for solving knowledge-intensive tasks like decision-making, strategic planning, or creative design.

Consequently, one of the first steps to support enterprise knowledge management is often to establish an electronically represented and accessible overview of people's special capabilities, experiences, and key knowledge areas (see, e.g., [1,16], or Davenport's case study for Teltech [10]). Such a *competence knowledge base system* (CKBS, or: "smart" *company yellow pages, skill database,* etc.) can be used for project team formation, troubleshooting in help-desk situations, coaching and advice transfer from experienced employees to newcomers, and also for strategic analyses in order to support long-term skill development in the company.

Practical approaches for building such a system usually rely on textual descriptions of the employees' skills and capabilities, or, in advanced *knowledge mapping* approaches, rely on two-dimensional visualizations of the underlying information space [11]. In our approach, we essentially regard an employee as a "knowledge container" (in a similar way as a book or a multimedia document) such that a personal competence can be described just like the other (tangible) contents of an Organizational Memory Information System (OMIS, shortly OM) [17]. This makes possible sophisticated retrieval mechanisms for searching competent employees and a deeper integration of the competence part into the overall OM system (see also [5]).

This paper is organized as follows: After a more detailed description of the envisioned CKBS usage scenario (Section 2), we describe our ontology-based modeling approach which associates the company's employees with formal concepts of a domain ontology describing their respective competences (Section 3). This section also illustrates ontology-based retrieval heuristics, the more technical formulation of which is described in Section 4. A short discussion of implementation issues (Section 5) and some concluding remarks (Section 6) end up the paper.

2 Application Scenarios for a Competence Knowledge Base System (CKBS)

Looking for people with specific expertise is a common problem in nearly every company. A prototypical example is a help desk where customers call in the case of trouble with a company's products. Such help desks often support a wide range of products or multiple domains. Individuals gain experience and thus develop expertise in particular domains over time. Computer systems try to capture this expertise to make it independent of the availability of a particular human expert (see [12] and [14]). For hard problems, however, an expert—for instance one of the product developers—must still be consulted. In this case, the particular expert must be identified very quickly—a typical application for a CKBS.

Another typical application for a CKBS is forming a project team that must be composed of people with the right expertise for the different tasks of the project. Here, the retrieving problem in a CKBS is further complicated by the fact that in some cases it might be preferable to find people with as many expertises as possible (even if they are not so deep) in order to keep the project team small. For solving a very difficult task, however, it might be advantageous to find experts with high competences—even if the project becomes large.

A related problem is to react on inquiries coming from customers or from other departments in the company. If a prospective customer asks for a solution to a specific problem the company has to direct the inquiry to an expert who can discuss possible solutions with the customer and in the end can make an offer.

Identifying people with a specific expertise in a CKBS is in some aspects different from retrieving information, e.g., in a document management system. There, it is possible to search in the information directly, e.g., by full-text search. In a CKBS, not the competence itself but a description of it is represented. But simple classification or a keyword approach are not sufficient for a CKBS. The specific competences of different people often differ in fine but significant details. Therefore a modeling approach is required that allows to describe people's competences accurately and to implement a retrieval strategy that allows to find a "nearly fitting" expert or multiple experts that together have the desired competence when a specific expert for a particular problem is not available. In the rest of the paper we will sketch an ontology-driven approach for describing and retrieving the competences of people in a CKBS. The presented ideas are prototypically implemented as a DFKI intranet component (Figure 1 shows a screenshot of its user interface).

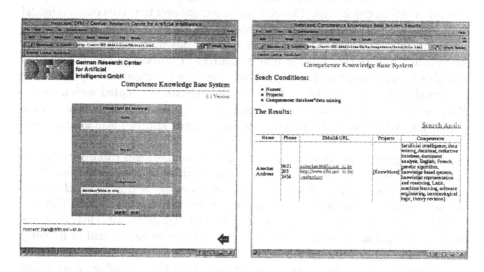

Fig. 1. Input and Output Window of the DFKI Competence Knowledge Base System

3 Ontology-Based Competence Modeling

A naive approach to build up a competence knowledge base would be to associate with each employee a number of index keywords describing his or her fields of knowledge; to search for employees competent in a given area would mean to simply look up this table. This would be analogous to keyword-based information retrieval (IR) approaches, thus inheriting all problems of such an approach:

keywords are not unequivocal; in a query situation the user often does not know exactly the keyword vocabulary; information needs are often vague or somehow orthogonal to the indexing vocabulary; keyword association is quite imprecise, etc.

In IR research, these problems led to a number of approaches aiming at, e.g., easier query formulation, automatic indexing, probabilistic matching between query terms and index keywords, incorporation of background knowledge into the retrieval process, and so on. One of the most powerful scenarios is defined by the *logic-based approach to IR* [18]: both queries and documents are represented in a formal, logic-based way, and finding a document which is likely to answer the query is understood as a process of logical inference. This view allows to have well-founded and theoretically understood retrieval mechanisms which can be supported by background knowledge represented as logical theories. On the other hand, we have the *conceptual IR approach* [21] which allows as index expressions only elements taken from a formal model of the domain of discourse structuring the concepts of this domain in an is-a/part-of hierarchy or something similar. If conceptual indexing and logic-based retrieval are combined, we can formulate generic as well as domain specific retrieval heuristics over the given domain model in order to support the retrieval inference [8].

In the KnowMore project, we take such a logic-based, conceptual IR approach for indexing and retrieval of the diverse sources of knowledge and information available in an enterprise. Heterogeneous sources are homogeneously described by formal information models. Information models are formulated with a vocabulary defined in some underlying ontologies on (i) logical structure and meta properties, (ii) creation and potential usage context, and (iii) semantic context [5, 6].

Following this idea, also personal (or, group) competences can be formalized as special kinds of "documents" mainly characterized by their owner and their content (i.e., the actual knowledge area). The advantage of this approach is that we can reuse algorithms and structuring ontologies from the overall KM/OM system and search/present competences and explicit (tangible) knowledge sources in an integrated manner. This comprehensive OM approach is still in its early stages and its description goes beyond the scope of this paper. Here, we will focus on some examples for competence retrieval with the help of ontology-based retrieval heuristics.

Example 1: Consider a part of a domain ontology describing the competences of the members of our DFKI research group shown in Figure 2. Suppose Tino to be our only employee, known as competent in the field of object-oriented databases. If we are now searching for a person competent in the field of databases, a simple keyword-based search would fail. However, if we can use the subsumption relationships between competence fields shown in Figure 2, together with a general search heuristics stating that people knowledgeable in a specific area should also be competent in the more general topics, we can expand our scope of search, thus finding Tino who will certainly have some knowledge in general database questions.

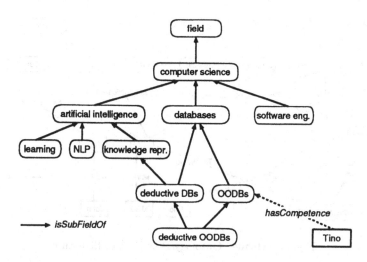

Fig. 2. Simple Ontology on Computer Science Competences

Example 2: In order to exemplify the use of a slightly more complicated search heuristics consider the following scenario. One source of knowledge which is readily available in every company describes which person works (or worked) in which project(s). If we make just the small extension of additionally representing which technologies were relevant in which projects, we can easily infer that people working in a project that deals with some technology are of course competent in this technology.

In Figure 3, we modified the above example accordingly by adding projects and the *worksIn* as well as the *usesTechnology* links in our model. If we are now looking for an expert in deductive, object-oriented databases (DOODB), we find the ESB project[1], and, via the *worksIn* link, we find Mike who is supposed to be competent in DOODB. If we also had to our disposal another general heuristic (similar to the one used in the prior example) which would state that someone competent in a more general area could also be knowledgeable in its specializations, we could again find Tino. However, this conclusion apparently is much more unsafe than the two other heuristics. Thus, it should be possible to formulate sort of a "cascading strategy" pursuing a sequence of search paths with decreasing certainty.

In this example, we exploited "sparse" indices with the help of intelligent traversal heuristics. Of course, the same effect could have been achieved with simple retrieval methods and a "complete indexing", putting all knowledge into the indices that is now heuristically inferred at runtime. At first hand, the reasons for choosing our approach were solely pragmatic: in a real-world enterprise,

---

[1] A DFKI application project which employs DOODB technology for contextually-enriched recording of maintenance experiences for a complex coal mining machine [9].

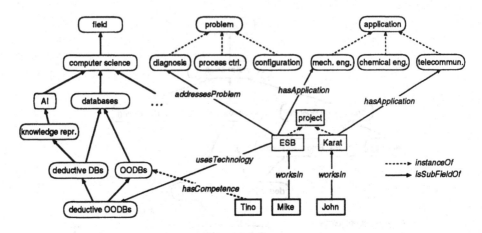

Fig. 3. Extended Ontology Plus Project Structure

we will always have to live with incomplete information, maintenance problems, and partly out-dated data. Under such circumstances, relying on a minimal extension—which must be put in and maintained—together with powerful completion methods seems to be the preferable approach. But, there is also a more fundamental reason: at least retrieval heuristics referring to the actual query context parameters can by no means reasonably be put into the index database. If, for instance, I want to retrieve people competent in a given area or any more general area which is still more specific than my own knowledge, this information can hardly be put into the indices in advance (for each possible querying employee).

Example 3: In the above two examples, one simple generalization/specialization hierarchy over topics accompanied by the project structure was sufficient for sophisticated competence retrieval. However, a natural, not biased approach to structuring our work did not lead to such a "single-hierarchy" view, but merely imposed a multiple-criteria structure on our work; the different (more or less) orthogonal dimensions were mainly glued together by projects which could be classified wrt. these different dimensions. The basic classification criteria identified were: (i) the *technological fields and approaches* adopted, (ii) the *generic problem class* tackled in a project, and (iii) the *domain of application* a project was situated in.

For instance, the ESB project mentioned above employed (i) DOODB, model-based information structuring, and case-based retrieval mechanisms for (ii) experience storage and diagnosis support in a (iii) mechanical engineering domain, namely coal mining machines [9].

We do not claim that this set of entity and relation types is a definite, optimal structure for organizing CKBSs. However, we have a strong feeling that such an organization—at least as a starting point—is quite intuitive in many company environments, that it is not necessarily more expensive to acquire than a "flat" keyword list for competence description, and that it offers much more benefits. Technically, a more complex structure requires more expressive knowledge representation means;[2] but it also offers more sophisticated means for heuristics formulation and more natural search interfaces.

Consider, for instance, a first customer contact by phone. Here, the application domain and the generic problem class are usually the first information pieces which can be acquired for further focusing the conversation. Depending on the actual topics, it might be useful to directly take into consultation a colleague experienced with the respective application domain—if this is so highly sophisticated that a further discussion already requires some domain knowledge, like, e.g., special areas in chemical industry. It is also often the case that "surprising links" are given by the system because IT experts usually mention only IT specific skills when describing their competence profile. However, via the project membership, we can again suspect that someone who was working in a project on fault diagnosis in a mechanical engineering domain has also some basic ideas on this mechanical engineering area. Since the links *between* independent classification dimensions (IT fields, projects, application domains, generic problem classes) use to be different—like *usesTechnology, addressesProblem*, etc.—from those *within* these dimensions—like *isSubFieldOf, isPartOf, isSubProjectOf, worksIn*, etc.— we can formulate much more exact search heuristics. For instance, if we want to group a brainstorming team for discussing the preferred approach for a project on configuration in electrical engineering, we could pick one member of each project that earlier tackled such a problem in a related domain, or we could select one expert for each technology used in such projects.

In the next section, we will give some more technical hints about how to formalize such retrieval heuristics as described above.

4 Ontology-Based Retrieval Heuristics

If we would do competence retrieval by hand, an intuitive way would be: take as input a graphical representation of the knowledge structures considered (illustrated as directed graphs in Figures 2 and 3), start with the given search items (i.e., marked nodes in the graph) and traverse this graph until a person is found which can be reached from the query items through a "reasonable" sequence of steps. In the examples of the previous section, the meaning of "reasonable sequence of steps" was illustrated by search heuristics describing graph traversal strategies which promise to lead from a competence field to a person which is supposed to know something about this field. Since we believe that such search heuristics are very much too domain and application specific to be formulated once forever and built into the system in a hard-wired manner, we propose a

---

[2] In fact, the question how to optimally represent and exploit ontological information for IR and competence retrieval seems still an open question to us. A more detailed discussion goes beyond the scope of this paper, but is under work. Related problems are investigated, e.g., in [19].

declarative heuristics specification formalism to be interpreted by the CKBS. A heuristics expression is a sequence of formulae of the following form:

$$f_1 \circ f_2 \circ \ldots \circ f_n$$

(denoting the functional composition of the f_i) with

$$f_i \equiv (\lambda)^\gamma$$

where λ is a link or an inverse link (written as $link^{-1}$) and γ is a "partial closure specification", i.e., one of the following path length specifications: n, $n..m$, $\geq n$, * (as abbreviation for ≥ 0), or + (as abbreviation for ≥ 1).

Such a formula takes as input a set of nodes of the directed graph under consideration and, for each node, follows the links specified in the formula in right-to-left order, in each step delivering an intermediary set of nodes as starting point for the next step. "Partial closure" means repeatedly following the same link type (in the case of $\gamma \equiv *$ generating the reflexive and transitive closure of the relation denoted by that link in the ontology). A heuristics formula makes sense if it delivers only **person** nodes as result set. A sequence of formulae is evaluated in its sequential order with the semantics in mind that less trustworthy heuristics should be denoted last.

Example 1: The first example of the previous section can then be specified as follows:

1. $(hasCompetence^{-1})^1$
   "First search for people directly linked to a search concept."
2. $(hasCompetence^{-1})^1 \circ (isSubFieldOf^{-1})^+$
   "Then look for people competent in some subfield."

For the sake of clarity, we have denoted two formulae here. An alternative formulation would have been: $(hasCompetence^{-1})^1 \circ (isSubFieldOf^{-1})^*$

Example 2: The second example can be denoted as follows:

1. $(hasCompetence^{-1})^1$
   "First search for people directly linked to a search concept."
2. $(worksIn^{-1})^1 \circ (usesTechnology^{-1})^1$
   "Then look for people working in a project applying the technology in quest."
3. $(hasCompetence^{-1})^1 \circ (isSubFieldOf)^1$
   "Finally look for people experienced in the direct superconcept of the topic in quest."

These examples show how heuristics expressions can provide a declarative means for tailoring and tuning the CKBS retrieval engine. The heuristics described should not be understood as prescriptive and valid in all environments. They shall just illustrate how ontology-based search heuristics could look like and how they can be written down in an intuitive, declarative, yet expressive way. Exactly the fact that heuristics may differ significantly from domain to domain, from company to company, or application situation to application situation makes such a declarative and easily adaptable formalism interesting and appropriate.

We illustrated the language constructs needed for formulating our sample heuristics. Of course, there are also boolean connectives useful; but only further work and experiments in a fielded application will show what expressiveness is really necessary in application examples. For a finalized, full-fledged search heuristics language, one could imagine, e.g., some kind of quantification, qualitative path length restrictions, or expressions over query context parameters.

Such a heuristics language is certainly more intuitive and flexible than directly coding search heuristics into the implementation of the retrieval machinery. It is necessary because in our opinion, practical applications cannot be sufficiently solved by few general search heuristics like the ones proposed in most papers on ontology-based IR. Of course, it is still not very easy to use such a language for an end-user, but (i) in practice it will be used by employees at the application programmer level, and (ii) it would be an interesting idea to provide both a graphical browser interface and an automatic retrieval engine and try to automatically derive (e.g., by explanation-based learning) search heuristics from user's manual interaction. It should also be noted that explicitly encoded factual knowledge about people's competences is superior—*if available*. What we propose is to enhance—in a cascading search stratgey—the retrieval facilities of a system which must also be robust in a dynamic and incompletely modeled world.

5 Implementation

The CKBS is implemented with JAVA [2] which allows it to be used on all JAVA-enabled platforms like UNIX, Macintosh, and Windows without porting efforts. The CKBS is designed as a client-server model, its architecture is shown in Figure 4.

In the input mask (cf. Figures 1 and 4), the tool allows to formulate queries over competence fields, project memberships, or (directly) employee names. Complex queries can be composed using "AND", "OR", and "NOT".

The actual knowledge base with persons and their competence indices, as well as the ontological structure of competence fields, project membership, etc., are stored in a conventional relational database (RDB) which is coupled to the JAVA system code via JDBC [3]. Details about how to efficiently store and access these object-oriented knowledge structures within the relational paradigm can be found in [4]. The relational storage approach together with some additional schema information (denoted in the picture as DB-signature) allows to implement an object-centered relational algebra (OCRA, see [4]) which provides an object-oriented view and access methods with special (weak) deductive capabilities for the underlying data. In detail, the OCRA directly implements the above

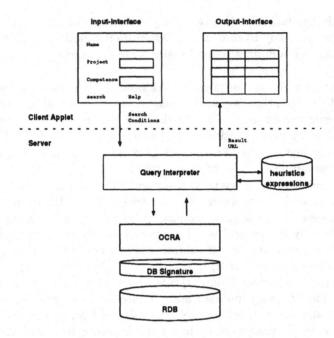

Fig. 4. The Architecture of CKBS

introduced "partial closure" operator, an essential part of heuristics expressions, which allows to efficiently follow a predefined number of links between objects.

Now, the heart of the CKBS retrieval machinery is a query interpreter which takes the user's complex query and maps it onto OCRA expressions, if needed, with the help of additional search heuristics. It goes beyond the scope of this application-oriented paper to sketch how complex queries (with boolean expressions) interact with retrieval heuristics to be translated into OCRA expressions.[3]

6 Conclusions

The study of organizational memories gains more and more interest although IT support is still in its premature stages. A main problem is the dichotomy of the general OM concept which can be understood either people oriented focusing on the intangible parts of the organizational knowledge assets, or document oriented focusing on explicit knowledge representations in documents and artifacts. This dichotomy is reflected, e.g., by the distinction between the process oriented and the product oriented view on Knowledge Management in [13]. It can also be

---

[3] In the current implementation, some parts of the system are much more "hard-wired" than described in the idealized view of Figure 4. However, in the near future we will deliver a full specification of the heuristics expression language and its mapping into OCRA queries.

found in many older works on the foundations of OM, see [7] for an extensive discussion of such categorial problems.

In this paper, we proposed a balanced approach which sees personal competences of employees as a "first-order knowledge source" in the OM which should be modeled and retrieved like other knowledge sources in the OM [5]. This requires, however, a sophisticated indexing and retrieval approach. While the semantical issues of well-understood ontology-based information modeling and retrieval are still an open question (see [19]), we were nevertheless able to implement a competence knowledge-base system fully operational in the DFKI Intranet, up to now containing the personal competences of the members of the Knowledge Management research group. Competences are described with respect to a domain ontology and accompanied by enterprise ontology information (project membership); complex queries are evaluated with the help of retrieval heuristics formulated over the structuring ontologies. We presented a first approach for declaratively specifying simple search heuristics and a generic architecture for processing them. Both will be further developed and specified in more detail if we have more practical experiences using the system to support our group internal customer care tasks.

Of course, there are many open questions which can only be clarified with practical experiences. The question how our approach scales up (with growing ontologies as well as large competence databases) seems not to be crucial. Technically, object-oriented databases and knowledge representation systems make rapid progress wrt. handling large ontological structures. Moreover, the number of personal competence profiles will always be neglectable compared with the document, data, and knowledge bases which must be managed in an OM anyway. A similar argument holds for the knowledge acquisition costs spent for ontology building. This is really a difficult problem if one wants to enable intelligent document and knowledge management in a company. However, if one wants to have this, one definitely has to build ontologies. So, these can also be used for competence management. From a user point of view, large ontologies can cognitively be better handled if there is a clear overall structure like in our approach.

Our system seems to be unique in that it treats documents and people in a similar way; other CKBS approaches use to be simple skill databases with full-text search facilities, or are designed for manual search and browsing. Within the ontology-based IR community (see, e.g., [15]) many approaches are designed for manual browsing, too, or propose only very simple ontological structures together with few generic search or query expansion heuristics. This seems too restrictive to us for real-world problems. So, we are working on the generic heuristics expression language for individual tailoring and tuning of ontology-based retrieval systems. Older work by Baudin et al. [8] already employed much more complicated retrieval heuristics than usual today, but only in a very specific domain and with more restricted ontological structuring mechanisms (the ontology contains only is-a and part-of links) than in our approach.

Minor extensions to our system in the near future will probably comprise an additional graphical presentation of the domain ontology in order to ease query term identification and a "fuzzy matching" facility for tolerating, e.g., small typos when searching for specific project or person names.

References

1. An interview with Tom Davenport and Larry Prusak, about their new book Working Knowledge: How Organizations Manage What They Know. Electronic Publication, http://www.brint.com/km/davenport/working.htm, 1998.
2. JAVA Hompage at SUN. http://java.sun.com/, 1998.
3. JDBC Homepage at SUN. http://java.sun.com/products/jdbc/, 1998.
4. A. Abecker, A. Bernardi, K. Hinkelmann, O. Kühn, and M. Sintek. Techniques for organizational memory information systems. DFKI Document D-98-02, February 1998.
5. A. Abecker, A. Bernardi, K. Hinkelmann, O. Kühn, and M. Sintek. Toward a technology for organizational memories. *IEEE Intelligent Systems*, May/June 1998.
6. A. Abecker, M. Sintek, and H. Wirtz. From hypermedia information retrieval to knowledge management in enterprises. In *IFMIP-98: First Int. Forum on Multimedia & Image Processing*, Anchorage, Alaska, May 1998. TSI Press.
7. L.J. Bannon and K. Kuutti. Shifting perspectives on organizational memory: From storage to active remembering. In *Proc. of the 29th IEEE HICSS, vol. III, Information Systems - Collaboration Systems and Technology*, pages 156–167. IEEE Computer Society Press, Washington, 1996.
8. C. Baudin, S. Kedar, and B. Pell. Increasing levels of assistance in refinement of knowledge-based retrieval systems. In G. Tecuci and Y. Kodratoff, editors, *Machine Learning and Knowledge Acquisition – Integrated Approaches*. Academic Press, 1995.
9. A. Bernardi, M. Sintek, and A. Abecker. Combining artificial intelligence, database technology, and hypermedia for intelligent fault recording. In *ISOMA-98: Sixth Int. Symp. on Manufacturing with Applications*, Anchorage, Alaska, May 1998. TSI Press.
10. Th.H. Davenport. Teltech: The business of knowledge management case study. Electronic Publication by Graduate School of Business, University of Texas at Austin, http://www.bus.utexas.edu/kman/telcase.htm, 1998.
11. M. Eppler. Knowledge Mapping. Eine Einführung in die Wissensvisualisierung. Presentation Slides, http://www.cck.uni-kl.de/wmk/, 1997. In German.
12. G. Kamp. Integrating semantic structure and technical documentation in case-based service support systems. In *Topics in Case-Based Reasoning – First European Workshop, EWCBR-93, Selected Papers*, number 837 in LNCS, pages 392–403. Springer-Verlag, June 1994.
13. O. Kühn and A. Abecker. Corporate memories for knowledge management in industrial practice: Prospects and challenges. In U.M. Borghoff and R. Pareschi, editors, *Information Technology for Knowledge Management*, pages 183–206. Springer-Verlag Berlin, Heidelberg, New York, 1998.
14. D. Logan and J. Kenyon. HELPDESK: Using AI to improve customer support. In A.C. Scott and Ph. Klahr, editors, *Innovative Applications of AI, IAAI-92*, pages 37–53, Menlo Park, Cambridge, London, 1992. AAAI Press / The MIT Press.

15. D.L. McGuiness. Ontological issues for knowledge-enhanced search. IOS Press, 1998. Int'l Conference on Formal Ontology in Information Systems (FOIS'98).
16. D. O'Leary. Knowledge management systems: Converting and connecting. *IEEE Intelligent Systems*, May/June 1998.
17. E.W. Stein and V. Zwass. Actualizing organizational memory with information technology. *Information Systems Research*, 6(2), 1995.
18. C.J. van Rijsbergen. Towards an information logic. In *Proc. of the 12th Annual Int. ACM SIGIR Conf. on Research and Development in Information Retrieval*, 1989.
19. C. Welty. The ontological nature of subject taxonomies. IOS Press, 1998. Int'l Conference on Formal Ontology in Information Systems (FOIS'98).
20. K.M. Wiig. *Knowledge Management: Foundations*. Schema Press, Arlington, 1993.
21. W.A. Woods. Conceptual indexing: A better way to organize knowledge. Technical Report TR-97-61, SUN Microsystems Laboratories, Palo Alto, CA, USA, April 1997.

Practical Evaluation of an Organizational Memory Using the Goal-Question-Metric Technique

Markus Nick and Carsten Tautz

Fraunhofer Institute for Experimental Software Engineering
Sauerwiesen 6, D-67661 Kaiserslautern, Germany
{nick, tautz}@iese.fhg.de

Abstract. Companies are recognizing the increasing importance of investing in the build-up of core competencies for their competitiveness. This is supported by the set-up and maintenance of an organizational memory. To justify such an investment, it must be evaluated according to the business case. Our evaluation approach uses the Goal-Question-Metric technique to systematically develop a measurement program for the evaluation of an experience base (an organizational memory for software engineering knowledge). Our approach has been applied to a publicly accessible WWW-based experience base for CBR systems, which supports the development of CBR systems. The measurement program not only helped evaluate the system but also provided guidance for the development of the system.

1 Introduction

Knowledge management (KM) has become a cornerstone for the competitiveness of companies, because

> in the long run, competitiveness derives from the ability to build, at lower cost and more speedily than competitors, the core competencies that spawn unanticipated products. [Here,] core competencies are the [result of] collective learning in the organization, especially how to coordinate diverse production skills and integrate multiple streams of technologies. [...] A company that has failed to invest in core competence building will find it very difficult to enter an emerging market. [14]

At the Fraunhofer IESE, we help our clients build up their core competencies in software development. Part of our transfer approach is to set up and run organizational memories for software engineering knowledge. The purpose of these KM processes is to "maximize the company's knowledge-related effectiveness and returns from its knowledge assets and to renew them constantly." [16, p2] The organizational memories explicitly store the core competencies in software development in the form of experience gained. In this paper, we refer to this special kind of organizational memory (OM) as an *experience base* (EB) [7]. It is set up and run by a logical and/or physical organization we refer to as the *experience factory*.

However, as with all investments, there has to be a positive balance between the benefits and the costs for setting up and running OMs [1]. Benefits are realized if the knowledge, which is stored in an OM, is exploited effectively.[1] The benefits of explicitly storing knowledge can be evaluated from various viewpoints (i.e., from that of a single user, a software development project, or the software development organization at large) with regard to various aspects (e.g., cost savings and reduced time-to-market of products). But all of the variations have in common that they are based on the business case, that is, on the way the OM is used in practice. Most existing evaluation approaches just provide a set of measures without a systematic, business-related rationale and, thus, cover the measurement space only partly. What is needed is a technique that reflects the business case [13]. Such a technique would systematically derive and select adequate measures based on the various "viewpoints" and environments. Therefore, a technique for evaluating an OM must be tailorable to company-specific objectives. There is no universal set of measures that can be used for all companies.

In the field of software engineering, an evaluation technique has been developed that can deal with these issues: the *Goal-Question-Metric (GQM) technique* [8, 15]. In this paper, we describe how this technique can be used for the evaluation of an experience base.

The paper is organized as follows. Section 2 gives an overview of our evaluation approach. Section 3 presents our evaluation approach in more detail and illustrates this with an application to a publicly available experience base [9]. Section 4 describes the relation to other work. The paper ends with a summary and a conclusion in Section 5.

2 Our Evaluation Approach

This section introduces the focus for the evaluation and the evaluation technique.

Evaluation focus. Basili, Caldiera, and Rombach propose that software development must be seen and treated as a professional business rather than an art. An experience factory is established to improve this business continuously by learning and reuse [7]. Since the obvious ultimate goal of a business is success – especially economic success –, an evaluation of an experience factory and its experience base must focus on its success. Then, such an evaluation can be used to justify the establishment of an experience factory. In this paper, we focus on the technical evaluation of the experience base.

Evaluation technique. GQM is an innovative technology for goal-oriented software engineering measurement [8, 11, 15]. GQM helps define and implement operational and measurable software improvement goals. It has been successfully applied in sev-

---

[1] This is a restrictive definition. In this paper, we will focus on the evaluation of the benefits of explicitly stored knowledge. However, knowledge management may also be used for tacit knowledge. The measurement of the benefits of tacit knowledge is beyond the scope of this paper.

eral companies, such as NASA-SEL, Bosch, Digital, and Schlumberger [10]. In GQM programs, the analysis task of measurement is specified precisely and explicitly by detailed measurement goals, called GQM goals, that reflect the business needs. Relevant measures are derived in a top-down fashion based on the goals via a set of questions and quality/resource models. This refinement is precisely documented in a GQM plan, providing an explicit rationale for the selection of the underlying measures. The data collected is interpreted in a bottom-up fashion considering the limitations and assumptions underlying each measure.

3 The GQM Technique and Its Application to CBR-PEB

This section describes the application of our approach to the existing system CBR-PEB. First, the system CBR-PEB is introduced. Then it is shown how GQM has been applied to evaluate CBR-PEB. Finally, it is stated how the evaluation can be rolled out for typical organizational memories (i.e., several domains and user classes).

3.1 The System CBR-PEB

CBR-PEB is an experience base that has been developed for supporting CBR system development [4]. Emphasis is placed on providing decision support for reusing existing CBR system know-how for the development of new systems. To make the system easily accessible by CBR developers all around the world, the system has been made publicly available via the WWW [9].

This experience base is based on a number of research efforts: Althoff et al. [2] developed the classification criteria for CBR systems. Bartsch-Spörl, Althoff, and Meissonnier [5] conducted a survey about CBR systems and made these experiences reusable by means of CBR technology, that is, each questionnaire has been represented as a structured case. Finally, an evaluation program was developed in order to show the usefulness of the system from the viewpoint of its users.

3.2 The GQM Process for CBR-PEB

This section introduces GQM in detail and shows how GQM has been applied to evaluate the existing experience base CBR-PEB.

GQM can be applied in cycles. Each cycle refines the measurement program and – as a side effect – the EB system as well. Figure 1 shows the complete GQM cycle and its steps in general, and its instantiation for CBR-PEB (the first iteration). The steps of the GQM cycle match the steps of the Quality Improvement Paradigm (QIP), which is compatible with TQM [6]. The single steps are described in detail in the following.

Prestudy. The first phase of a GQM program has the objective of collecting information relevant to the introduction of a GQM-based measurement program. This includes

Fig. 1. Standard GQM cycle and its instantiation for CBR-PEB

a description of the environment, "overall project goals", and "task of the system". This helps the person(s) responsible for the measurement program become familiar with the topic making it possible to appear in interviews as a competent person and partner. Usually, the participants of the measurement program are also trained in this phase.

In the prestudy for CBR-PEB, a usage process model for CBR system development with CBR-PEB was developed to allow identification of definite points for measurement. It was also proposed that the public installation in the WWW will lead to certain problems with the collection of measurement data, that is, it must be possible to distinguish between measurement data from surfers and from real use.

Identify GQM Goals. The objective of identifying goals is to get a list of well-specified and ranked goals. First, informal goals are collected. Second, they are formalized according to the template for GQM goals (see Figure 2 "Goal" for an example). Third, the goals are ranked, and, fourth, the ones to be used in the measurement program are selected.

The resulting GQM goals focus on the technical and economic utility of the retrieved information (Goal 1 and 2) and on the user friendliness of the EB system (Goal 3). The viewpoint is represented by the interviewees and the context by environment and task of the system. Here, it is obvious that the other goals have the same viewpoint and context as Goal 1.

Develop GQM Plan. The objective of this step is to develop a GQM plan for each goal, that is, an operational refinement of a GQM goal via questions into measures including the interpretation models that specify how the measurement data is analyzed to answer the questions. This is done as a two-step process:

First, people representing the viewpoint according to the GQM goal are interviewed to make their implicit, relevant knowledge about the GQM goal explicit. For this purpose, *abstraction sheets* are filled out in an interview (e.g., see Figure 2 for the abstraction sheet of Goal 2 for CBR-PEB). An *abstraction sheet* represents the main issues

Goal:	*Analyze*	the retrieved information	**Names:** M.M., N.N.
	for the purpose of	characterization	**Date:** 97/10/01
	with respect to	economic utility	
	from the viewpoint of	the CBR system developers	
	in the context of	decision support for CBR system development.	

Quality factors:	**Variation factors:**

1. similarity of retrieved information as modeled in CBR-PEB **(Q-12)**
2. degree of maturity (desired: max.) [development, prototype, pilot use, daily use] **(Q-13)**
[...]
	1. amount of background knowledge
	   a. number of attributes **(Q-8.1.1)**
	   [...]
	2. quality of the case source [university, industrial research, industry]
	[...]

Baseline hypothesis:	**Impact of variation factors:**
1. M.M.: 0.2; N.N.: 0.5 (scale: 0..1) [...] The estimates are on average.	1. The higher the amount of background knowledge, the higher the similarity. **(Q-8)** 2. The more "industrial" the case source, the higher the degree of maturity. **(Q-9)** [...]

Fig. 2. Abstraction sheet for Goal 2 "Economic Utility". The numbers of the related questions in the GQM plan are included to improve traceability (here limited to questions addressed in the paper).

and dependencies of a GQM goal in four quadrants: The "quality factors" describe the measured properties of the object in the goal, the "baseline hypothesis" describes the current knowledge with respect to the measured properties, the "variation factors" are factors that are expected to have an impact on the measured properties. This impact is described under "impact of variation factors". Variation factors should only be listed if their impact is stated as well.

Second, for each goal a *GQM plan* is derived from the abstraction sheet. For each issue addressed in the quadrants "quality focus" and "impact of variation factors", a top-level question is derived. For each of these top-level questions, an interpretation rule (called "model"), the hypothesis, and a data presentation are also given. The top-level questions are refined as necessary. For example, the question for the variation hypothesis 3 for Goal 2 is refined into questions for the involved variation factor "quality of case source" and the involved quality factor "degree of maturity" (see Figure 3). So, the GQM plan documents all relevant and necessary information for the evaluation and, thus, shows a rationale for the measurement program.

Measures in GQM plans can be qualitative (e.g., quality of case source) and quantitative (e.g., completeness and similarity) as well as subjective (e.g., completeness estimated by the user) and objective (e.g., similarity automatically collected by the system).

Derive Measurement Plan. The objective of this step is to implement the data collection. Thus, the GQM plans must be linked with the usage processes of the EB system.

Q-9   What is the impact of the quality of the case source on the degree of maturity?

Q-9.1 What is the quality of the case source?

M-9.1.1 **per retrieval attempt:** for each chosen case: class of case source [university, industrial research, industry]

Q-9.2 What is the degree of maturity of the system?

M-9.2.1 **per retrieval attempt:** for each chosen case: case attribute "status" ["prototype", "being developed", "pilot system", "application in practical use"; "unknown"]

Model: Distribution of retrieval attempts by degree of maturity and class of case source — see data presentation below.

The percentage of retrieval attempts per degree of maturity m (including "unknown") and class of case source c is calculated as follows:

$$att\%_{maturity}(m, c) = \frac{\sum_{k=1}^{\#retrieval\ attempts} \frac{\#chosen\ cases\ in\ attempt\ k\ in\ (m,\ c)}{\#chosen\ cases\ in\ attempt\ k}}{\#retrieval\ attempts}$$

A *chosen case* is a retrieved case that is regarded useful by the user.

Hypothesis: The more "industrial" the case source ("industry" is more industrial than "industrial research" is more industrial than "university"), the higher the degree of maturity.

That is, there should be a cumulation on the diagonal from (prototype, university) to (practical use, industry) in the data presentation below.

Data presentation:

degree of maturity	class of case source			
	university	industrial research	industry	unknown
development				10%
prototype	51%			
pilot use				
practical use			30%	
unknown	9%			

Fig. 3. Excerpt from GQM plan for Goal #2 "Economic Utility", Question 9. The data presentation contains the results from the usage trials for this question.

This is documented in the form of a *measurement plan* that describes for all measures from all GQM plans of the measurement program what measurement data is collected when, how, by whom, and who validates and stores the data. Finally, the data collection procedures are implemented, that is, questionnaires (paper-based or on-line – see Figure 4 for an example) and automatic data collection procedures are developed.

Data Collection. For the first iteration of the measurement program, only data from usage trials with the experts and some other persons were collected. This helped validate the data collection procedures and get first results. For the second iteration of the measurement program, data from real use are being collected.

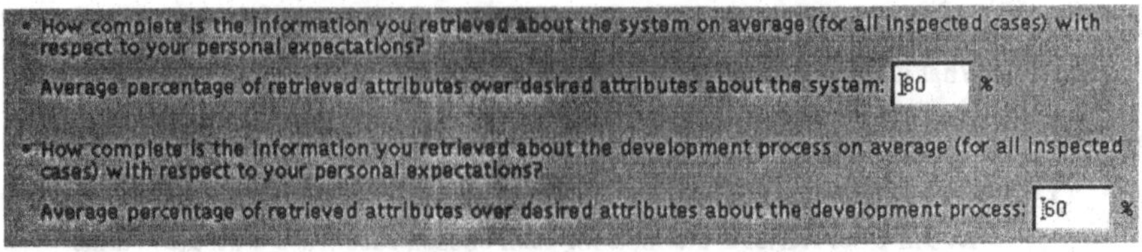

Fig. 4. Excerpt from on-line questionnaire for Question 5 (completeness).

Interpret Collected Data. The collected data is interpreted in *feedback sessions* with the experts (for exemplary data see Figure 3 "Data Presentation"). Thus, the objectives of these feedback sessions are the interpretation of the results of measurement data analyses, the verification of the hypotheses stated in the GQM plans, the evaluation of the measurement program, and the identification of the possibilities for improvement of both the software system and the measurement program [11, p151].

In case of CBR-PEB, possibilities for improvement of both the measurement program and the retrieval process (i.e., the EB system) were identified. For the measurement program and the on-line questionnaires, for example, one should try to receive feedback from the Internet by means of a subjective rating of the whole system by the user and a text field for comments about the system. This feedback should be evaluated by the experience factory staff and during future feedback sessions. For the EB system, the experts suggested to improve the on-line help regarding certain terms which are not obvious.

Package. Some of the experience gained in the measurement program was packaged as lessons learned to make it explicit. These lessons learned can be used as guidelines for creating and maintaining a successful experience base. For example:

- High-quality artifacts are required and the information about these artifacts should be as up-to-date and as complete as possible.
- An effective retrieval mechanism is needed for identifying suitable (i.e., relevant) artifacts for reuse (e.g., with the 60 attributes of CBR-PEB, an exact match would be pure chance and very rare). This relevance must be modeled appropriately.
- The first iteration of the GQM process for CBR-PEB showed that the GQM approach is useful for evaluating an experience base and led to a meaningful result.

3.3 Analysis of the Measures Used in the GQM Plans

In general, the measures used are simpler than expected. For example, we expected that the experts would ask for recall and precision for measuring completeness and correctness. Instead, a very simple subjective definition for completeness was given.

None of the measures used in the GQM plans refers to cost or benefit in dollars or effort. The quality factors from the goals related to utility are believed to have an impact on economic cost or benefit (i.e., CBR system development costs).[2] Thus, the analysis of the measures shows that practitioners tend to use indirect measures for which data can be easily collected, that is, early with low collection effort.

3.4 Roll-Out of the GQM Program

Although, in the case of CBR-PEB our approach has only been applied to one domain (CBR system development) and one class of users (CBR system developers), it can be easily rolled out to the general case with several domains (e.g., management processes, documents, experiences) and several classes of users (e.g., line and project managers) by defining GQM goals for each context and viewpoint according to domain and user class. Thus, the measurement program can be scaled according to a company's needs by refining domain and/or user class.

4 Related Work

In [2], existing CBR systems were evaluated to derive the requirements for the INRECA system [3], which was the basis for several industrial CBR systems combining the benefits of existing CBR systems. Although the goal of this study was a different one, the context was the same as for CBR-PEB, and the procedure and the kind of expected results were similar to the GQM process: The evaluation criteria were categorized and refined. The existing CBR systems were analyzed according to the evaluation criteria to derive the requirements for the INRECA system. Several iterations were necessary to get the final results.

In [12], it was proposed to use evaluation to guide the incremental development of knowledge-based systems. An experimental methodology for this guidance was developed. It was stated that people (knowledge engineers and users) need to be involved in development and evaluation. This is similar to the involvement of experts in GQM interviews and feedback sessions.

In [13], the need for business-level evaluations was underlined. An approach using critical success metrics (CSMs) for such evaluations was presented. CSMs indicate success if some number inferred from the system passes some value. This approach was applied to a knowledge-based system used in the petrochemical industry. In contrast to GQM, the approach does not allow subjective measures, which are typical for more complex applications like experience bases, and allows only small changes to a running system.

5 Results and Conclusion

Most of the existing evaluation approaches for knowledge-based systems in general and organizational memories (OM) in particular are difficult to adapt to company-spe-

---

[2] This was stated by the experts in the GQM interviews.

cific needs [13]. To be useful in practice, evaluation techniques need to be able to cope with various environments, viewpoints, and measurement objectives. A detailed evaluation can also guide the development of an OM. Our approach uses the Goal-Question-Metric (GQM) technique to evaluate an OM for software engineering knowledge. GQM is a technique for software engineering measurements, especially designed to deal with practical needs. It does so by involving the data collectors (in this case the users of the OM), as they are considered to be the experts in developing and/or applying the measured objects.

We described the application of GQM using an experience base for case-based reasoning systems (CBR-PEB). CBR-PEB was developed as a repository for CBR systems. A CBR system stored in CBR-PEB can be used as the basis for a new CBR system and, thus, reduce the development costs for new CBR systems.

Starting with the predefined (but vague) measurement goal of "evaluating the success of CBR-PEB from the viewpoint of the developer of a CBR system", the users refined the goal to measuring the "technical and economic utility of the retrieved information" and the "user friendliness of the system". This means that the users were not interested in the success of the OM at large, but rather in the success of each single retrieval attempt. A study of existing evaluation approaches performed beforehand led to the hypothesis that cost savings in dollars or man hours for developing a new CBR system would be appropriate measures for evaluating the success. However, during the application of GQM we had to learn that practitioners tend to use indirect measures (such as number of assets in the OM, completeness and accuracy of their characterizations). In contrast to cost figures, the data for measures identified by the practitioners can be collected very early (i.e., at retrieval time). Cost data can only be collected at the completion of the development. Savings in cost cannot be measured objectively, because it is difficult to predict the costs for developing systems from scratch. Moreover, the users applied CBR-PEB in unanticipated ways (e.g., as an information system for performing feasibility studies). Therefore, the measurement of success must also consider the usages, not anticipated by the developers of OMs.

From these results we conclude that the application of the GQM technique was successful, that is, the application led to an evaluation fulfilling the "information needs" of a practitioner. This is in line with the experience gained so far [10].

Currently, we are evaluating CBR-PEB (continuing the use of GQM) in a field study based on the initial results presented in this paper. In the future, we will apply the GQM technique to OMs containing various kinds of knowledge about software development. Moreover, we will detail and simplify (wherever possible) the GQM application process for evaluating OMs for software development. As part of this work, "core measures" will be identified that will help in the guidance of the development and maintenance of OMs for software development.

6 Acknowledgments

We thank Klaus-Dieter Althoff, Frank Bomarius, and Sonnhild Namingha for reviewing an earlier version of this paper.

References

[1] A. Abecker, S. Decker, N. Matta, F. Maurer, and U. Reimer. *Building, Maintaining, and Using Organizational Memories (Proceedings of the Workshop on Organizational Memories at ECAI-98)*. Aug. 1998. http://www.aifb.uni-karlsruhe.de/WBS/ECAI98OM/.

[2] K.-D. Althoff. Evaluating case-based reasoning systems: The Inreca case study. Postdoctoral thesis (Habilitationsschrift), University of Kaiserslautern, 1997.

[3] K.-D. Althoff, E. Auriol, R. Bergmann, S. Breen, S. Dittrich, R. Johnston, M. Manago, R. Traphöner, and S. Wess. Case-based reasoning for decision support and diagnostic problem solving: The INRECA approach. In *Proceedings of the Third German Conference on Knowledge-Based Systems (XPS-95)*, 1995.

[4] K.-D. Althoff, M. Nick, and C. Tautz. Concepts for reuse in the experience factory and their implementation for CBR system development. In *Proceedings of the Eleventh German Workshop on Machine Learning (FGML-98)*, Aug. 1998. http://demolab.iese.fhg.de:8080/Publications/fgml98/.

[5] B. Bartsch-Spörl, K.-D. Althoff, and A. Meissonnier. Learning from and reasoning about case-based reasoning systems. In *Proceedings of the Fourth German Conference on Knowledge-Based Systems (XPS97)*, Mar. 1997.

[6] V. R. Basili. The Experience Factory and its relationship to other improvement paradigms. In I. Sommerville and M. Paul, editors, *Proceedings of the Fourth European Software Engineering Conference*, pages 68–83. Lecture Notes in Computer Science Nr. 717, Springer–Verlag, 1993.

[7] V. R. Basili, G. Caldiera, and H. D. Rombach. Experience Factory. In J. J. Marciniak, editor, *Encyclopedia of Software Engineering*, volume 1, pages 469–476. John Wiley & Sons, 1994.

[8] V. R. Basili, G. Caldiera, and H. D. Rombach. Goal Question Metric Paradigm. In J. J. Marciniak, editor, *Encyclopedia of Software Engineering*, volume 1, pages 528–532. John Wiley & Sons, 1994.

[9] Cased-Based Reasoning Product Experience Base CBR-PEB. 1998. http://demolab.iese.fhg.de:8080/.

[10] T. CEMP Consortium. Customized establishment of measurement programs. Final report, ESSI Project Nr. 10358, Germany, 1996.

[11] C. Gresse, B. Hoisl, and J. Wüst. A process model for GQM-based measurement. Technical Report STTI-95-04-E, Software Technologie Transfer Initiative Kaiserslautern, Fachbereich Informatik, Universität Kaiserslautern, D-67653 Kaiserslautern, 1995.

[12] S. Kirchhoff. *Abbildungsqualität von wissensbasierten Systemen: eine Methodologie zur Evaluierung*. Verlag Josef Eul, Bergisch Gladbach, Germany, 1994.

[13] T. Menzies. Evaluation issues with critical success metrics. In *Proceedings of the Eleventh Workshop on Knowledge Acquisition, Modeling and Management*, Feb. 1998.

[14] C. K. Prahalad and G. Hamel. The core competence of the corporation. *Havard Business Review*, 68(3):79–91, May-June 1990.

[15] H. D. Rombach. Practical benefits of goal-oriented measurement. In *Proceedings of the Annual Workshop of the Centre for Software Reliability*, pages 217–235. Elsevier, Sept. 1990.

[16] K. M. Wiig. Knowledge management: Where did it come from and where will it go? *Expert Systems With Applications*, 13(1):1–14, 1997.

On Texts, Cases, and Concepts

Mario Lenz[1] and Alexander Glintschert[2]

[1] Dept. of Computer Science, Humboldt University, D-10099 Berlin, Germany
lenz@informatik.hu-berlin.de
[2] infopark online service GmbH, Kitzingstr. 15, 12277 Berlin, Germany
alex@infopark.de

Abstract. The management of textual information is getting more and more attention within the case-based reasoning community. In this paper, we will address the question of how a case base can be obtained from a given textual description and how this representation scheme can be enriched by higher level concepts.

Keywords: Textual Case-Based Rasoning, information extraction, text classification.

1 Introduction

Traditionally, case-based reasoning research has been very much directed towards structured representations of data. This is still true for many of today's applications as, for example, in electronic commerce scenarios. In addition, however, the management of less structured information is receiving more and more attention.

First of all, this covers the management of information contained in textual documents in the sense of reusing existing documents for problem solving and performing an inference based on given documents in order to answer an information request, such as the question posed by a user.

On the other hand, CBR also touches special aspects of knowledge management (KM) in so far as it may be used to implement subtasks of KM, such as knowledge dissemination and knowledge reuse [7]. This is the case, for example, when implementing Textual CBR applications designed for in-house usage as was the case in the FALL-Q project [9].

In this paper, we will address the question of how a formally represented case base can be obtained from documents mainly containing textual descriptions and how this representation scheme can be enriched by higher level concepts. For the latter, we will demonstrate how techniques developed within the Information Extraction community can be exploited in order to obtain a structured representation of the semantics of a given text without performing deep natural language processing. We will briefly describe the THEMESEARCH system which implements these techniques and sketch possible application areas.

2 Textual Case-Based Reasoning

2.1 Considering cases as documents

In Textual Case-Based Reasoning, existing documents are interpreted as cases containing information worth to be reused for future problem solving episodes [11]. A specific problem that has to be solved is the identification of an appropriate index vocabulary in terms of the knowledge container model [12, 13]. Also, a similarity model has to be constructed which reflects the relationships among the various index terms, such as synonymous phrases.

For acquiring the necessary knowledge, several *knowledge layers* can be used some of which represent knowledge about a particular set of terms (such as general purpose terms or domain-specific phrases). Other layers can be used to encode relationships among these terms as well as a more general domain model for a targetted application. Filling these knowledge layers requires a strong focus on a domain in order to be able to build up a similarity model describing the domain as precisely as possible. Hence, a careful knowledge engineering process is required [6].

CBR-ANSWERS is a system built at Humboldt University, Berlin, in cooperation with *tecInno*, Kaiserslautern. The system implements an interpretation of Textual CBR where cases are seen as a specific *view* on existing textual documents rather than having a separate case base in addition to these. Very briefly, specific keywords and phrases are being represented as *information entities* (IEs) which, in turn, may be connected by links according their semantic relationships. Taken together, these components can be represented by a Case Retrieval Net [8] allowing for an efficient and flexible case retrieval.

2.2 Applications of Textual CBR

A number of successful applications of these techniques already exist, such as the SIMATIC KNOWLEDGE MANAGER which aims at providing an automatic hotline via the World Wide Web to technicians maintaining Siemens products [1, 11]. The basic idea here is to reuse existing documents, such as FAQs and problem reports, and to try answering user requests by finding relevant documents. The major benefit for the user is that they have permanent access to information independently of whether the actual telephone hotline is busy or whether problems have to be solved outside the office hours. On behalf of Siemens, the goal is primarily *call avoidance*: the highly skilled hotline staff should not be bothered with questions that often reoccur and that have been solved before.

The major difference of the techniques implemented in CBR-ANSWERS to traditional Information Retrieval models is that assessing the relevance of a document to a user's query requires extensive knowledge about the domain and cannot rely on a pure keyword matching strategy. Rather, domain-specific knowledge has to be taken into account, such as information about products, their components and devices, and which products are compatible and which not.

2.3 The need for higher level concepts

Despite the success of the approach taken by CBR-ANSWERS, an obvious short-coming is that there is no real analysis of the structure of phrases and sentences. Rather, the textual descriptions contained in the documents are represented as *sets* of IEs — that is, any *structure* present in the text will be lost and relation-ships among the detected IEs can not be recognized.

One first sight, an obvious solution to this problem is to apply sophisticated techniques known from Natural Language Procssing (NLP) and to really parse the texts according to a given (formal) grammar. This approach, however, is not feasible because of several reasons:

- In real-world applications, huge amounts of data have to be dealt with. According to our experiences, state-of-the-art NLP techniques are too com-plicated to handle these efficiently.
- In particular in technical domains, unknown terms will occur in virtually every sentence. In contrast, many NLP techniques require a *complete* dictio-nary and would reject sentences in which just one unknown word is present.
- Very often, documents do not contain complete sentences in a correct gram-mar. Rather, many brief notes and comments are inserted and tables are widely used to represent information. Thus, the language being used is differ-ent from, for example, novels where each sentence is grammatically correct.

Due to these shortcomings, an extension of the techniques used so far in the CBR-ANSWERS system has been developed which originates in the techniques developed within the Information Extraction community [14, 3]. The basic idea is to perform a more *shallow* analysis of the structure of sentences than in NLP; this analysis is heavily pattern-driven in that typical phrases and stereotypes are used to identify the different roles of the various objects in a sentence. In the following section, we will describe this approach in more detail.

3 From IEs to Concepts

The fundamental idea underlying the THEMESEARCH system is to enrich a Tex-tual CBR system as described in the previous section with a pattern-matching component that, in a certain sense, abstracts from some of the less important components of a sentence, identifies the main phrases, and recognizes the existing structures between these.

3.1 Reoccuring phrases and expressions

This approach is motivated by the observation that, at least in the application domains considered so far, stereotypical expressions are very common. Very often this is due to the fact that a fairly small group of people is responsible for writing the documents and, hence, there is a natural tendency to use *cut–and–paste* techniques whenever possible.

As an example consider so-called *Design Change Request* (DCR) documents in which the desire of a client for an additional functionality in a purchased product is expressed. In most situations, these documents contain a number of of expressions which can easily be mapped to IEs referring to

- the name of the client;
- the current version of the product;
- a desired functionality;
- a purpose the functionality is required for.

These could be interpreted as *actors* in the given expression.

In addition, only a small number of verb phrases are in most situations, such as forms of **ask** and **request**. Given this, and knowledge about the above described actors, only a fairly small number of *patterns* is possible, that is only a limited number of word forms that may occur and of the ordering of these words. This is in particular true for English texts where stronger rules for word ordering apply than, for example, in German.

Consequently, a pattern-driven approach where texts are matched against the most likely patterns in a current context is promising in so far as it suffices to analyze the most essential parts of the given texts.

3.2   Concept nodes

In the very heart of the approach are so-called *concept nodes*. These are structures which become activated by a *trigger* which is, in most cases, a specific word. However, in addition to this trigger, a concept node is only being activated if it occurs within a predefined linguistic context. To specify this context, the concept node also has a number of *activation conditions* which have to be satisfied in order for the concept node to be activated. These activation conditions describe the required structure of a sentence in terms of words that must be present, of the ordering of the various parts of the sentence, or of grammatical forms of verbs and nouns.

Very briefly, a concept node has the following components:

- a unique name;
- a specific trigger word which is most often a verb;
- a list of patterns that could be used to match a sentence;
- a list of slots each of which is used to match a word or group of words and lists the positions on which this word may occur in the above listed patterns.

A pattern is an abstraction of a set of potential sentences which can be obtained by one or more of the following techniques:

- replacing a word by a more abstract concept, such as a specific name of a person by the concept **proper_name**.
- replacing a word with its *Part-of-Speech* tag (which we obtained by using the TREETAGGER tool [1]);
- replacing a word or group of words with a wildcard;

---

[1] http://www.www.ims.uni-stuttgart.de/Tools/DecisionTreeTagger.html

3.3   The matching process

Matching starts by handing over a given text to the TREE TAGGER which splits the input into sentences and adds part-of-speech information to each word. This includes information about the possible word forms and the base form. Given this, a sentence is scanned for potential trigger words and the corresponding concept nodes are checked as to whether their ativation conditions expressed are satisfied. If such a matching concept node is detected, the information contained in that sentence may be extracted and represented in a frame–like form.

During this matching process, the lingustic context expressed in the concept node definitions helps to overcome the *ambiguity problem*, i.e. that certain keywords and phrases may have completely different meanings in different situations. At the same time, the *paraphrase problem* known from Information Retrieval techniques is avoided as a concept node may be used to capture more than one lingustic context. While the basic constituents of the concept nodes remain the same (in particular the trigger), the order of words and phrases may change and the occurence of words may differ, such as when rewriting an active sentence in its passive version.

4   THEMESEARCH

The goal of the THEMESEARCH system [4] is to provide a *thematic* search engine for the World Wide Web. By using the above described concepts nodes, documents that have been collected by a robot should be classified as to whether or not they really describe a topic related to the predefined domain. The difference to existing systems is that classification of documents should be based on *contents* rather than on the language of the document or the internet domain where it has been found.

4.1   General architecture of THEMESEARCH

The general architecture of the THEMESEARCH system is shown in Figure 1. For the purpose of this paper, only the DOCUMENT EVALUATOR and the DOCUMENT RETRIEVAL COMPONENT are of further interest as they are based on the above described techniques of Textual CBR and the utilization of concept nodes.

The general idea of THEMESEARCH is to apply a filter to the documents collected by the DOCUMENT FINDER such that only those documents are inserted into the internal database which appear to be relevant to the domain. Relevance is determined based on the number of instanciated concept nodes that could be found in a document (for details on this see [4]).

4.2   Applications of THEMESEARCH

In a first implementation, THEMESEARCH addressed German documents about sights in Berlin. A vast amount of related documents exist and even more would

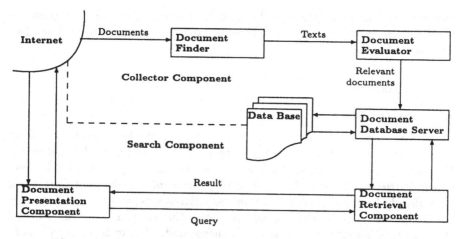

Fig. 1. General architecture of THEMESEARCH (taken from [4])

be considered as relevant by a pure keyword-based approach simply because they mention the name of a sight in some place. If, however, concept nodes are applied, then

- the precision may be greatly improved by discarding those documents which, by pure coincidence, mention a term that seems related to Berlin sights but does not otherwise express one of the typical concepts;
- information about the documents may be extracted in represented in a more structured form, such as frames.

As an example consider the example

The Brandenburg Gate has been built by Carl Gotthard Langhans in 1871.

which would match a pattern

    * BUILDING MODAL_VERB BUILD_PASSIVE "by" PERSON "in" YEAR.

As should be obvious, having matched this pattern successfully allows for classifying the text as relevant to the domain of Berlin sights. In addition, knowledge about *who* built *which* sight *when* can be extracted.

As it turned out during the development of the THEMESEARCH system, verbs appear to be most useful as triggers in concept nodes. Furthermore, for the particular domain a relatively small number of highly significant verbs could be identified, such as *to build* or *to be situated*.

4.3 Further application areas

THEMESEARCH has been designed primarily for the classification of documents as either relevant or non-relevant to the given domain. As already pointed out, however, similar techniques may be used for extracting information from the texts and using this for further improving existing Textual CBR systems (see Section 5.2 below).

5 Discussion

5.1 Current State

As already mentioned, the THEMESEARCH system has been implemented for classification tasks. With respect to Figure 1, the *Document Evaluator*, the *Database*, and the *Document Database Server* are fully implemented. The *Document Retrieval Component* as well as the *Document Presentation Component* have already been implemented within the CBR-ANSWERS system. Thus, only the *Document Finder* remains as an open issue. Currently, a major shortcoming of the system is that the dictionary of concept nodes has to be built manually, tools for this currently do not exist.

With respect to classification accuracy, THEMESEARCH has been evaluated by means of the Berlin sights domain; details can be found in [4].

5.2 Future Work

In the near future we will address three main issues:

- the integration of concept nodes into the CBR-ANSWERS system;
- the application of this approach to other domains;
- the implementation of the *Document Finder*;
- machine learning techniques for automatically acquiring potential concept nodes based on a given document collection (see, for example, [2]).

Concerning the first point it is not necessarily required to represent concept nodes as part of the Case Retrieval Nets used to index the documents. Rather, recognition of concept nodes may be performed in a second stage *after* the retrieval based on traditional IEs has been performed because the IEs that describe the contents of the concept nodes have to be present in the document and, thus, the process of actually recognizing the concepts nodes may be seen as a filter functionality.

A more difficult problem is how to recognize concepts in queries because these in most cases do not provide sufficient information for more than a shallow analysis. A three-stage process seems promising here which

1. performs retrieval based on IEs,
2. analyzes the retrieved documents with respect to concept nodes,
3. queries the user for these concepts (apart from showing the results of the actual retrieval process).

The latter point also raises an interesting question as to what the result of a CBR retrieval process should be. In theory, it is a preference ordering of cases. In practice, however, various pieces of information may be desired based on the analysis of the user's query and relevant cases. This is beyond what is traditionally considered retrieval of cases.

5.3   Related Work

As already discussed in Section 2, NLP techniques might be considered as potential alternatives to the approaches discussed in this paper. Due to the mentioned shortcomings, however, we did not further investigate into this direction. Nevertheless, we realized that there might be strong relationships. For example, verbs appear to be highly useful as triggers for concept nodes due to their position being relatively fixed within a sentence. Similarly, HPSG formalisms known from NLP are very much verb phrase driven.

Another area of research, from which in particular the idea of using concept nodes has been borrowed, is Information Extraction (IE) the goal of which is the identification of structural information in given texts [3]. THEMESEARCH goes a step further, though, in that the information extracted from the documents is afterwards used for a particular purpose, namely text classification. On the other hand, state-of-the-art IE systems are probably more advanved with respect to feature extraction than THEMESEARCH currently is. Unfortunately, we have not yet managed to get access to a running IE system which we could test for our purposes.

References

1. K.-H. Busch. Customer Support for Siemens Products on the Internet and CD-ROM. Talk at EWCBR-98 Industry Day, 1998.
2. C. Cardie. A case-based approach to knowledge acquisition for domain-specific sentence analysis. In *Proc. AAAI-93*, 1993.
3. H. Cunningham. Information extraction - a user guide. Research Memo CS-97-02, University of Sheffield, Sheffield, 1997.
4. A. Glintschert. ThemeSearch: Aufbau einer intelligenten, themenspezifischen Suchmaschine im WWW. Master's thesis, Humboldt University Berlin, 1998.
5. D. B. Leake and E. Plaza, editors. *Case-Based Reasoning Research and Development, Proceedings ICCBR-97*, Lecture Notes in Artificial Intelligence, 1266. Springer Verlag, 1997.
6. M. Lenz. Defining Knowledge Layers for Textual Case-Based Reasoning. In Smyth and Cunningham [15], pages 298–309.
7. M. Lenz. Managing the Knowledge Contained in Technical Documents. In U. Reimer, editor, *Proc. Practical Aspects of Knowledge Management (PAKM-98)*, 1998.
8. M. Lenz and H.-D. Burkhard. Lazy propagation in Case Retrieval Nets. In Wahlster [16], pages 127–131.
9. M. Lenz and H.-D. Burkhard. CBR for Document Retrieval - The FALLQ Project. In Leake and Plaza [5], pages 84–93.
10. M. Lenz, H.-D. Burkhard, B. Bartsch-Spörl, and S. Wess. *Case-Based Reasoning Technology – From Foundations to Applications*. Lecture Notes in Artificial Intelligence 1400. Springer Verlag, 1998.
11. M. Lenz, A. Hübner, and M. Kunze. Textual CBR. In *Case-Based Reasoning Technology – From Foundations to Applications* [10], chapter 5, pages 115–138.
12. M. M. Richter. The knowledge contained in similarity measures. Invited Talk at ICCBR-95, 1995. http://wwwagr.informatik.uni-kl.de/~lsa/CBR/Richtericcbr95remarks.html.

13. M. M. Richter. Introduction. In *Case-Based Reasoning Technology – From Foundations to Applications* [10], chapter 1, pages 1–16.
14. E. Riloff and W. Lehnert. Information extraction as a basis for high-precision text classification. *ACM Transactions on Information Systems*, 12(3):296–333, 1994.
15. B. Smyth and P. Cunningham, editors. *Advances in Case-Based Reasoning*, Lecture Notes in Artificial Intelligence, 1488. Springer Verlag, 1998.
16. W. Wahlster, editor. *Proceedings 12th European Conference on Artificial Intelligence ECAI-96*. John Wiley and Sons, 1996.

Integrated Case-Based Neural Network Approach to Problem Solving

Brian Lees and Juan Corchado

Applied Computational Intelligence Research Unit
Department of Computing and Information Systems
University of Paisley, High St., Paisley, PA1 2BE, Scotland, UK
lees-ci0@paisley.ac.uk

Abstract. Case-based reasoning can be a particularly useful problem solving strategy when combined with other artificial intelligence reasoning paradigms or with some other computational problem solving method. An approach is presented in which the machine learning capabilities of an artificial neural network are used to enhance the reuse of past experience in the case-based reasoning cycle. This approach has been found to be effective in the application of case-based reasoning to forecasting.

1 Introduction

Although case-based reasoning (CBR) may be employed on its own as a method of artificial intelligence (AI) problem solving, it can be particularly useful when combined with some other AI problem solving paradigm, for example artificial neural networks, constraint satisfaction or rule-based mechanism. As well as being used in conjunction with other AI problem solving paradigms, case-based reasoning may also be integrated with other computer-based technologies.

The structure of the paper is as follows. The combination of CBR with some other method of problem solving is considered, first through the combination of CBR with some other non-AI computational problem solving method, and then through the combination of CBR with another AI method. Then the particular combination of CBR and artificial neural networks is discussed. A model for the integration of CBR and neural network operations, which has been investigated by the authors, is then presented. The application of this approach to the problem of forecasting, and the ensuing results, are then described.

2 CBR in Hybrid Problem Solving

2.1 Combining CBR with a Non-AI Method

As well as operating in conjunction with other AI reasoning methods, CBR may, to good effect, also be used in support of some other computer-based technology or theory. CBR has, for example, been integrated with Decision Theory, to provide a case-based assistant to help in the design of pharmaceuticals [1]. This approach is reported to have demonstrated its usefulness in the evaluation of design alternatives and choices, based on user-defined criteria, by combining the heuristic descriptive reasoning of CBR with the formal reasoning of Decision Theory.

CBR has been applied in support of Quality Function Deployment (QFD), a product development methodology which is aimed at increasing customer focus throughout the product development process. The methodology involves a number of stages in which the means for achieving a set of requirements are identified, culminating in a set of production operations to create the product. Problems are frequently encountered because of the nature of the decisions that need to be made in QFD, which depend heavily on the previous experience of the designer. Because of this reliance on previous experience and the subjective nature of the decisions which are required in the early stages of QFD, it is believed that Case-Based Reasoning may be an effective approach in providing computational decision support to the designer in applying QFD. A prototype system is being developed to support the early stages of QFD, which employs previous design experience and relevant customer feedback [2].

The concepts of CBR and QFD have also been combined to assist in software design by supporting the attainment of quality in software development. Advice is given on which metrics are appropriate for assessing the quality of the software being designed [3]. The system incorporates a library of cases holding past software quality histories. To apply QFD in software development it is necessary to determine the software requirements (quality factors) which need to be specified by the customer, e.g. efficiency, maintainability, portability, and also to measure the software metrics during the different stages of development. The quality assessment model which has been developed is designed to measure the overall *quality deviation* (i.e. the deviation from the customer requirements) as a useful overall measure of software quality. The results obtained using data drawn from industrial case studies suggest that the combination of quality function deployment and case based reasoning can provide an effective means of supporting the assessment of software quality.

2.2 Combining CBR with another AI Method

This section considers the combination of two or more AI problem solving methods in order to produce a hybrid problem solving approach. Much work has been carried out elsewhere, especially in combining rule-based and connectionist approaches to problem solving. In the particular case of hybrid case-based reasoning, Hunt and Miles [4] identify two approaches to combining the separate reasoning methods: the tightly-coupled approach, in which the lines of communication and the control process are defined algorithmically; and the loosely-coupled approach, in which the system components are not closely linked and the control mechanism may be determined dynamically. Whilst the former approach may provide more efficient operation, the latter approach has the potential of providing a more flexible problem solving capability.

The incorporation of another AI method may be to support one or more of the processes of the CBR cycle, with the aim of strengthening the CBR problem solving behaviour. For example, case adaptation may be guided with the aid of a rule-based component, through access to a collection of adaptation rules. Used as such, the second problem solving method may be regarded as being subservient to the CBR method. Alternatively, the CBR mechanism may be used, either in parallel with, or in support of some other problem solving method. In this paper, attention is directed to the combination of artificial neural networks and case-based reasoning, possibilities for which are discussed in the next section.

3 Combining CBR and Neural Networks

Case-Based Reasoning and Neural Networks may be considered to be complementary problem solving methods [5]; CBR systems are able to reuse information from past experience, whereas neural networks can generate adaptive structures using large data sets. Many complex tasks that a human being can perform with apparent ease, for example distinguishing among visual images, patterns or sounds, are not so easily performed by computers using traditional algorithmic methods. Neural networks are a more appropriate means of carrying out such tasks, since their structure and processing operations are modelled on those believed to be present in the human brain [6]. ANNs are able to analyse large quantities of data to establish patterns and characteristics in situations where rules are not known and, in many cases, can make sense of incomplete or noisy data.

CBR systems have the potential to provide, by reference to previous learned experiences, some of the human characteristics of problem solving that are difficult to simulate using the logical, analytical techniques of knowledge-based systems and standard software technologies. CBR has much potential application in engineering, particularly design. An underlying premise in such research is that in providing intelligent computer-aided support for design, a strategy of enabling access to and reuse of previous design experience may be more effective than attempting to reason from domain knowledge alone. The aim in applying CBR to engineering design may be to meet one of various design goals: to support quality assurance, to learn from previous design processes, or to facilitate design traceability [7].

3.1 Hybrid CBR and ANN Systems

There is current interest in the application of hybrid CBR and ANN systems in various domains, including engineering and healthcare. For example, a fuzzy logic-based neural network in a case-based system, as a means of diagnosing symptoms in electronic systems has been proposed by Liu and Yan [8], the aim being to overcome the problem that descriptions of symptoms are often uncertain and ambiguous. In the domain of medical diagnosis, Reategui et al. [9] have used an integrated case-based reasoning and neural network approach: the task of the neural network is to generate hypotheses and to guide the CBR mechanism in the search for a similar previous case that supports one of the hypotheses. The model has been used in developing a system for the diagnosis of congenital heart diseases and has been evaluated using two cardiological databases with a total of over two hundred cases. The hybrid system is able to solve problems that cannot be solved by the neural network alone with a sufficient level of accuracy.

An important task in the design of case-based systems is the determination of the features that make up a case and also of ways to index those cases in the case-base for efficient and correct retrieval. Main *et al.* [10] consider the use of fuzzy feature vectors and neural networks as a means of improving the indexing and retrieval steps in case-based systems. A neural network has been employed as a basis for calculating a measure of similarity between a new problem case and each stored candidate [11]. It is claimed that the neural network provides a mechanism to retrieve cases using information that in other models would require a parallel architecture. The connection between both case-based and rule-based reasoning mechanisms and high level connectionist models has been investigated by Sun [12] in the process of exploring the use of such models for approximate common sense reasoning.

3.2 Design Support with Neural Networks and CBR

The field of engineering design, in particular, has attracted the attention of CBR researchers. An algorithm for neural network based analogical case retrieval and a strategy of constraint networks based object scheme evaluation and modification are proposed by Quan *et al.* [13] who have applied such an approach to industrial steam turbine design.

Artificial neural networks have been applied to many civil and structural engineering problems, where their ability to solve unknown functional mappings has been exploited to solve complex problems. As an example, a hybrid AI approach to masonry panel design support has been developed at the Universities of Strathclyde and Edinburgh [14]. Because of the lack of an adequate theoretical model for such designs and also the availability of a considerable amount of experimental results, the situation lends itself well to the application of CBR and neural networks. The role of CBR is to identify a theoretical method of analysis which is most suitable for the current problem, whilst the neural network is employed to obtain a solution with substantial savings in computer processing time. The hybrid system combines ANN and CBR to obtain the failure pressure of masonry panels. The CBR system stores cases derived from experimental tests at various research centres. The experimental failure pressure results are analysed using a finite element plate bending program incorporating the biaxial failure criterion [15]. By comparing the experimental results with theoretically predicted results, it is possible to deduce which method would be expected to produce the most reliable results in any particular situation.

A case base containing several such panel analyses is used to assist the user in determining which method should be used. Each case contains the experimental results from the analysis of panels, using different boundary conditions, together with theoretical results for the various cases and an appraisal of the recommended method of analysis.

The operation of the hybrid model in calculating the failure pressure of a panel is as follows. First the neural network is trained with data generated from existing methods of analysis. After training, the performance of the net is evaluated by testing it against a separate set of problems. When a new panel is to be analysed, the user supplies its parameter values to the CBR component. The CBR system identifies the best matching stored case, which, as well as the experimental results, also records the theoretical predictions of the failure load and the most reliable method of analysis. The method that previously produced the closest result to the experimentally obtained failure pressure is then displayed. After studying the results, the user can decide which method to adopt for the current problem.

4 Integrating ANN in CBR

The introduction of a neural network in a hybrid CBR system may be with the aim of supporting one of the processes in the CBR cycle. It is this approach which is being investigated in the current research and which enables the learning capabilities of a neural network to be used in making effective reuse of information contained in several cases which closely match the current problem situation.

An appropriate type of network for this, and the one which has been employed in the current research, is the *Radial Basis Function* network [16], in which the input layer is a receptor for the input data, whilst the hidden layer performs a non-linear transformation from the input space to the hidden layer space. The hidden neurons form a basis for the input vectors; the output neurons merely calculate a linear combination of the hidden neurons' outputs. Activation is fed forward from the input layer to the hidden layer where a Basis Function is calculated. The weighted sum of the hidden neurons' activations is calculated at the single output neuron. Radial Basis Functions (RBF) are better at interpolating that at extrapolating and are less sensitive to the order in which data is presented to them than is the case with other neural network models, such as Multi-Layer Perceptrons. Furthermore, Radial Basis Functions are of potential use in hybrid systems because of their fast learning capability.

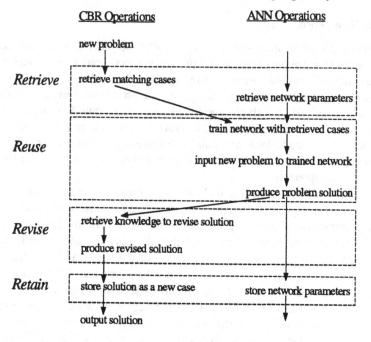

Fig. 1 Involving neural networks in the CBR cycle

A model for the incorporation of an RBF network in the *Reuse* phase of the CBR cycle is depicted in Figure 1. The parameters of a previously trained network (i.e. the network's centres and weights) are stored. On input of a new problem, the closest matching cases are retrieved from the case base. Then the stored network parameters are retrieved and the network is trained with the data values in the retrieved cases. After training, the corresponding values of the new problem are presented to the network inputs, in order to produce a problem solution. This provisional solution may need to be modified, using other stored knowledge, to produce the final output solution. Finally, the revised parameters are recorded for use in solving future problems.

5 Practical Application

The hybrid CBR problem solving method outlined above is being investigated in collaborative work between the University of Paisley and Plymouth Marine Laboratory (PML) in which the aim is to develop a methodology for predicting the values of physical parameters of the ocean (in particular, sea temperature at a given depth) at some point ahead of a moving vessel from data acquired in real time, and also from past records of sea temperature (and possibly other oceanographic parameters). This information may also then be used to provide a forewarning of an impending oceanographic *front*, i.e. a boundary between different large water masses. The approach builds on earlier collaborative into the application of knowledge based methods for the analysis of oceanographic data [17].

5.1 Real-Time Forecasting

The raw data (on sea temperature, salinity, density and other physical characteristics of the ocean) which are measured in real time by sensors located on the vessel, consist of a time series of sampled parameter values. These data values are supplemented by additional data derived from satellite images, which are received weekly. Temperature values are sampled along a single horizontal dimension, thus forming a set of data points. This data must be pre-processed in order to eliminate noise, to enhance interesting features, to smooth stable areas and to transform the data set into a form which may be represented on an absolute scale. Figure 2 gives an outline of the forecasting system and its components.

In order to produce a forecast in real-time, a *problem case* is generated every 2 km, which consists of a sequence of N sampled data values (after suitable filtering and pre-processing) immediately preceding the data value corresponding to the current position of the vessel. The problem case also includes various other numerical values, which include the current geographical location of the vessel and the time and date when the case was recorded. The set of N data values forms an *input vector*, which is then used to produce a forecast of the ocean temperature, ahead of the vessel.

The forecasted values are created using the neural network enhanced case-base reasoning approach, presented in the preceding section. The CBR mechanism allows the experience recorded in previous forecasting situations to be reused. The role of the neural network lies in the case adaptation process.

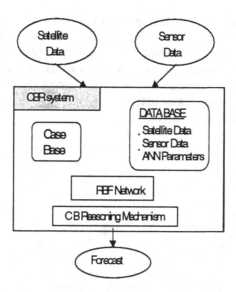

Fig. 2 Forecasting system outline

5.2 Case Representation

Each case represents the 'shape' of a set of temperature values, together with temporal and geographic data. Two different types of cases are used:

Cases of *Type A* consist of:

(i)   a 40 km temperature input profile $x_0, x_1, .., x_k$ (where k = 40)

representing the sampled water temperature values at 1 km intervals between the present position of the vessel and its position 40 km back;

(ii) a 10 km temperature output profile $y_0, y_1, .., y_q$ (where q = 10)

representing the forecasted water temperature values at 1 km intervals up to 10 km ahead of the present position ;

(iii) the latitude and longitude of the position of the vessel, together with the time, day and year in which the data were recorded, and the tow orientation (i.e. North-South, South-East, etc).

Cases of *Type B* consist of:

the same fields as Type A, with the difference that the profiles extend over a distance of 160 km

i.e.   Input profile: $x_0, x_1, ..,x_k$ (k = 160)

and a 40 km temperature profile

Output profile: $y_0, y_1, ..,y_k$ (q = 40).

Type A cases are used to forecast up to 10 km ahead and Type B up to 40 km ahead of the current location. The case base which is composed of a large number of data profiles recorded by the Plymouth Marine Laboratory during the last decade, during many scientific cruises. The case base also holds additional cases that have been created from satellite images, to create a collection of cases representative of the whole of the Atlantic Ocean. Cases may also be created from data obtained from a temperature sensor operating in real time.

5.3 System Operation

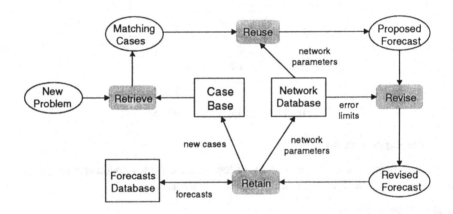

Fig. 3 Neural network supported CBR for forecasting

The forecasting system uses data from two sources: (i) the real-time data are used to create a succession of problem cases, characterising the current forecasting situation; (ii) data derived from satellite images are stored in a database (which, for simplicity, is not shown in Fig. 3). The satellite image data values are used to generate cases, which are then stored in the case base and subsequently updated during the CBR operation.

The cycle of forecasting operations (which is repeated every 2 km) proceeds as outlined below.

- First a new problem case is created from the pre-processed real-time data.

- A set of k cases, which most closely match this current problem case, is then obtained from the case base during the CBR *retrieve* phase, using nearest neighbour matching.

- In the *reuse* phase, the values of the weights and centres of the RBF neural network used in the previous forecast are retrieved from the neural network knowledge base. These network parameters together with the k closest matching cases are then used to create a forecast of the temperature 5 km ahead. At this point the parameters of the network are modified by taking into account the information contained in the retrieved cases. The effect of this is to allow the system to learn from all these k cases (rather than simply using the single adjudged closest matching case) in making a new forecast.

- The revised forecast is then retained in a temporary store – the forecasts database. When the vessel has travelled a further 5 km, the actual value of the water temperature at that point is measured. The forecasted value for the temperature at this point can then be evaluated, by comparison of the actual and forecasted values, and the error obtained. A new case, corresponding to this forecasting operation is then entered in the case base. Knowledge of the forecasting error is also, at this point, used to update the error limits of all the k cases that were reused to obtain that forecast.

6   Conclusion

The hybrid system has been tested at sea, on a research cruise in the Atlantic Ocean, which crossed several water masses and oceanographic fronts. The results obtained were very encouraging and indicate that the hybrid system is able to produce a forecast with a low average forecasting error. Experiments have also been carried out to evaluate the performance of the hybrid forecasting approach in comparison with several separate neural networks and statistical forecasting methods and also with a CBR system alone. The hybrid CBR-neural network method produced a lower forecasting error than any of these other methods.

The experimental results obtained to date are encouraging and indicate that the neural network supported approach is effective in the task of predicting future oceanographic parameter values. It is believed that the approach may be applicable to the problem of parametric forecasting in other complex domains using sampled time series data.

Acknowledgement

The authors are grateful for the support of Prof. Jim Aiken and Nigel Rees of the Plymouth Marine Laboratory in this research.

References

1. Tsatsoulis, C., Cheng, Q., Wei, H-S.: Integrating case-based reasoning with decision theory, IEEE Expert, 12(4) (1997) 46-55

2. Adams, D.A., Lees, B., Irgens, C., MacArthur, E.: Using cases to utilise feedback in Quality Function Deployment, Procs. ES'97, Cambridge, December (1997)

3. Hamza, M., Lees, B., Irgens, C: Providing software quality advice through the integration of quality function deployment and case based reasoning methodologies, Procs. 7th European Software Control and Metrics Conference, Cheshire, U.K. April (1996)

4. Hunt, J., Miles, R.: Hybrid case-based reasoning. The Knowledge Engineering Review, 9(4) (1994) 383-397

5. Corchado, J., Lees, B., Fyfe, C., Rees, N.: An Automated Agent-Based Reasoning and Learning System. Procs. SEKE'97, 9th International Conference on Software Engineering and Knowledge Engineering, Madrid, June (1997)

6. Rumelhart, D.E., McClelland, J.L.: Parallel Distributed Processing, Vol. 1, Foundations. MIT Press, (1996)

7. Lees, B.: Engineering design support through case-based reasoning, Procs. Colloquium on Intelligent Design Systems, IEE, London, 25th February, Digest no. 97/016 (1997) 8/1-8/3

8. Liu, Z.Q., Yan F.: Fuzzy neural network in case-based diagnostic system, IEEE Transactions on Fuzzy Systems, IEEE 5(2) (1997) 209-222

9. Reategui, E.B., Campbell, J.A., Leao, B.F.: Combining a neural network with case-based reasoning in a diagnostic system, Artificial Intelligence in Medicine 9(1) (1997) 5-27

10. Sun, R.: Commonsense reasoning with rules, cases, and connectionist models: a paradigmatic comparison, Fuzzy Sets and Systems 82(2): (1996) 187-200

11. Main, J., Dillon, T.S., Khosla, R.: Use of fuzzy feature vectors and neural networks for case retrieval in case based systems, Procs. Biennial Conference of the North American Fuzzy Information Processing Society - NAFIPS, IEEE, (1996) 438-443

12. Garcia Lorenzo M.M., Bello Perez R.E.: Model and its different applications to case-based reasoning, Knowledge-Based Systems 9(7): (1996) 465-473

13. Quan Mao, Jing Qin, Xinfang Zhang, Ji Zhou.: Case prototype based design: philosophy and implementation, Procs Computers in Engineering 1 (1994) 369-374

14. Mathew, A., Kumar, B., Sinha, B.P., Pedreschi, R.F.: Analysis of masonry panel under biaxial bending. Project report, Dept. of Civil Engineering, University of Strathclyde (1997)

15. Sinha, B.P., Ng, C.L., Pedreschi, R.F.: Failure criterion and failure of brickwork in bi-axial bending, Journal of the Materials in Civil Engineering 9(2): (1997) 70-75

16. Bishop, C.R.: Neural Networks for Pattern Recognition, Oxford University Press (1995)

17. Lees, B., Rees, N., Aiken, J.: Knowledge-based oceanographic data analysis. In: Attia F et al. (eds) Procs. Expersys-92, IITT International, Paris, October (1992) 561-65

PRO_PLANT
Experiences with a Knowledge-Based System for Plant Protection

Karoline Epke

pro_Plant, Gesellschaft für Agrar- und Umweltinformatik mbH, Nevinghoff 40,
D-48147 Münster, Germany
k.epke@proplant.de
http://www.proplant.de

Abstract. The knowledge-based consulting system PRO_PLANT for
the environmentally friendly use of plant protection agents in agriculture is being used practically in agriculture since 1993 and shows by
the large number of installed versions its high level of acceptance with
the user. The knowledge-based techniques used have allowed a constant
maintenance and extension of the system since the start of development.
Crucial to its success is the integration of different system components,
the integration in the system environment of the user and the technical
support of the users.

1 Introduction

PRO_PLANT is a consulting system for environmentally friendly plant protection in agriculture. The analysis of the weather-dependent infection events of
fungi and the infestation development of parasites allows an exact determination of the time of spraying and reduces, with simultaneous high yield certainty,
the number of sprayings to be carried out and their application rates.

PRO_PLANT is conceived as decentrally organized program that is executable on the farms own PC. A detailed representation of all program components
is contained in [1]. The import of current and forecasted meteorological data
from the German Weather Service (Deutscher Wetterdienst) takes place via an
interface to T-Online. Data from automatic weather stations can also be used.

The knowledge-based diagnostic system determines in different crops, for a
cultivated area, pathogen or parasite-specific controlling decisions, which are
integrated to a total recommendation, for which an product selection then takes place. The factual knowledge concerning crop variety resistances, efficiency
characteristics of crop protection agents, as well as data about recommendati-
ons already carried out, necessary for the treatment decision and the product
selection, are administered by a database management system.

The explanation component of the diagnostic system as well as the query
and logging possibilities of the plant protection-relevant data used, make the
decisions of the system comprehensible. The interactive graphic system visualizes

the results of the weather data analysis and functions as a warning service and quick consultation. Multimedial information systems concerning the biology and the control possibilities of oil seed rape parasites and weeds support the user with field checks. Further information concerning the system architecture can be taken from [19].

2   Course of the project

- 1989 - 1991: Development of the prototype Expert system for the control of fungal diseases in grain ' as MS-DOS version at the Institute for Agrarian Computer Science of the WWU Muenster promoted by the Ministry for Environment, Area Planning and Agriculture (MURL).
- 1991 - 1995: Development of a comprehensive consulting system for plant protection in arable farming at the Institute for Agrarian Computer Science of the WWU Münster promoted by MURL (Windows version).
- since 1996: Updating and further development by the pro_Plant GmbH in Münster.

3   Integration with the users

PRO_PLANT is conceived for different groups of users:

Farmers and contractors predominantly use the field-specific diagnostic system, in order to lower their plant protection costs by the optimization of application rates and dates of spreading and to receive competent consultation. PRO_PLANT integrates itself well into the operational process. Representatives of practical agriculture inform themselves daily during the season about the infection and infestation events on their fields. The diagnostic system explains its decisions, so that the users can co-ordinate their fertilization, growth controller application and plant protection measures.

Official and private advisors, on the other hand, use mainly the database and the graphic system in order to obtain descriptions of the newest crop varieties and plant protection agents and to determine region-specific infection and application dates. For this group of users, PRO_PLANT provides special functions to support advisory activities, which are carried out particularly on the telephone. These consist of diagrams, which provide a fast overview of the infection situation and the respective efficiency characteristics of the plant protection agents.

Trade and industry pursue seasonal features with the graphic system, in order to make customers aware of plant protection problems and to be ables to react upon demands of the market.

Training colleges and universities use PRO_PLANT in their teaching.

Finally, PRO_PLANT serves research centres as an important tool for experimental design and interpretation of test results.

The PRO_PLANT user guidance is adapted to the demands of the user. The attention of the user is directed to the problems, which should to be dealt with more urgently (see fig. 1).

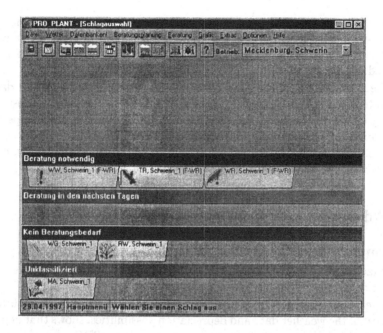

Fig. 1. *The PRO_PLANT-surface orders fields by necessity of advice*

Differentiated demands result from different levels of familiarity of the users with the system and from different levels of previous plant protection knowledge. This is taken into account, with a more or less strict user guidance and a functionality consisting of field-specific consultation and clear diagrams.

4 Integration into the application environment

Even after short training period, all user groups began using PRO_PLANT successfully. The user installs using a simple installation program from diskette or CD-ROM.

Different technical conditions apply for putting the system into operation, depending upon the source of the weather data: for the predominantly used weather data from the German Weather Service and for the call-up of forecast data, as well as to fill in gaps in the weather data in case of the failure of an in-house automatic weather station, T-Online access must be available. Otherwise, the existence of raw data files from the automatic weather station and a description of the data format, provided by the respective weather station manufacturer, suffices. Interfaces to these third-party systems are integrated into the program and do not result in additional work for the user. However, frequent version modifications of the T-Online software require constant program adaptions. The user maintains a field card index, merged into PRO_PLANT, which administers plant protection-relevant data. Experiences with interfaces to other field card-indexes used in agriculture has shown that different development specifications of software firms lead quickly to inconsistency problems. Currently no index-card interfaces are supported. A publication of the interface parameters is planned.

The maintenance of the plant protection agent and crop varieties database takes place centrally via pro_Plant GmbH. Here the newest research results concerning efficiency characteristics and crop varieties are compiled independently of producers. Database and program updates are sent at least once a year via diskette. The user uses the Hotline all year round, smaller problems are solved immediately by file transfer via the Internet.

5 Advantages for users and client

PRO_PLANT is of economic advantage for users. Independent test results showed that on average 1 spraying a year can be saved. This reduced use of plant protection agents results in an increased profit of 50 DM/ha.

An economic calculation which takes into account initial costs, maintenance fees, cost of the weather data and depreciation possibilities, shows that depending upon size of the arable farming area to be manages, PRO_PLANT amortizes itself after a short time and makes a profit (see fig. 2).

The amount of time the user spends using the programme varies according to his interest in the technical basis of plant protection and his enthusiasm for computers. It is not, however, extensive enough that it would have to be taken into account in an economic analysis, above all because the practical agriculture even without PRO_PLANT would strive for some other form of consultation.

Efficiency of PRO_PLANT calculated for three years
e.g.: a grain-licence for a farm with 100 ha arable area

Item	Per year	For three years
Licence fees	530 DM	1590 DM
Costs of weather data and T-Online	290 DM	870 DM
Maintenance fees (first year free)	230 DM	460 DM
Total costs for three years		2920 DM
Profit (average increased profit of 50 DM/ha)	5000 DM	15000 DM
Profit for three years		12080 DM

Fig. 2. *Economic calculation of PRO_PLANT*

Not only the economic advantage determines the satisfaction of the user with the system, the user appreciates the ecological aspect and the knowledge gain, because plant protection-relevant correlations are pointed out and shared with the user.

The successful conclusion of the PRO_PLANT project in 1995 meant a high prestige gain for the Ministry for Environment, Area planning and Agriculture of the state of North Rhine-Westphalia as a client. PRO_PLANT is one of the few projects, which has managed the leap from a research level into agricultural practice. This consulting system has established itself permanently in practice and produces demand beyond the national boundaries. With PRO_PLANT, current plant protection consultation is always available in agriculture. The Ministry has shown that it promotes the development of modern software technology and makes a large contribution to environmental protection at the same time.

6 Experience report

The knowledge-based component of PRO_PLANT is of substantial importance for the fast success and the maintenance of the system. The diagnostic system alone contains more than 10000 rules. This amount of rules could not be developed and mainatained over the course of ten years with other software techniques. The dialog with the experts is supported by the use of knowledge-based techniques. The necessity to use a common terminology and to have to decisions explained, contributes to the structuring of the unclear domains and minimizes knowledge loss.

For the creation and maintenance of the diagnostic system a rule compiler was developed, which translates a defined rule language into Prolog code. This code is bound together with a specially-developed expert system shell to Dlls [21]. These rule bases produce explanation texts, which are stored outside of application. An overlay concept and the rapid development on the processor market could solve the initial resource problems regarding storage space and performance.

The PRO_PLANT consulting system was developed in close co-operation with the experts at the Institute for Plant Protection at the Chamber of Agriculture Westfalen-Lippe. Through this co-operation, an increase in know-how even of the experts was achieved, new control strategies were successfully introduced into agricultural practice with PRO_PLANT [23].

The administration and maintenance of the program is guaranteed for by pro_Plant GmbH in Münster, which aside from PRO_PLANT naturally undertakes further software development. Two agricultural engineers observe the agricultural market, and define, on the basis of the newest trial and research results, the technical specification for modifications and further developments of the program and man the Hotline to answer technical questions of an agricultural nature. Three software engineers take care of the maintenance, the programming and undertaking of the technical Hotline.

1998 are almost 500 versions in use distributed across the sectors of practical agriculture, consultancy, industry, research and teaching (see fig. 3). Nationwide almost all advisory boards use PRO_PLANT, the area covered by PRO_PLANT is therefore accordingly large. Abroad, Europe is increasingly interested in the system, since no comparable programs exist in the neighboring countries.

PRO_PLANT-licences

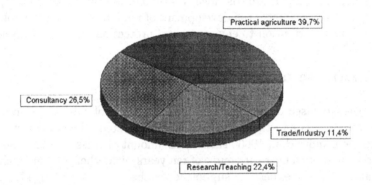

Fig. 3. *Destribution in sphere of activity, September '98*

The large success of the system lies in the integration of the different system modules (attachment to T-Online, multimedia, graphic system, database, diagnostic system), the straight-lined architecture, the up-to-date nature of all knowledge components and the ergonomic user guidance. The consulting system is of modular construction. According to his own requirements, the user can put together his own program system do away with unnecessary overhead [15].

Crucial to the acceptance of the program is the existence of a technical and agricultural Hotline. The clientele consists predominantly of inexperienced computer users, who require assistance even for smaller technical problems. Exchange of experiences and the discussion on the technical level are in addition, particularly important. The response to the Hotline offer is surprisingly large.

Problems of acceptance with PRO_PLANT users are present particularly in the area of data import to the system. Despite automation of the weather data import, problems can occur particularly at the beginning of the season, enquiries concerning interfaces to market-dominating plot card indexes are obtained again and again. Acceptance problems with non PRO_PLANT users lie in the price of the programme and the offers of official and private industrial consultants that put the results of PRO_PLANT at their cusomers disposal.

There are aspects, whose meaning were falsely estimated at the start of the project. Every knowledge-based system strives for transparency by its explainability. The explanation component of the PRO_PLANT diagnostic system manages this only to a limited extent. The static, partially very clumsy, composition of explanation texts receives little attention from the user. On the contrary, somewhat experienced users would gladly do without the dialogue control and therefore without explanations, if they could enter the necessary field information only once into a form and directly obtain the spray product list as a result. However the amount of the user input, which becomes necessary when no situation-specific diagnosis takes place, tends to be underestimated. Users incur a knowledge gain above all from the diagrams, which show correlations between weather, parasite or pathogen and the efficiency of plant protection agents.

In the last few years, the emphasis of the maintenance work lay in making the administrability of the PRO_PLANT system possible, by moderisation and reduction of the progamming languages used. Futher activities lay in the extension of the graphic system and modifications to the system, which became necessary because new plant protection agents with new activity characteristics required modified control strategies. For the future, the introduction of more crops into the consultation capabilities, an internationalisation of the programme and a version for internet use are planned.

The extensive amount of text, which a knowledge-based system produces via dialogs, help and explanations, stand in the way of internationalization. The technical feasibility is not being questioned here, however the translations in these special domains and the updating of these texts causes substantial work.

Further problems during the introduction of international versions would be caused by the legal and economic basic conditions of interested countries, e.g. different permits for plant protection agents and crop varieties, attainable prices for grain. Also the Hotline requirement to the necessary extent is not possible.

In order to minimize maintenance costs of internationally used versions, an Internet solution presents itself. A prerequisite for this is among other things, the replacement of the interactive diagnostic system. Legal questions regarding the use of the users technical data and possibilities for the paying system are to be still clarified.

References

1. EPKE, K., MICHEL, S. & VOLK, T. (1996): Entwicklung des wissensbasierten Beratungssystems PRO_PLANT für den umweltschonenden Einsatz von Pflanzenschutzmitteln in der Landwirtschaft. Forschung und Beratung Reihe C, Heft 50, 154 S.
2. FALKE, F. & EICKELBERG, S. (1998) Insektizidanwendung im Raps: Haben sich Computerprognosen bewährt? top agrar 3, S. 76-79
3. FRAHM, J., HANHART, H., KLINGENHAGEN, G., JOHNEN, A. & VOLK, T. (1998): Strobilurins in cereals: integration in the decision support system PRO_PLANT. 7th International Congress fo Plant Pathology (ICPP98), Edinburgh (Scotland) 9-16 August 1998, Abstracts of invited & offered papers, 5.6.2

4. FRAHM, J., & KLINGENHAGEN, G. (1996): PRO_PLANT as a tool for advisory work, timing of herbicides. In SECHER, B. & FRAHM (ed.): Proceedings of the workshop on Decision Systems in Crop Protection. Münster, Germany 4-8 November 1996. SP report No. 15. S. 31-38.

5. FRAHM, J. & VOLK, TH. (1994): PRO_PLANT - a computer-based decision-support system for cereal disease control. Proceedings EPPO Conference on Computerized Advisory Systems for Plant Protection 1992. EPPO Bulletin 23: 685-693.

6. FRAHM, J., VOLK, T. & JOHNEN, A. (1997): Development of the PRO_PLANT decision-support system for plant protection in cereals, sugarbeet and rape. Proceedings EPPO Conference on Forecasting in Plant Protection, Potsdam 1995-11-21/24, Bulletin OEPP/EPPO Bulletin 26: 609-622.

7. FRAHM, J., VOLK, TH. & U. STREIT (1991): PRO_PLANT - A knowledge based advisory system for cereal disease control. In SECHER, B. et al. (ed.): Computer-based Plant Protection Advisory Systems. Danish Journal of Plant and Soil Science, Report No. S 2161; 101-109.

8. FRAHM, J., VOLK, TH. & STREIT, U. (1995): The decision-support system PRO_PLANT for cereal disease control: scientific background and practical experiences. European Journal of Plant Pathology, Abstracts of the XIII International Plant Protection Congress, The Hague, The Netherlands, 2-7 July 1995, 935.

9. HINDORF, H., KRASKA, T., JOHNEN, A. & THIERON, M.(1998): Disease forecast systems optimizing fungicide application in Germany with special reference to PRO_PLANT. Proceedings of the 12th International Symposium on Systemic Fungicides and Antifungal Compounds : Castle of Reinhardsbrunn (Thuringia), May 24.-29.1998 (be printing).

10. JOHNEN, A. & EPKE, K. (1995): Gezielte Bekämpfung von Rapsschädlingen mit PRO_PLANT. Raps 4: 140-145.

11. JOHNEN, A., VOLK, T., FRAHM, J., BERG, G. & BOUMA, E. (1998): Erfahrungen aus dem Einsatz des Beratungssystem PRO_PLANT im europäischen Ausland. Mitt. BBA 357: 197-198.

12. JOHNEN, A., FRAHM, J. & GRÜNEWALD, M. (1995): New ways in controlling oil seed rape pests with the aid of the decision support system PRO_PLANT. European Journal of Plant Pathology, Abstracts of the XIII International Plant Protection Congress, The Hague, The Netherlands, 2-7 July 1995, 939.

13. MORITZ, H. (1996): Cercospora & Co. - mit dem PC sicherer im Griff? top agrar 6: 54-57.

14. PFEIFFER, R. (1993): Importation and Management of Meteorological Data in the Decision-Support-System PRO_PLANT. Proceedings of the Workshop on Computer-based DSS on Crop Protection, Parma, Italy 23-26 November 1993. SP report No. 7. S. 125-130.

15. RÜCKER, P., Wolff, CH. & HARTLEB, H. (1997): Mit ProPlant den Fungizideinsatz planen. top Spezial 4: 29-26.

16. SCHEPERS, H.T.A.M., BOUMA, E., FRAHM, J. VOLK, TH. & SECHER, B.J.M. (1997): Control of fungal diseases in winter wheat with appropriate dose rates and weather-based decision support systems. Proceedings EPPO Conference on Forecasting in Plant Protection, Potsdam 1995-11-21/24, Bulletin OEPP/EPPO Bulletin 26: 623-630.

17. VISSER, U. & HELL, K. (1997): PRO_PLANT Information System - Canola Pests ICCIMA'97 - International Conference on Computational Intelligence and Multimedia Applications, 10-12 February 1997, Gold Coast, Australia edited by B. Verma and X. Yao, S. 59 - 63

18. VISSER, U., VOGES, U. & STREIT, U. (1994): Integration of AI- Database- and telecommunication-techniques for the plant protection expert system PRO_PLANT. Industrial and engineering applications of artificial intelligence and expert systems. Proceedings of the Seventh International Conference, Austin, Texas, May 31 - June 3, 1994. S. 367-374.

19. VISSER, U., VOGES, U., EPKE, K., PFEIFFER, R. & STREIT, U. (1993): Umweltschonender Pflanzenschutz mit Hilfe des Expertensystems PRO_PLANT. KI, Heft 3. S. 34-43.

20. VOGES, U. (1989): Konzeption einer Micro - shell als Entwicklungswerkzeug für das wissensbasierte System PRO_PLANT. Werkstattbericht Umwelt-Informatik, H. 2; Abteilung Landschaftskologie des Institutes für Geographie der Univ. Münster, 17 S.

21. VOGES, U. & K. EPKE (1992): PRO_PLANT, ein Beratungssystem für den umweltgerechten Pflanzenschutz: Shell-Entwicklung und Wissensrepräsentation. Informatik für den Umweltschutz, 6. Symposium, München, 4.-6. Dezember 1991, S. 577-585.

22. VOGES, U., VISSER, U., JOHNEN, A. & HELL, K. (1993): PRO_PLANT - Pflanzenschutz mit Hilfe eines Expertensystems. KI, Sonderheft zur 17. Fachtagung für Künstliche Intelligenz, S. 80-81.

23. VOLK, TH. (1993): Das Pflanzenschutz-Beratungssystem PRO_PLANT als Ergebnis einer engen Zusammenarbeit mit der landwirtschaftlichen Praxis. Berichte der Gesellschaft für Informatik in der Land-, Forst- und Ernährungswirtschaft, Band 5: Referate der 14. GIL-Jahrestagung in Leipzig 1993 S. 184-188.

24. VOLK, TH. (1993): Reduced dosages of fungicides for controlling cereal diseases in North-West Germany. Proceedings of the Workshop on Computer-based DSS on Crop Protection, Parma, Italy 23-26 November 1993. SP report No. 7. S. 95-102.

WEkI
A Knowledge Based System of Suva for the Assignment of Companies to Risk Related Groups

Gregor Kaufmann[1], François Braun[1], Kurt Egli[2], and Marc Hodel[3]

[1] SYNLOGIC AG, Rottmannsbodenstrasse 30, CH-4102 Binningen, Switzerland
info@synlogic.ch
[2] Suva, Abteilung Informatik, Postfach 4358, CH-6002 Luzern, Switzerland
[3] Suva, Abteilung Versicherungstechnik, Postfach 4358, CH-6002 Luzern, Switzerland

Abstract. Suva in cooperation with SYNLOGIC AG developed a knowledge based system for the assignment of companies to risk related groups. The system is fully integrated in the preexisting information infrastructure and almost transparent for the occasional user. The architecture of the system is characterized trough the orthogonal use of a generic model of knowledge and a small set of parametrizeable rule types. The system implements a client server model in which the rule base is held centrally. Rule sets are loaded on demand from the inference engine residing on local PC. The rule based is maintained by domain experts using a specially developed rule editor. The system went operational starting in July 1998 and has since been used routinely. A list of realized benefits is provided.

1 Introduction

The Swiss National Accident Insurance Company (Suva) is the primary provider of insurance cover for occupational accidents in Swiss industrial companies. It insures two third of all Swiss employees against occupational accidents, occupational diseases and non-occupational accidents. 22 agencies located all over Switzerland take care of the around 1.7 million insured individuals and around 100'000 insured companies.

Suva decided in 1991, based on its IT-strategy, to conduct a study to identify potential benefits of the knowledge based technology. Several areas of interest have been identified. One of these areas was the creation and maintenance of a system of risk related groups and the assignment of companies to these groups.

1.1 Risk Related Groups

About 200'000 occupational accidents and occupational diseases cause cost of about 1.1 billion Swiss franks p.a., which have to be covered by the net premiums collected.

Since the Suva is a governmental agency[1], the premium rates have to be fixed in such a way that the total amount of premiums paid and the total costs of insurance are balanced. The net premiums should be related to the risk faced by companies and help to promote work security measures.

The requirement for risk related premiums calls for the creation of homogeneous risk related groups. The understanding of occupational accidents suggests to partition the set of insured companies according to their industry affiliation and similar objective risk factors faced by companies with similar activities. Suva therefore maintains a hierarchical, multileveled system of risk related groups. The whole set of insured companies is partitioned into classes and subclasses. The latter build the actual risk related groups. Classes represent the companies affiliation to industries. Classes and subclasses are linked to actual premium rates. The system of risk related groups has to be regularly adjusted due to changed economical conditions or evolutions of the legislation.

The attributes of a company – typically specified by a Suva inspector visiting the company - represent typical activities and tasks, which are carried out by the its employees. Company attributes may also represent machines and equipment on which these are executed. They are risk relevant. The attributes of a company are registered together with the percentage of the total amount of wages of the employees assigned to these activities and machines on so called company description forms. A company description form describes the company attributes. The attributes may relate the company to several classes.

1. 2   Situation Preceding the Introduction of WEkI

The adjustment of risk related groups as well as the assignment of companies was largely carried out manually at Suva. The rules for the assignment were recorded in a so called assignment key, a voluminous folder. Responsible for the construction and maintenance of the risk related groups and the assignment key were the domain experts of the department "Versicherungstechnik"[2] (VT) at the head office. Responsible for the assignment of companies in simple cases were the employees of the agencies, but the experts had to finally supervise the decisions proposed by the agencies. The more complicated cases were reserved to the domain experts. The amount of work spent for the construction and maintenance of the risk related groups was enormous, and the time needed for the assignment of a company was rather long (see § 4).

---

[1] This term should be understood as the English translation of the German term "Anstalt".
[2] "Insurance Engineering"

2 Development of a knowledge bases System

2. 1 The Prototype

Following the 1991 study, a prototype [1],[2] with limited functionality for the automatic assignment of companies to risk related groups has been developed in 1993/1994. The primary aim of the prototype was to demonstrate the capabilities of the knowledge-based technologies, investigate its impacts, and to collect experience. Moreover the prototype should be used to support the domain experts in the adjustment of a certain class of the system of risk related groups.

The system used a KADS [3] compatible model of knowledge, which has been constructed throughout a series of interviews with three domain experts. The model tried to imitate the way these experts used to work. During these interviews, it became clear that the variations in the way the experts worked were not easy to model. The overall experience gained with the prototype was positive.

2. 2 Development of a operational System

After a long period of intense discussions between the experts of the VT department and between the experts and the IT department, and based on the lessons learned as well as the experience gained from the prototype, a joint decision was made to develop a new knowledge based system, called WEkI with the goal to put it into operations.

2. 3 Requirements

The goals of the system were two fold :
1. Handle the routine assignment of companies in the agencies (the "Online" mode);
2. Support the domain experts in the maintenance of the risk related groups (the "Batch" mode). The system should be constructed in such a way that the domain experts be able to build and maintain the assignment rules by themselves.

Additional requirements were, that

- the system should be almost totally transparent to the employees in the agencies,
- the system should be tightly integrated in the existing insurance application,
- the rules should be kept centralized on a database on a mainframe,
- the system should not necessitate changes in the existing IT-infrastructure,
- the system should be developed with PLATINUM's AionDS.

These additional requirements were placed to assure a smooth introduction of the system and therefore to minimize possible causes of failure.

The feasibility of a tight integration of a system developed with AionDS in the existing infrastructure and well as its possible influences have been studied in summer 1997 prior to the start of the actual development.

2. 4 Architecture

Based on the lessons learned from the prototype, a more generic KADS compatible model of knowledge has been developed in a first stage. This model no longer tries to imitate the workings of individual "model experts" as exactly as possible but represents a general view of the assignment process. The model does not adhere closely to the way the (three) domain experts interviewed during the prototype project were working. Instead, it provides a standard frame in which the individual ways of working of all the domain experts can easily fit[3]. The advantage of developing such a model is manifold:

- It allows the rules to be organized, thus easing the maintenance task.
- It allows an expert to understand and follow at a meta level the way the system works, thus easing the debugging and fine tuning of the rules.
- A guidance in the writing of rules can be provided due to the types of rules that can be found at a given stage.

In addition, a small set of parametrizeable rule types have been developed. The rule types are orthogonal to the model of knowledge. The primary advantage expected from defining rule types – possibly at the expense of less flexibility in the writing of rules – is to allow the specification and development of a context specific rule editor that can be used by domain experts having no knowledge of the low-level handling of the rules by the underlying inference engine. This combination of a generic model of knowledge and, orthogonal to it, of parametrizeable rule types, results in a very flexible, expressive but nevertheless easily understandable system. In principle, a rule conceived by a domain expert independently of WEkI should fit into its model with only minor changes. In other words, the domain experts do not have to vastly adapt their way of working to the system. The applicability and validity of this solution have been extensively verified through simulations, before and during the developments. These testing works led to a fine-tuning of the initial generic model.

To support the work of the domain experts a rule type sensitive rule editor and a test environment for the rules were developed. Using the type-guided rule editor, a domain expert is able to enter, adapt and delete specific rules. The test environment for the rules eases the generation and maintenance of test cases and allows the effects of changes to the rule base to be verified.

Each rule in the database is assigned with it a period of validity, a version number and the visa of the responsible domain expert. These attributes allow for extensive testing and simulation of the effects of changes made to the rule base through the responsible domain expert before the changed rules become operational.

The inference engine implements the model of knowledge. It is relatively small and is installed on the local PCs of the users. The inference engine is constructed as a Subsystem and can only be invoked from other applications. When it is invoked, it gets as input the company attributes, as well as other relevant information such as the total amount of wages paid by that company. Depending on the company attributes, the inference engine selects and downloads the relevant rule sets from the database on

---

[3] the generic model still adheres to the KADS-1 concepts of inference and task layers.

the mainframe over a WAN managed by the Suva. It then assigns the company to a class and subclass of the system of risk related groups and delivers this assignment as output back to the invoking application.

The separation of the rule base from the inference engine, the centralized storage of the rules as well as their systematical download for each new assignment case, allow the knowledge to be always kept up-to-date. As soon as a rule change has been decided by the responsible domain expert, the modification is made immediately active and available throughout Suva. The inference engine itself stays valid, as long as the basic paradigm used does not change. These architectural decisions vastly simplify the maintenance of WEkI.

2. 5 Examples

The following "school cases" highlight the concepts presented so far[4]:

Class/Subclass :

The "micro-mechanics" industry can be seen as a (simplified) class, the "production of micro mechanical devices" then as a subclass, and 3 ‰ the standard premium rate assigned to this type of industrial activity.

Process steps[5] : about 10 process steps have been defined, such as

"pre-processing" :   during which attributes are filtered and recomputed in % among other elementary activities;

"simple assignment" : a very simple company with a single – pure – industrial activity is classified here without complex processing;

Rule types : 8 rule types have defined such as

"Combination and sum rule" : such a rule creates a variable which value is the sum of attributes, when a number of comparisons in the if-part hold;

"Stop rules" : simple rules that prevent WEkI to further process a case and provide results; this happens if another rule previously fired and generated a result that enables a "Stop" rule to fire.

2. 6 Implementation

After a development time of only four months, one of which has been reserved for system tests, WEkI went into operations in July 1998 and has been since routinely used.

---

[4] Detailed real examples cannot be provided because of their confidential character and their complexity.
[5] Knowledge sources in KADS terminology

3 Current State of the WEkI System

WEkI is used in two different ways:

Online mode :   It is used in the agencies to automatically assign companies to the classes and subclasses of the system of risk related groups
Batch mode :   It supports the domain experts in the maintenance of risk related groups as well as the creation of new risk related groups.

In August 1998, the rules for about one third of all classes and subclasses of the system of risk related groups were already entered into WEkI and made operational. The implemented rules handle the most important classes. WEkI can therefore already process a majority of the Swiss companies without manual intervention. The rules for the rest of the classes are being added at a fast pace.

3. 1   Typical Use at the Agency Level

An employee of an agency enters into the insurance application the attributes of a company gathered in the company description form. Then, a dropdown menu selection "assignment" allows the inference engine to be invoked.   The insurance application hands the company attributes over as input to the inference engine. The inference engine then downloads the relevant rules from the database on the MVS-mainframe over the WAN, according to the company attributes. It normally assigns the company to a class and subclass of the system of risk related groups and delivers this assignment as output back to the invoking insurance application. The insurance application displays the assignment and the employee can carry on with her/his work. The only thing the employee usually perceives from the process is the wait time required for the assignment. Therefore no additional training has been needed for the employees of the agencies.

This process works independently of the complexity of the individual case as long as the necessary rules exist and allow for a proper assignment. If WEkI cannot reach an assignment, for whatever reason, a notice is automatically posted by email to the responsible domain expert and the case handed over to him for manual inspection.

As mentioned, prior to the introduction of WEkI, the assignment of companies was only carried out in simple cases by the employees of the agencies. In all other cases, the company description form was sent to the domain experts by mail. This resulted in lengthy processing times for a significant number of cases (3 to 5 days typically) and a lot of rather boring routine work for the experts. Moreover, the manual assignment was not totally reproducible because of slight differences in the interpretation of the rules. Here the benefits of WEkI are obvious.

3. 2   Expert Use

The domain experts are responsible for the creation and maintenance of the system of risk related groups. Each domain expert is personally responsible for part of the system and therefore for part of the rule base of WEkI. If an expert wants to change some of the rules under his/her responsibility, including adding new rules or deleting obsolete ones, the system creates a personal copy of the rule base. The expert uses then the rule editor to make the intended changes.

At any moment, a class expert can test the effects of the changes made by use of the test environment, typically when the classification policy should be modified for one class. Here a number of appropriate cases are selected among a library. The inference engine is then automatically invoked once for each of the test cases. In this environment it uses the experts personal copy of the rule base. The results of the assignments are then displayed in the test environment. The expert can finally compare the obtained results to stored reference assignments. If the changes made to the rules are satisfying, the expert can commit these changes into the operational rule base. Apart from rules, the experts can also define, alter and delete test cases on their own. They are responsible for managing an appropriate set of test cases.

The test environment is also used, when a revision occurs for every class. Such a revision is a major undertaking and has a strong influence on the financial results of the Suva. With the help of WEkI, the experts are able to simulate the financial effects of such a revision. They adapt the rules in their personal copy of the rule base to the revised class structure. The stored attributes of all possibly affected companies are then passed through WEkI within the test environment. The obtained results are finally analyzed and used to compute the expected amount of premiums to obtain. If the result is to low or to high, the revision has to be fine tuned.

Combining a generic model of knowledge with rule types seems to allow the domain experts not to largely deviate from their own way of building classes and subclasses. Moreover, the guidance provided by the rule types seems an interesting compromise between ease of use and flexibility. These two factors explains that the experts only needed minimal training prior using WEkI. In fact, no formal training has been provided. Instead the three experts which were involved in the development from the early beginning of the prototype system 1993/1994 acted as tutors for the other experts. Since they were already intimately familiar with the way of thinking and working habits of domain experts, they provided a very efficient support. As the experience shows, this was a good decision.

Prior to the introduction of WEkI, the domain experts had no simple way of exhaustively testing their rules. In particular, they could not systematically check the consistency of the rules, and ambiguities occurred. If an expert noticed such irregularities, he/she usually improvised a case-based solution instead of adapting the rules. The introduction of WEkI brought more rigors to the creation of rules. The usual irregularities can now be detected almost instantaneously. Furthermore, the simulation of the result of a revision had to be carried out manually. This simulation often took several months. The process of revising classes could thus only be carried out infrequently. A total revision of the whole system of risk related groups took between ten and fifteen years to complete. However, constant evolutions in the structure of industries nowadays demand a systematic revision every three to five years. The Suva experts are now convinced, that only with the support of WEkI can these revision deadlines be met.

4 Realized Benefits

All involved parties benefit from the use of WEkI. In overall, the Suva gained a clear competitive edge. Here a short list of the observed benefits:
"Online" mode :

- shortened processing paths for client files,
- shortened processing time for client files, typically reduced from an overall process duration of several days to a few minutes, as a consequence of the first benefit,
- experts unburdened from routine work, typically 70% of the processing is performed at the agency stage with WEkI,

"Batch" mode :

- improved control of the expected results during the maintenance of risk related groups,
- shortened time required for a complete revision of the risk-related groups; the Suva expects to speed up the revision process of all classes by a factor of 4,
- shortened reaction time to changes in the environment,
- minimization of assignment errors.

5 Special factors for success

Some of the particularities of the architecture and of the development history of WEkI pointed out above proved to be essential for its success. These particularities are summarized in the following list:

- WEkI uses a generic – KADS compatible – model of knowledge. This model does not try to imitate the workings of individual "model experts" as closely as possible but provides a general framework for the assignment.
- Orthogonal to the knowledge model, a system of parametrizeable rule types has been specified. The combination of a generic model with the specification of rule types result in a very flexible tool. The domain experts can keep their individual, usual way of writing rules for an assignment. They are supported in their task by the knowledge model as a general path, and are guided by a rule editor to maintain their rule sets.
- The use of WEkI did not require a change in the existing infrastructure of Suva. The rules are held in a database on a mainframe, outside the inference engine, which in turn incorporates the knowledge model and resides on local PCs. This allows the Suva to develop tools to analyze and maintain the rule base in the environment they are used to. The inference engine is completely integrated in the client environment in the agencies. After an employee at an agency enters the attributes of a company, he/she can choose to automatically assign the company. In this case, the inference engine is transparently invoked and loads in real time the necessary rules from the mainframe, based on the company attributes. As output, WEkI delivers an assignment. The centralized storage of the rules and their

systematical download in case of use allows the knowledge to always be kept up-to-date. The inference engine is small, stays independent of the knowledge and remains always valid.

- The responsibility for the construction and maintenance of the rule base is fully assigned to the domain experts. They have a rule type and inference model sensitive rule editor and a test environment for the rules at their disposal, that have direct access to the database on the mainframe. The rule editor and test environment allows the experts to experiment with several variants of the rules and to optimally adapt the rules to their ways of thinking. Such a procedure was impossible prior to the introduction of WEkI, due to the immense amount of work necessary.
- The environment, the mission and the technology used were well known to all participants of the project. A prototype was already developed years ago. Then, a knowledge model was developed. Important lessons could be learned, and the initial model was rejected in favor of a less "expert-friendly" but more "expert-independent" i.e. generic one as a result. Finally, the feasibility and consequences of a tight integration of a system developed with the selected inference development tool in the existing infrastructure was investigated.
- All participants of the project, especially the involved domain experts, were convinced of the project potential benefits, and of its successful completion during the whole development process. The project never faced internal resistance.
- The experts involved in the development of the prototype served as tutors for the other experts. All participants used the same vocabulary right from the beginning.
- The short elapsed duration from the project start to the productive use of WEkI prevented the occurrence of any fatigue or demotivation among the participants.

6 Conclusions

With the introduction of WEkI, Suva has now a knowledge-based system at its disposal that efficiently supports its employees in tasks that were recognized to be difficult to support with traditional IT-technologies. Since its introduction, WEkI proved its reliability and showed a number of clearly identifiable benefits. WEkI is seen as a major success at Suva.

The most important lesson learned is, that it is only through the joint effects of different factors that WEkI became a success. Besides the observed and expected benefits, technical and psychological points have been identified. Taking into account the different needs of the individual participants, by introducing a generic model of knowledge or by developing a rule editor dedicated to the experts, showed to be crucial.

7 Key figures[6]

- Classes (total)   113
- Subclasses (total)   ca. 250
- Classes (implemented in WEkI)   27
- Subclasses (implemented in WEkI)   80
- Rules (in WEkI)   521
- Assignments (total p.a.)   ca. 10'000
- Assignments (until now using WEkI)   ca. 1'200
- Assignments (needing no further work from the experts)   ca 1'000
- Experts   9
- Agencies   22

References

1. E. Lebsanft & al., 1995. "Ein wissensbasiertes System für das Versicherungs-wesen", Informatik- Informatique Magazine, 6/1995
2. E. Lebsanft, 1994. "WEKI calculates premiums for Swiss insurance company". AI Watch magazine, November 1994
3. G. Schreiber, B. Wielinga & J. Breuker, 1993. "KADS, a principled approach to knowledge-based system development". Academic Press

Acknowledgments

The authors would like to acknowledge the important contributions of I. Bulgarelli, K. Meyer, E. Bucher of Suva and E. Lebsanft and N. Tribut of SYNLOCIG AG without which WEkI would not have been the success it is.

---

[6] as of end of August 1998

Expert System Technology in Aircraft Fleet Management - The Development of SAREX

Henrik Imhof

Atraxis AG, COVE, CH-8058 Zurich-Airport
himhof@sairgroup.com

Abstract. Aircraft check planning and flight assignment are closely interrelated. We describe an expert system supporting both tasks. Search and Constraint techniques from the realm of Artificial Intelligence are paired with Scheduling methods based on certain mathematical models. The objective of Check Planning is to optimise the Maintenance Check Yield across the whole fleet. The problem is how to accommodate the frequently changing user requirements in an expert system environment. Those requirements can be expressed as constraints regarding e.g. fleet availability, hangar space, work load, or time restrictions. In contrast to classical constraint technology, where these problems are solved by instantiating variables and checking consistencies, we make use of a direct link of constraints into scheduling algorithms. As a main advantage, the basic scheduling algorithm could be left unaltered while new constraints were permanently added during the development process. For most of the constraints, SAREX offers dedicated interfaces to edit these planning rules in an easily readable format. This paper gives an overview of the applied technology and of the history of its implementation. For more technical details the reader is referred to [3].

1 The purpose of SAREX

Recovery from schedule irregularities plays a vital role in the day to day operation of an airline. The causes for irregularities can be manifold - weather conditions, technical delays, traffic congestion, additional production etc. Since 1991 Swissair relies on SAREX (Swissair Aircraft Reassignment Expert System) for decision support regarding the deployment of their fleet. A new release, introduced in 1998 for Singapore Airlines, also covers fully automated check planning. This module, tightly integrated with the aircraft assignment functionality, optimises the Maintenance Check Yield, i.e. the utilisation of check intervals, in the long and mid term planning. It also supports schedule recovery in the day to day operation by virtue of rescheduling functions.

Both the flight assignment and the check-planning module incorporate a substantial amount of expert knowledge, ranging from available resources over minimum ground times to check regulations imposed by the aviation authorities. Most of this knowledge is, and has to be, easily accessible by the users of the system. These expert users are always able to override the proposals of the system in order to cope with unforeseen situations. In case of conflicts, warnings are flagged to the user, thereby facilitating the training of new staff.

2 The Architecture

Different organisational units are linked via the client/server architecture and have access to the same central database. The units involved typically are Commercial Flight Planning, Flight Operation, and the Engineering Department. This way, a direct online communication is established. The system also automates a variety of existing communication channels, such as electronic message dispatching and generating graphical printouts. Of course, there is also a link for online exchange of flight schedule data.

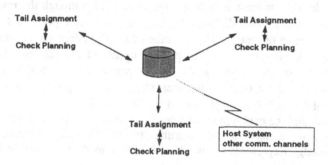

Integration of organisational units

On the system level, as well as in the check-planning module itself, there is a close interaction between two technological paradigms. On the one hand, Expert Systems technology such as Constraint Programming and search techniques from Artificial Intelligence; dedicated scheduling algorithms on the other hand. The latter rely on mathematical models and are usually considered as Operational Research technology. The following picture gives an overview of the problems dealt with and the methods used.

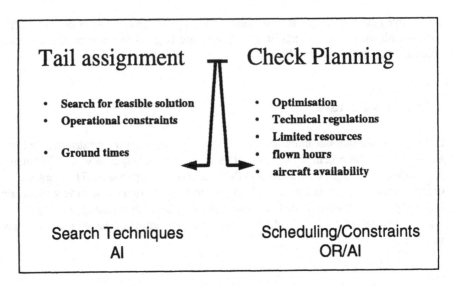

Connecting the flight assignment and check planning modules within one system facilitates the fleet management to a large extent. Even though the responsibilities for these tasks remain with different departments, it is now possible for either side to judge the impact of their decisions on the other. The client server architecture allows working with temporary solutions prior to update of the database. In fact, different scenarios of aircraft assignment can be compared to each other. The best one is selected or manually refined by the user. Here, and to support the search process, the concept of *Multiple Worlds* [4] is used (cf. Section 4).

To maintain the evolving set of rules and constraints for check planning, a new approach of integrating classical scheduling techniques with less conventional methods of Knowledge Representation is taken. It is described in [3] and, briefly, in the next section.

3 Combining new technologies with traditional approaches

Check Planning can be regarded as an instance of Scheduling with Constraints. It is worthwhile to note that the list of constraints cannot be regarded as fixed but is usually evolving throughout the development phase. This is because rules change over time, and customers often come up with examples which point at constraints that were not initially recorded in an abstract form.

This situation demands an architecture wherein the domain knowledge, expressed through constraints, allows open access to the developer and, for the most part, to the user of the system. Constraint Programming offers such a framework. All constraints are simply expressed in some abstract constraint language, and the problem is then passed to a general Constraint Satisfaction solver. Solving scheduling tasks in this declarative way has been described, for instance, in [2]. However, when it comes to scheduling, classical scheduling techniques [1] usually provide more efficient algorithms due to the fact that they often exploit inherent mathematical properties of the problem instance. Unfortunately, these properties, and along with them, the efficient solution, are easily lost when the constraints environment changes. This dilemma is expressed in the following diagram.

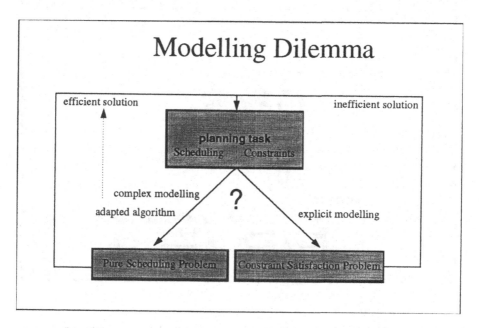

To overcome the dilemma, it is, at least in many cases, possible to analyse the structure of a scheduling algorithm, and thus to arrive at a 'constraints variant' of it. The constraints are then expressed independently and are easy to maintain. For SAREX, the link between the constraints and the scheduling algorithm is defined in a fixed library of CLOS classes and functions, to be reused also by other applications.

As a main advantage, constraints can now be changed by the programmer, or, through dedicated interfaces, by the user, without losing control over the efficiency of the scheduling algorithm. At Singapore Airlines, several hundred checks can be scheduled within 4 to 5 seconds, thereby optimising the utilisation of check intervals, and taking into account hangar availability and suitability, fleet operation, and daily work load restrictions.

Apart from this automated scheduling, the employed data structures also support manual rescheduling. In a graphical interface, checks can be rearranged in a drag and drop fashion with resulting conflicts being immediately flagged. To achieve this real time conflict detection, a *scalable degree of data abstraction* is crucial. That is to say, higher performance in constraints checking may be traded in for more accurate conflict description. The following screen dump shows a situation where a check is moved to an inappropriate hangar.

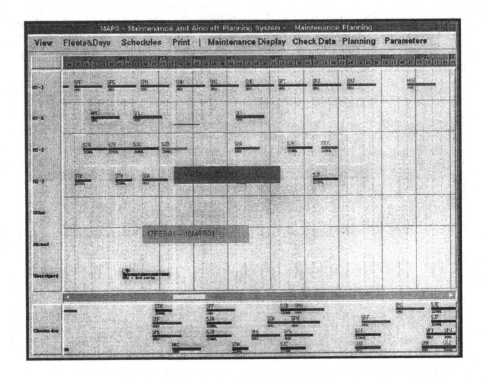

The concept of joining the constraints part with the scheduling algorithms as two independently accessible components is illustrated in the following diagram.

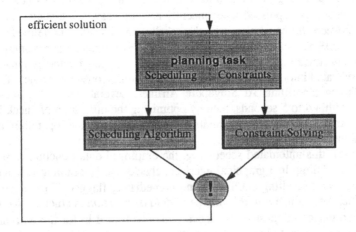

4 From prototyping to the productive system

The history of SAREX dates back to studies carried out by Elina Rantakallio at the ECAI Madrid of Unisys in the 1980s. She invented SAREX for Swissair and is now heading the development team at Atraxis. A first prototype was based on Intellicorp's expert system shell, KEE, running on dedicated AI hardware, TI Explorers, with a pure LISP operating system. The advantages of this approach were manifold. First of all, KEE realises deKleer's Multiple Worlds Concept. It is used in the search process for aircraft (re-)assignment. Solutions can be compared, and partial solutions can be analysed. Graphical tools facilitate this task enormously. Another advantage of the prototyping was the early co-operation with the expert users. In the initial phase, the system was by no means completely specified, and it hardly could have been, due to the complexity of the problem and the increasing number of links to other systems. Making the user work with a prototype and listening to their comments has proved superior to detailed system specifications, especially for a completely new type of system.

In a second phase, the functions of SAREX were re-implemented in an object-oriented dialect of LISP, on the mentioned hardware platforms. From 1991 to 1998, this configuration was in production and being continuously extended.

Between 1997 and 1998, a migration to UNIX workstations, along with large extensions of the capabilities, took place. Programming language of the now productive system is CLOS, the standard object oriented LISP version. The flight schedule and a lot of other data are kept in an Oracle database. In a version for Singapore Airlines, the automated check planning facility was first implemented. The close co-operation with the users from the very beginning, already very fruitful for the aircraft assignment component, formed the basis for the success of the new system. On the technological side, the evolving user requirements could be permanently added to the system thanks to the flexible architecture described in Section 3.

Apart from the technological difficulties sketched above, there were others – of organisational nature – to overcome. First of all, as with all major IT projects the role of the new system and its relation to legacy systems had to be defined. This ranges from questions of which system is responsible for which scope of data down to the specification of user access rights.

More specific, however, in the field of expert systems, is the following problem: On the one hand, the universality of being deployed by completely different departments (companies, in fact), is a great asset of SAREX (cf. Section 2). On the other hand, this flexibility can be a burden because any changes to the system affect a wide range of users each of them with their own preferences. This goes far beyond GUI customisations. Much rather it is to do with information filtering according to business needs. To give just one example, not all users would like to see a stand-by aircraft in the Gantt chart of aircraft activities.

Where no compromise between the users could be found, individual customisations had to be made. A rule-based approach can simplify this task a lot and make it more transparent. At present, the system behaviour is partly represented in rules, partly in the code of the functions, and to some part halfway in between – that is by extremely simple, transparent, functions (cf. Section 3). The future development, driven by the need for smooth maintenance as well as reusability for other customers, will aim at increasing the proportion of explicit representation of system behaviour.

At Swissair, the annual savings due to improved fleet management with SAREX are estimated to range between 2.5 and 3 Mio. CHF. Further savings are expected through the check-planning module but no figures are available as yet.

5 The road ahead

The current optimisation processes in SAREX are based on operational, as opposed to economical, criteria. The main purpose is, and will be, the smooth operation of the fleet (implicitly, though, the optimised Maintenance Check Yield is also an optimised economic objective). The economic decision of *Fleet Assignment* is carried out in other systems and several departments. The department concerned with the current season is also using SAREX, whence it would be only natural to take profitability data (cost and revenue) into account for the aircraft assignment. This extension, if it is to come, will turn SAREX into a full scheduling tool, for which, at least in the European market with frequent fleet reassignments, there should be a high demand.

6 References

[1] Dincbas, M., Simonis, H. and van Hentenryck, P, Solving Large Combinatorial Problem in Logic Programming, J. Logic Programming 8:75-93 (1990).

[2] Brucker, P., *Scheduling Algorithms*, Springer, 1995.

[3] Imhof, H., Combining OR and Expert System Technology in Check Planning, in *Proceedings of the 38th AGIFORS Symposium*, 1998, to appear.

[4] Nardi, A. and Paulson, E. A., Multiple Worlds with Truth Maintenance in AI Applications, in *Proceedings of the 7th European Conference on Artificial Intelligence*, Brighton, 1986.

Experiences with a Knowledge–Based Tutoring System for Student Education in Rheumatology

S. Schewe[1], B. Reinhardt[2], and C. Betz[2]

[1] Med Poliklinik, Univ. Munich, schewe@pk-i.med.uni-muenchen.de
[2] Dept. Artificial Intelligence, Univ. Wuerzburg,
{reinhard|betz@informatik.uni-wuerzburg.de}

Abstract A knowledge–based tutorial computer system in rheumatology had been integrated in a standard course of internal medicine for students in their fourth year of medical curriculum. The tutoring software is based on the expert–system shell–toolkit D3 and its tutorial component D3Trainer. Based on the knowledge base "Rheuma", which is also used for consultation, the "Rheumatrainer" is generated with the D3Trainer. The students visit the course two weeks in groups of two or three twice a week. After taking the medical history from patients, students turn to the tutorial programm "Rheumatrainer" for other parts of the diagnostic process for training of the ensuing diagnostic work up. Using the software, students learn recognition and interpretation of symptoms and findings, indication of further tests and deduction of diagnoses in a trial–and–error environment while the system is able to criticize all decisions of the student.

1 Introduction

The trend in medical school education is towards problem based learning with curricula organized around real or typical cases the students should solve on their own. The aim of this teaching approach is a higher motivation level as well as a better transfer from knowing to doing. The students should be integrated into everyday medical practice as early as possible. Since knowledge–based systems for various domains are readily available it seems obvious to apply this knowledge to teaching. In this paper we first explain this approach in detail and discuss some of the available systems, before presenting evaluation results available.

2 D3Trainer

The expert system tool kit D3 [Puppe et al. 1996] integrates a teaching component (D3Trainer) for tutorial use of knowledge bases developed originally for diagnostic problem solving. The D3Trainer ([Puppe & Reinhardt 1995], [Reinhardt 1997]) draws on various knowledge sources including the static knowledge of the knowledge base, the dynamic knowledge of the problem solver and a case base, to generate intelligent training environments for students to practice diagnostic problem solving. The main didactic idea of training systems is to provide a learning environment, in which students operate self responsible and maintain control. Regarding the basic tasks of diagnostic problem solving, *recognition and interpretation of raw data, selection of new data* and *deduction of diagnoses,* a training system should allow students to perform all of these actions within a case scenario. Based on these requirements, the D3Trainer presents a case description and offers the following options to the students:

1. ask for new information and explain the choice,
2. recognize findings in a multimedia document,
3. suggest diagnoses and cite findings supporting them.

All students' actions can be criticized based on a comparison to the underlying expert system's knowledge (Fig. 1).

For recognition of findings in a multimedia document a new authoring tool had to be added enabling the domain expert to create a collection of images presenting the case. To allow critque of students' interpretation of these images, they have to be connected to knowledge base elements.

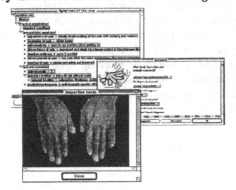

The idea of using an existing knowledge base was introduced by Clancey in Guidon [Clancey 1987], where the Mycin knowledge base was applied to teaching. Another example is the intelligent computer-assisted instruction system (ICAIS) [Fontaine et al. 1994] for clinical case teaching based on And/Or–networks. However, in both systems the knowledge base for consultation had to be extended

Figure1. Case–presentation, picture for recognition and feedback of the D3Trainer

with special teaching knowledge, like tutoring rules (Guidon) or a separate adjunct network (ICAIS). Furthermore there was no possibility to integrate multimedia elements, so recognition of findings in images could not be provided. There are some conventional coded systems like "Trouble in Thorax" [Eitel & Arends 1994] or "Thyroidea" [Fischer et al. 1994], which use media elements making the system more attractive and teaching recognition of findings as well. The architectures of "Trouble in Thorax" and "Thyroidea", built with the authoring system Casus [Holzer et al. 1998], are based on a linked order of knowledge parts, while possible student actions and feedback are specifically modeled by the case authors. A disadvantage of full coded, non knowledge–based teaching systems is their restriction of students' actions. Every possible action has to be coded for every single case situation, so the effort for providing near–complete scenarios exceeds the reasonable costs. In the D3Trainer there is no need to consider any single student action because the underlying expert system with its comprehensive problem solving capabilities does this job.

3 The Evaluation Scenario

The tutoring software is generated from the knowledge base of the consultation system "Rheuma" ([Gappa et al. 1993], [Puppe & Schewe 1997]). An evaluation of this rheumatologic knowledge base in different stages of development was performed over years in several studies by comparing the results of the expert system with those of specialized physicians [Schewe & Schreiber 1993]. Preliminary evaluations of the training system generated with this knowledge base were carried out in similar scenarios [Schewe et al. 1996]. A modified system is currently being used and evaluated in the context of continued medical education [Rienhoff 1998].

The Rheumatrainer has now been applied over five semesters as an integral part of medical school education of stu-

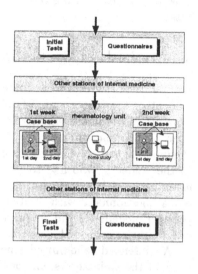

Figure2. Structure of courses for rheumatology

dents in their fourth year. Each term 14 to 27 students were trained within the following scenario for practical instruction. This was established over several years without major changes as shown in Fig. 2: groups of two or three students received four training lessons, lasting 1.5 hours each. The first day, students were faced with an out–door patient in the rheumatology unit of Munich medical–school. During approx. 30 min, students took the medical history and did the physical examination. This is the conventional teaching method in the other parts of the course, e.g. cardiology. After the patient examination the case is discussed with a professor of rheumatology with respect to examination techniques and different strategies for ordering further tests without getting their results. During the next day the same patient is presented to the students in the computer based training system with the full range of findings (e.g. symptoms, lab data, images).

In discussion with their tutor the students decide on a diagnosis, which is then compared to the solution of the knowledge–based system. In addition to this case the students have to solve another case with similar symptoms but a potentially different diagnose. In the time between the second and the third lesson (approx. a week) the students have time to learn and deepen the differential diagnostic aspects of these cases. In both summer terms '97 and '98 a CD with the Rheumatrainer with 25 additional cases was given to the students for supporting their studies at home or in the clinic, where some PCs were offered for students who do not have access to a computer at home.

After the week of private study, the students return to the rheumatology unit and for presentation of another patient to be examined by the students, followed by a discussion with the professor. During the fourth and last day the students diagnose two cases using the Rheumatrainer software without the support of a tutor.

4 Methods of Evaluation

A total of 82 students participated in the study over a period of four years (22 students in the winter term '94/'95, 19 in the summer term '95, 27 in the summer term '97 and 14 in the summer term '98). At the beginning and the end of winter term '94/'95 and summer term '98 a test was given, each with two up to four rheumatological cases. For each case the presenting symptoms were forwarded to the students, who had to ask for additional findings from history, physical examination, laboratory and images. In addition to these tests the students filled out a questionnaire with 46 items ranked from 0 (most negative) to 10 (most positive judgement) and seven yes–or–no–questions. The essential parts of the questionnaire remained constant during the four years.

An intended randomized study of comparing the learning success with or without the training system could not be performed due to organizational reasons: both groups of students (with and without training system) would have to be observed under identical learning conditions. This seperation was not possible due to the integration of this rheumatology scenario into the curriculum for internal medicine important for the acceptance among students and lecturers.

5 Results

The results collected over the past four years as shown in detail in Table 1 exhibit that the integration of tutoring software in higher education is appraised very positivly (7.6±1.94) and that the ranking of the Rheumatrainer as an optimal computer based training program is surpassing (6.1±1.9). The score is particularly high for the application in self–education and the use of the Rheumatrainer in addition to a course (6.44 ± 2.34), whereas it is rejected as a replacement for a practical class or a human teacher.

Learning with systems like the Rheumatrainer is judged reasonable, esp. for training in special fields (like rheumatology). It can also motivate learning in new domains. The power of the Rheumatrainer clearly lies in the systematic analysis of cases and the knowledge transfer, esp. for learning how to take a medical history and diagnostic capabilities. The students appraise the tangibility, the structuring as well as the legibility of the texts as positive.

The judgement of the ease of learning how to use the Rheumatrainer is most outstanding, as the understandability of the decisions of the knowledge–based system is. The pleasure working with the Rheumatrainer, combined with the fact that working with it is not boring leads to the statement, that the students are motivated to do further training with that software.

Nevertheless there were technical difficulties with the Rheumatrainer. Students with technical problems using the Rheumatrainer as expected gave lower rankings for the application of tutoring software in common and especially of the Rheumatrainer and some other points concerning the its use. Neither the sex nor the accessibility of a PC at home had significant influences on the opinions of the students. Throughout the different terms the answers of the students only changed marginally.

An increase of knowledge could be observed both for winter–term '94/'95 (compare to [Schewe et al. 1996]) and for summer–term '98. In two different cases with an estimated connective tissue disease there were significant more correct statements for history, physical, laboratory and technical examinations since the start of the class until the end of the term. There were also notable more correct answers in clarification of two cases of monarthritis; while by the clarification of gout no differences could be proven. The target criterion of ordering a test for antinuclear antibodies as basical for diagnosing the group of connective tissue diseases was reached of 11 more students at the end of the class compared to the beginning vs. one student who missed it. Five other students selected it correctly both on start- and end–test of the course.

6 Conclusion

The Rheumatrainer was well accepted by the students particularly with regard to the integration in the conventional education scenario as described in this evaluation. Students will always prefer the confrontation with a real patient instead of a computer program, because they can experience the personal world of the patient and repeat the most important clinical examinations. On the other hand, with the computer program they benefit from the chance to choose all possible examinations and to learn by trial–and–error. So the integration of a computer based training system in conventional teaching seems a good solution for problem based education.

Unlike many other evaluation studies for computer based training systems (e.g. [Fischer et al. 1994], [Schulz et al. 1997]) this evaluation took place in a real education situation. The disadvantage of this approach is the difficulty to provide a statistical sound control group, but the advantages prevail. The real world situation as well as representative student participants (without special interests in neither computer based training nor rheumatology) make the whole evaluation more realistic. Surprisingly neither the sex nor the previous computer–experience had any influence on the assessment of the training system.

Apparently a part of the students (10 %) rejected the computer as an educational tool. Reasons were technical problems with the handling of the program, related partly to hardware restrictions of the students' computers and partly to the absence of printed user information. Both problems are solved by now so that the current evaluation study in the winter term '98/'99 is expected to show better results in this respect.

The critique concerning the lack of clarity expressed by some students and physicians is understandable but unavoidable given the complexity of rheumatology. There is some technical help, for example dynamic hierarchies or coloring of pathological findings. However, since 70% of the diagnostic informations can be derived from medical history, its presentation has to be very detailed, especially in an educational environment.

The measurable learning success documented in test results (immediately after the class as well as in the finals, sometimes months after the class) [Schewe et al. 1996] supports the conclusion that the learning goals could be achieved during the class. This holds particularly for areas, in which the students lacked knowledge prior to the class, less for areas with considerable pre-knowledge.

The effort for building a teaching case, from real documentation of the medical history up to the provision of diagnostic images with multimedia elements, is considerable higher than for the preparation of a conventional class. The expected benefit from multiple usage of the system, e.g. in a planned internet version, could not yet be confirmed.

As shown in other evaluations ([Gräsel 1997], [Arends & Eitel 1998]), computer based training systems can be a useful addition to problem based learning, but cannot be the only source to learn with. To get an optimal result the systems have to be integrated in the existing curriculum, so the time spent with real patients can be used effectively while the students can follow a more trial-and-error way of learning with the training systems.

References

[Arends & Eitel 1998] W. Arends und F. Eitel: *Programmierung und Evaluation eines interaktiven computerunterstützten Selbstlernprogrammes Rundherd in der Lunge, Trouble im Thorax.* In: M. Adler, J. Dietrich, M. Holzer und M. Fischer (Hrsg.): *Computer Based Training in der Medizin*, Seiten 1–20. Shaker, 1998.

[Clancey 1987] J. Clancey: *Knowledge-Based Tutoring - The GUIDON Program.* MIT Press Cambridge, 1987.

[Eitel & Arends 1994] F. Eitel and W. Arends: *Trouble im Thorax - Diagnostik, Differentialdiagnostik und Therapie des solitären Lungenrundherdes.* Zentralblatt Radiologie, 1:282–283, 1994.

[Fischer et al. 1994] M. Fischer, C. Gräsl, R. Gärtner und H. Mandl: *Thyroida: Konzeption, Entwicklung und Evaluation eines fallbasierten Computerlernprogramms in der Medizin.* In: E. Schoof und Glowalla (Hrsg.): *Hypermedia in Aus- und Weiterbildung*, 1994.

[Fontaine et al. 1994] D. Fontaine, P. Beux, C. Riou, and C. Jacquelinet: *An intelligent computer-assisted instruction system for clinical case teaching.* Methods of Information in Medicine, 33:433–345, 1994.

[Gappa et al. 1993] U. Gappa, F. Puppe, and S. Schewe: *Graphical knowledge acquisition for medical diagnostic expert systems.* Artificial Intelligence in Medicine, 5:185–211, 1993.

[Gräsel 1997] C. Gräsel: *Strategieanwendung und Gestaltungsmöglichkeiten.* Hofgrefe Verlag für Psychologie, 1997.

[Holzer et al. 1998] M. Holzer, J. Konschak, S. Bruckmoser und M. Fischer: *Wissensdiagnostik in medizinischen Lernprogrammen am Beispiel des Autorensystems CASUS.* In: M. Adler, J. Dietrich, M. Holzer und M. Fischer (Hrsg.): *Computer Based Training in der Medizin*, Seiten 51–55. Shaker, 1998.

[Puppe et al. 1996] F. Puppe, U. Gappa, K. Poeck und S. Bamberger: *Wissensbasierte Diagnose- und Informationssysteme*. Springer, 1996.

[Puppe & Reinhardt 1995] F. Puppe and B. Reinhardt: *Generating Case-Oriented Training From Diagnostic Expert Systems*. Machine Mediated Learning, 5(4):199–219, 1995.

[Puppe & Schewe 1997] F. Puppe und S. Schewe: *Mehrfachverwendung von diagnostischen Wissensbasen in der Medizin*. Künstliche Intelligenz, 3:15–23, 1997.

[Reinhardt 1997] B. Reinhardt: *Generating Case Oriented Intelligent Tutoring Systems*. In *Technical Report*, volume FS-97-01 of *Papers from the 1997 AAAI Fall Symposium*, pages 79–85. AAAI Press, November 1997.

[Rienhoff 1998] O. Rienhoff: *Ärztliche Fortbildung und Qualitätssicherung*. In: *Forum Info 2000*, Band 105 der Reihe *Schriftenreihe des Bundesministeriums für Gesundheit*, Seiten 114–117. Bundesministeriums für Gesundheit, 1998.

[Schewe et al. 1996] S. Schewe, T. Quak, B. Reinhardt, and F. Puppe: *Evaluation of a Knowledge-Based Tutorial Program in Rheumatology*. In C. Frasson, G. Gaulthier, and A. Lesgold (eds.): *Proceedings of the Third International Conference ITS'96*, pages 531–539. Springer, June 1996.

[Schewe & Schreiber 1993] S. Schewe and M. Schreiber: *Stepwise development of clinical expert system in rheumatology*. The Clinical Investigator, 71:139–144, 1993.

[Schulz et al. 1997] S. Schulz, T. Auhuber und R. Klar: *Kontrollierte Evaluationsstudie von MicroPat - Interaktiver Atlas der Histopathologie*. In: H. Conradi, R. Kreutz und K. Spitzer (Hrsg.): *CBT in der Medizin - Methoden, Techniken, Anwendungen*, Seiten 117–123. GMDS, 1997.

Table of Results

Table1. Table of judgements of all students combined (level of significance refers to mean difference between the rankings and an indifferent score of 5).
level of significance $p < 0.01$ + + resp. - - for negative values,
$p < 0.05$ + resp. -, n.s. not significant

Item	mean value	standard deviation	No. of cases	level of significance
value of rheumatology for the study	6,61	1,68	82	+ +
value of rheumat. for a later profession	6,22	2,14	82	+ +
technical problems	3,35	2,68	81	
self assessment of knowledge before	3,10	1,42	82	- -
self assessment of knowledge afterwards	5,69	1,51	80	+ +
tutoring programs are reasonable	7,61	1,94	82	+ +
this program is optimal in CBT	6,07	1,87	82	+ +
using the program during the lessons	6,44	2,34	81	+ +
using the program on a PC at university	5,01	2,66	82	n.s.
using the program at home	7,30	2,58	81	+ +
using it in a group	3,52	2,49	80	n.s.
using the program for self-studies	7,42	2,32	82	+ +
complementary to a course	6,99	2,56	82	+ +
as substitution of a course	1,55	1,21	82	- -
preparation for a test	5,58	2,70	82	n.s.
for training in special fields	6,61	2,67	82	+ +
motivation to explore unknown domains	6,05	2,74	60	+ +
learning with the program is reasonable	6,55	2,32	82	+ +
working with the program is not boring	6,88	2,06	82	+ +
eligibility for case analysis	6,81	1,99	80	+ +
applicability to clarify terms	5,59	2,30	81	+
qualification to learn how to take history	6,00	2,43	81	+ +
diagnostic capabilities	6,73	2,29	81	+ +
learning pace	4,53	2,36	81	n.s.
support for diagnostic	6,30	2,28	81	+ +
learning motivation	6,31	2,43	81	+ +
diagnostic process	5,63	2,56	81	+
knowledge transfer	6,76	2,13	81	+ +
relation to practical use	5,09	2,68	81	n.s.
replace the human tutor	1,79	1,38	81	- -
help for lecturers	6,86	2,25	81	+ +
training of factual-knowledge	4,85	2,31	81	n.s.
think autonomous	6,36	2,81	81	+ +
tangibility of texts	7,17	1,63	77	+ +
structuring of texts	6,71	1,92	77	+ +
legibility of texts	6,32	2,24	77	+ +
graphical representation	5,49	2,23	77	n.s.
easy to learn	7,26	2,10	77	+ +
roboustness	5,34	2,82	77	n.s.
clarity	5,47	2,34	77	n.s.
do further training with the program	6,43	1,96	77	+ +
understandability	6,78	2,04	77	+ +
explanation of own hypthesis	5,66	2,32	77	+
pleased by working with the trainer	6,51	2,06	77	+ +
concentration on the work	5,88	2,28	77	+ +
utility for study	6,84	2,37	77	+ +

Computer Assisted Editing of Genomic Sequences – Why and How We Evaluated a Prototype

Thomas Pfisterer[1] and Thomas Wetter[2]

[1] German Cancer Research Centre, Dept. Molecular Biophysics, Heidelberg, Germany
[2] University of Heidelberg, Institute for Medical Biometry and Informatics, Heidelberg, Germany

Abstract. After sequence data is obtained from the laboratory there is still a lot of time consuming manual post-processing necessary until the data is ready for submission to one of the sequence databases. One of the most time consuming activities called *editing* is to find and correct faulty base calls in the sequences by looking at the original electrophoresis trace data. Our efforts in this project aim towards developing appropriate methods and tools to reduce the time the editor (our expert) has to spend for this post-processing. Therefore we intend to automatically perform as much of this sequence editing as possible. A first prototype with limited competence was implemented and evaluated. This paper discusses the issues involved in this evaluation. We elucidate why it can be reasonable to evaluate a system at a very early point in time, explain how this evaluation was conducted and present the results obtained.

1 The Domain

Usually nucleotide sequences are obtained by gel or capillary electrophoresis. But electrophoresis is able to 'read' only sequences of a few hundred bases of length (normally $300-800$ bases with the required precision) until the signal becomes more and more blurred. Thus a lot of these short sequences (called *reads*) have to be combined to achieve larger sequences. At the moment this is usually done by random shotgun sequencing [3].

For a typical project with a sequence length of 50,000 base pairs (50 kbp) 600 to 1200 reads are necessary. These reads are random fragments of the sequence we want to examine. Because they are random fragments they are partially overlapping. We can assemble these reads into larger structures (called contigs) by searching these overlaps (see [9] for further detail, and figure 1 for an example). Assembly must be fault tolerant due to the $1\% - 2\%$ of sequencing errors (local error rates can be much higher).

We need enough reads for an average $4/, -6$ fold coverage of the region we want to sequence. But gaps still remain and we obtain a lot of these contigs instead of a single sequence. If assembly is based on very loose criteria it often puts reads into a wrong position (this is called a misassembly). A very strict assembly oversees correct overlaps and ends up in lots of contigs whose mutual overlap remains undetected.

After the assembly we have a couple of reads on a single position of our sequence. This redundancy allows us to uncover base-calling errors[1] and misassemblies whenever a nucleotide letter deviates from another in the same place (column). The aim of sequence editing is to examine and resolve these conflicting situations by editing the read or removing it from the contig. This decision is made by looking at the original electrophoresis data.

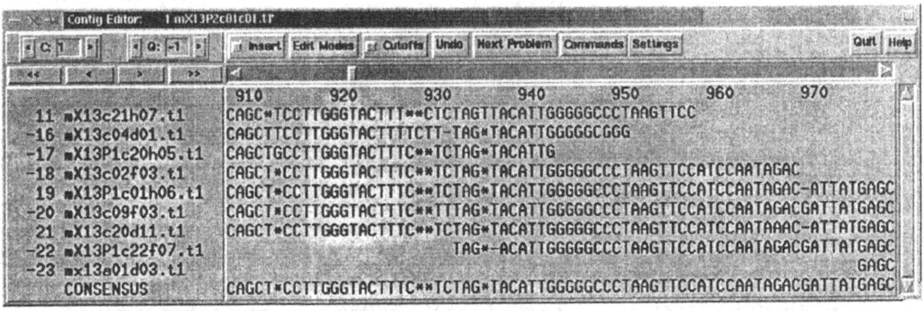

Fig. 1. Fraction of an assembly. Symbolic level of sequence editing. Each row represents one gel electrophoretic read. Bottom line contains the consensus sequence build out of the above reads.

In comparison with existing efforts our system is the so far first attempt to tackle the problem of sequence editing by a knowledge-based system. Current systems either use base qualities (e.g. PHRAP [5]) to obviate much of the necessary trace checking activities by overriding bases weakly supported by the raw data. Base qualities can be used to calculate estimates for the probability of the consensus base [1]. If available the original electrophoresis trace data can be examined. This is the way most human editing is performed. The automatic editor from Sanger Centre [4] calculates and evaluates signal parameters. Other groups calculate confidence values for sequence readings [7] or they use linear discriminant analysis to assign specific error probabilities to each position in the primary sequences data [6]. Another possibility is to align a sequence with its trace data using dynamic programming [8]. At the moment these systems emphasise the finishing of the sequence data and neglect other editing activities.

2 Problem Solving Method

According to the modelling paradigm for knowledge acquisition (following traditional KADS [11]) we built a model of the human expertise in rating the signal

---

[1] Base calling is a preprocessing step where the electrophoresis signals are examined in order to find out which bases are called.

traces, deciding about the editing problems and in performing the necessary operations. Ideally an interpretation model from a KADS library (e.g. [2]) would have been used for the inference layer. But the necessary mixture of diagnostic and repair inferences was not available.

Beside decisions of high quality we aim towards reproducible, flexible and modular decision functions for ubiquitous *atomic* problems. With these activities we intend to lay a cornerstone towards noticeably extending the supported activities in the future. The same decision functions are e.g. used to improve the quality of the assembler. When a read is incorporated into the assembly we examine all mismatching bases if they can be explained by the trace data.

For the problem at hand there is a variety of different subtasks (not all of them can or should be solved using formal knowledge representation techniques). The most important ones are:

- hypotheses' generation: which faults in the reads would explain the discrepancy found?
- rating hypotheses: there is theoretically an infinite number of hypotheses – but only a few of them are reasonable.
- describing the electrophoresis signals: which properties or parameters can be extracted from the signal and how can we 'link' them to the concepts intuitively used by the expert.
- decisions about hypotheses: how can we come to a decisions about the fault hypotheses based on the signal analysis and additional information (e.g. effects of the chemical processes applied)

When we began there wasn't any experience with the knowledge based approach to the problem of computer assisted editing. Hence we could not predict how far the components mentioned above have to be elaborated. Which set of signal parameters could yield a sufficient foundation for the decision functions? Is it important to deal with complex hypotheses – are we able to decide among them?

Both identifying possible faults by means of the base sequences (symbolic data) and the visual examination and evaluation of the electrophoresis signals (the traces) is done very intuitively. The experts could only give very sparse and unclear descriptions about their decisions and the verbal explanations were unclear and did not discriminate very well between the possibilities. On the other hand it was possible to protocol and analyse the training of a junior knowledge engineer in sequence editing. This was essential to provide a correct mapping between the concepts used in the domain and the signal parameters which were required to decide the hypothesis.

Because the system was intended to support and not to replace the human editor it was not necessary for us to solve all problems. An applicable system can pass the problems it is not able to solve or the decisions it is not certain about back to the human editor. Therefore it lent itself to thoroughly model the overall problem solving method and then to start applying it to a circumscribed class of easy to solve fault hypotheses. By analysing these experiences we expected to gain the information necessary to select the components which promise the greatest improvement of the total system. It was also important to prove for each step of the refinement that the decisions actually made have sufficient quality to be accepted by the users.

This situation gave rise to the idea of a scalable design [10]. Its inference structure persists whereas distinct components and knowledge sources are replaced by more powerful ones to improve the system's overall performance. This is possible because the main tasks can be described quite independent from each other.

3 Questions examined in the evaluation

In order to carry out a scalable design consistently, it was however necessary to actually perform an evaluation at quite an early point in time. This was done to determine the components that should be developed with top priority in order to attain a comprehensive and efficient system fast. The system we evaluated could handle only a subset of the fault classes we build. This subset was chosen for different reasons. The hypotheses were easy to generate and the faults were named by the experts to be so annoying that some of the editors solve these problems as a first stage of editing.

The inspection of the quality of the results was an important point of the evaluation because sufficient quality is a prerequisite for routine use.

Furthermore it was important to determine whether there are already considerable savings of time. We expected the time saved to be slightly lower than the proportion of problems solved. This is due to the fact that easy problems are more likely to be solved automatically and that the expert solves easy problems faster than sophisticated ones.

Although an agreement is usually achieved about the predominant part of the decisions, there are nevertheless cases where different editors arrive at different decisions. Thus it is necessary to consider the variations between different editors as well. We supposed that the cases of disagreement result mainly from being more bold or being more cautious and we hoped that completely different decisions were seldom. But about this matter there was no information available. Our investigations also aimed at revealing if there is a real problem to assess the correctness of an editing action performed by the automatic editor.

4 Realization

It is possible to examine the two main questions *sufficient quality* and *time saved* separately.

4.1 Time saved

In order to find out if we can already save any time we wanted to compare the time which was required to edit a project using the system and the time required to edit it conventionally. The difference between these two values is the time that can be saved. But of course you cannot use the same project twice because the expert would remember the project. Using different editors for the same project would also be problematic because of their different editing styles[2] and editing speeds. Using different projects would also measure the differences between these projects. Assuming that disturbing effects are randomly distributed they would be equalised in the long run. But it was unrealistic to collect such an amount of data. So we decided to balance the conditions by ourselves:

The **differences between projects** were minimised by composing two artificial projects out of typical original data. The two projects were stratified in such a way that all known important causal variables were taken into account: the length of the project in number of base pairs, the number of contigs, the number of faults, and the length distribution of the contigs etc. (see table 1). We constructed both artifical projects out of a single real project to have comparable signal qualities, specimen properties etc. All editing was done on the same computer. This computer was set free from other processes that could have had impact on its performance.

To eliminate the **differences between the experts** we used a cross-over study design which is known to give good results even if there is only a small number of cases available. Every expert edited a project conventionally and another one which had already been automatically edited. Which of the projects was conventionally edited was assigned by random. Because each project was edited by all editors[3] we were able to compare if there would be any differences between them.

4.2 Quality

To measure the quality of the decisions made we took a number of representative projects sent to us in the original assembled state and after the first stage of editing. The only additional work for the experts to be done was to send us the projects and to make a brief minute about problems or cases of doubt encountered during the manual editing. We aimed at collecting a great amount of data for this part of the evaluation because real errors of the system were supposed to be quite seldom. All projects that had been submitted and the results of the manual editing had been commented were also edited by our system and the results compared. Due to the system's use as a preprocessing stage (after the reads are assembled and before they are edited) we counted only the false positive decisions. Because of the individual differences and the different severity of the errors we decided to discuss each of them. We had no fixed percentage of errors we would tolerate for routine use. This would heavily depend on their severity. We established for each project a small web page where we published the cases of doubt. The problems and their underlying signal traces were put up for discussion.

---

[2] E.g. how many tags are set (tags are a kind of comment for the edit operations).
[3] or to be more precise at least every problem not solved by the automatic editor was edited by everyone

5 Results

Our projects where put together by only looking at the values which where important to stratify them and without looking at the data itself or any results of the automatic editor. Hence it could happen that one of the contigs (unfortunately the longest one) of project P_1 was misassembled. Although such misassemblies occasionally happen this one distorted the results a little bit (both, of the assembly and the evaluation). A great deal of multiple faults our prototype could not handle led to an under average performance for this project (see table 1 compared with the results from table 3).

Table 1. Characteristic parameters of the two artifical projects used.

project	length kbp	contigs	faults	solved
P_1	22.1	9	112	40
P_2	20.8	9	101	51

Looking at the time needed for editing the projects great variances can be noticed. Fortunately our stratified artificial projects and the cross-over design could eliminate a good deal of the individual differences and led to useful and quite homogeneous results. Because we could recruit only 5 experts during the two days of the study we had not enough data for doing any statistical testing. Albeit we can not really prove that there is an effect in general, we can observe that we saved 30% of the time. This is slightly less than the percentage of problems solved.

Table 2. Time differences. Differences were calculated by subtracting the time needed for conventional editing from the time needed with assistance from the automatic editor. The first index is the editor-id, the second index is the project-id.

expert	projects edited by expert	time elapsed (min)		time difference (min)
		assisted	conventional	
1	$t_{1.1} - t_{1.2}$	19	32	-13
2	$t_{2.1} - t_{2.2}$	31	28	3
3	$t_{3.1} - t_{3.2}$	23	35	-12
4	$t_{4.2} - t_{4.1}$	9	14	-5
5	$t_{5.2} - t_{5.1}$	16	26	-10

When comparing the different editors of the cross-over part of the evaluation we could find only small differences in the decisions made. 15 minor discrepancies due to a different opinion or editing style could be found in the 1065 decisions made altogether (about 1.5%). But to our surprise we could also find a notable number of 26 faults due to neglicence when actually performing the edit operations[4]. The small number of serious differences between the editors allows us to compare our system with a single editor to measure its quality. For the two projects of the evaluation our system made no questionable edits.

The examination of the quality of the decisions made showed an error rate of below 1% (the positive predictive value is over 0.99). Although at first sight about 2% of the edits made by our system had differences of any kind a good deal of them had simply been forgotten to examine by the editor. To summarise, we could easily show that quality was no problem for this first prototype. This was not a surprise because we had intended to implement a quite conservative system.

Table 3. Evaluation of decision quality (data from sequences of the mouse chromosome Ids-DXHXS1104. Sequenced at the Genome Sequencing Centre, Jena).

Project	faults	solved	differences
mX11	513	241	3
mX13	262	122	0
	775	363	3

Table 4. Results standardised to the time needed to solve 100 faults.

expert	difference projects	difference time (min)	time difference (relative)
1	$t_{1.1} - t_{1.2}$	15	0.47
2	$t_{2.1} - t_{2.2}$	0	0.00
3	$t_{3.1} - t_{3.2}$	14	0.40
4	$t_{4.2} - t_{4.1}$	-4	0.31
5	$t_{5.2} - t_{5.1}$	-7	0.30
	Sum of all	-40	0.31

The quality of the decisions the system did make was quite good and needed no improvement in the short run. Most problems the system didn't decide were due to the hypotheses generation, which we had limited to single fault hypothe-

---

[4] In figure 1 e.g. in read mX13c04d01.t1 the bases at the positions 927 and 929 must be deleted and not the C at position 928.

ses, and not due to the decision functions. This was very encouraging because we can now go ahead and extend the scope of hypotheses generation and we can begin to handle other fault classes as well. Improving signal analysis and decision functions would have little effect at the moment.

6 Conclusion

It has shown up that an early evaluation was reasonable. We obtained both information to guide the further development of the system and the certainty that a routine use of the system is already possible. We are also able to show that it is worthwhile using the system because time savings can be expected (even if we have not enough data to make a statistical test reasonable or significant).

We could limit the necessary time for the evaluation by using a cross-over design to reduce the variablity between different editors and projects. Especially for the experts the temporal load of the evaluation was quite low.

7 Acknowledgements

The research presented in this article was conducted in close cooperation with the Genome Sequencing Centre of the Institute for Molecular Biotechnology, (IMB) Beutenbergstraße 11, 07745 Jena, Germany. The authors special thanks go to M. Platzer and his colleagues who made this evaluation actually possible.

This work is supported by the Bundesministerium für Bildung, Wissenschaft, Forschung und Technologie by grant number 01 KW 9611.

References

1. J. K. Bonfield and R. Staden. The application of numerical estimates of base calling accuracy to DNA sequencing projects. *Nucleic Acids Research*, 23(8):1406–1410, 1995.
2. J. Breuker and W. Van der Velde, editors. *CommonKADS Library for Expertise Modelling*. IOS Press Amsterdam, 1994.
3. D. Casey. Primer on molecular genetics. US Department of Energy, 1992. http://www.ornl.gov/hgmis/publicat/primer/intro.html.
4. S. Dear, R. Durbin, L. Hillier, M. Gabor, J. Thierry-Mieg, and R. Mott. Sequence assembly with CAFTOOLS. *Genome Research*, 8:260–267, 1998.
5. B. Ewing and P. Green. Base-calling of automated sequencer traces using PHRED. II. error probabilities. *Genome Research*, 8(3):167–94, 1998.
6. C. B. Lawrence and V. V. Solovyev. Assignment of position-specific error probability to primary DNA sequence data. *Nucleic Acids Research*, 22(7):1272–80, 1994.
7. R. J. Lipshutz, F. Taverner, K. Hennessy, G. Hartzell, and R. Davis. DNA sequence confidence estimation. *Genomics*, 19(3):417–24, 1994.
8. R. Mott. Trace alignment and some of its applications. *Bioinformatics*, 14(1):92–97, 1998.

9. J. Setubal and J. Meidanis. *Introduction to computational molecualar biology*. PWS Publishing Company, 1997.
10. T. Wetter and T. Pfisterer. Modeling for scalability - ascending into automatic genome sequencing. In *Eleventh Workshop on Knowledge Acquisition, Modeling and Management (KAW'98)*, Banff (Canada), April 14-18, 1998.
11. B. J. Wielinga, B. J. Schreiber, and J. A. Breuker. KADS: a modelling approach to knowledge engineering. *Knowledge Acquisition*, 4(1):5–54, 1992.

Experiences of Using a Computer-Aided Therapy Planning for Pediatric Oncology in Clinical Routine

Petra Knaup[1], Timm Wiedemann[1], Andreas Bachert[2], Ursula Creutzig[3], Reinhold Haux[1], Michael Schäfer[1], Freimut Schilling[4]

[1] University of Heidelberg, Institute for Medical Biometry and Informatics, Department of Medical Informatics, Im Neuenheimer Feld 400, 69210 Heidelberg
{Petra_Knaup, Timm_Wiedemann, Reinhold_Haux} @ukl.uni-heidelberg.de
from 1.1.99: {...} @med.uni-heidelberg.de
[2] HMS GmbH, Heidelberg
[3] Gesellschaft für Pädiatrische Onkologie und Hämatologie, Hannover
[4] Olgahospital Stuttgart

Abstract. A system for computer aided therapy planning in pediatric oncology (CATIPO) is introduced, which is in routine use in about 20 clinics all over Germany. The system mainly consists of a knowledge acquisition tool for entering protocol-specific knowledge and a decision support tool for deriving a patient-specific therapy plan. The benefit of the system is that mistakes can be avoided and the effort for deriving a particular therapy plan can be decreased. The limitation of CATIPO is that is offers basic decision support for therapy planning and is not yet integrated in a comprehensive electronic patient record. It can be assumed that the success of CATIPO is based on the fact that there has been an enourmous demand for this kind of decision support and that it has been developed in tight cooperation with future users.

Introduction

Subject and Relevance

In Germany the treatment of childhood cancer has been relatively successful the last decades. According to the report of the German Childhood Cancer Registry [1] the recurrence-free survival rate increased to an average about 70%. This varies in dependence of the particular diagnosis. So, the recurrence-free survival rate ranges from 36% for acute non-lymphatic leukemia to 95% for retinoblastoma. It is expected that nationwide multicenter trials have considerably contributed to this success. For the 18 most common diagnoses of childhood cancer trial centers have been established which release therapy protocols for the treatment of the respective children. About 90% of the children with cancer in Germany are treated according to these protocols. The research questions of the multicenter trials focus currently not only on the survival rate but also on minimizing side effects of the intensive therapy.

Problems and Motivation

The core of treating childhood cancer is in most cases chemotherapy. Dosing cytostatic drugs is dependent on age, height and weight of the patient. Therefore, the guidelines of each therapy protocol have to be adjusted to an individual patient. These calculations are rather time-consuming and complex (cf. e.g. [2]). An error would have severe consequences [3]. Due to this, the department of Medical Informatics of the University of Heidelberg has developed in cooperation with the German Society of Pediatric Oncology and Hematology (GPOH) an application system for Computer-Aided Therapy Planning in Pediatric Oncology (CATIPO) [4]. CATIPO is currently in routine use in about 20 pediatric-oncologic clinics all over Germany.

Aims of the paper

The aim of the paper is to report on our experiences of applying CATIPO in the various clinics with the help of answering the following questions:
- What is benefit and what are the limitations of CATIPO?
- What are the reasons that CATIPO is really in routine use?
- Which general conclusions can be drawn from this experiences for the applicability of decision support systems in clinical routine?

Computer-aided therapy planning in pediatric oncology

Available approaches

Several information systems for supporting protocol-guided therapy in oncology have been introduced in the last two decades (e.g. [5-7], [3]) and their benefit has been evaluated. Most of the systems are designed for the treatment of cancer in adults. Typical problems are decision support for the eligibility of a patient for a certain protocol or for further medication based on the the response of earlier treatment and changes in vital parameters or laboratory findings (cf. for example [8-10]).

This problems are not predominating in pediatric oncology in Germany. In most cases the adequate protocol can be assigned unambiguosly, because there is in general just one protocol for each of the most common diagnosis. Furthermore, the physician treating the child is not alone responsible for this decision, he will get support from the German Childhood Cancer Registry [11] and the respective trial centers.

Additionally, children can - in contrast to adults - tolerate a high-dose chemotherapy rather well. Therefore, often the proposed chemotherapy cycle can be applied like he has been calculated. Daily decisions on therapeutic actions normally affect only supportive medication.

Another reason why most of the available systems are not applicable for widespread use in pediatric oncology in Germany is the necessity for a flexible and easy to use knowledge acquisition tool. The protocol-specific knowledge has to be entered by the physicians in the clinics where the patients are treated. Most of the 18 multicenter trials last about 5 years, so that every year 3-5 new protocols are delivered.

A system that is well directed to the needs of pediatric oncology is THEMPO [12]. Besides representing and calculating therapy plans it allows the representation of causal, temporal and other clinical contexts [13]. But THEMPO has been developed in the NEXTSTEP environment, so that it is not yet applicable for widespread use in clinics all over Germany.

CATIPO

Knowledge acquisition: Defining therapy protocols

A prerequisite for deriving a patient-specific therapy plan is that the respective therapy protocol has been defined. Therefore, CATIPO provides a knowledge acquisition tool that inheres general knowledge about chemotherapy cycles in pediatric oncology which is independent from a particular therapy protocol. Knowledge acquistion itself takes place in the hospitals, where the physicians can enter the protocol-specific knowledge on chemotherapy cycles. This is knowledge on, among others:

– particular drugs, the way they are applied and the way their dosage is calculated
– how a solution with the active agent is composed
– the composition of infusions
– the sequences of drug applications
– criteria that have to be fulfilled in order to be able to apply the chemotherapy cycle to a patient.

Because the hospitals' conventions (concerning e.g. the usage of drugs) vary between the hospitals the knowledge acquisition process can not take place in the trial centers.

Decision support: Deriving a patient-specific therapy

For deriving a patient-specific therapy plan that adheres to a protocol definition the patient-specific data are necessary. The physician treating the child has to
– record age, heigth, weight and sex of the patient

– determine the starting point of the chemotherapy cycle
– select the therapy protocol and chemotherapy cycle according which the patient has to be treated.

Additionally, the criteria which are necessary for including a patient in a selected chemotherapy cycle have to be confirmed.

Because of the toxic reactions on previous radiotherapy or chemotherapy the physician may decide that the complete dosage proposed by the therapy protocol should not be administered to the child. In this case he has the opportunity to reduce the dosage either for all or just for certain drugs. If the physician decides during the administration of a chemotherapy cycle that the following doses of this cycle should be reduced he can calculate a new therapy plan starting with the respective day of the current cycle and with reduced dosage.

The derived therapy plan can be printed as a structured document and can serve as an aid for organisation and documentation.

To summarize, figure 1 shows the architecture of CATIPO.

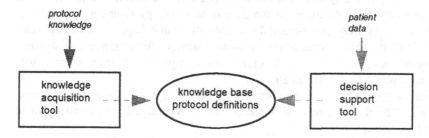

Fig. 1. Architecture of CATIPO. The physician specifies protocol specific knowledge with the help of the CATIPO-knowledge acquisition tool. The knowledge is also accessed by the decision support tool which derives patient specific therapy plans. For that the CATIPO-decision support tools needs certain data about the patient.

Discussion of experiences

Benefit

The main task of CATIPO is to support physicians with deriving patient-specific, protocol-guided therapy plans for patients with childhood cancer. Due to the complexity and scope of therapy protocols of multicenter trials (cf. e.g. [14]) CATIPO can help to avoid mistakes which could have severe consequences. CATIPO is now in routine use for several years. All dosages of cytostatic drugs in pediatric oncology are calculated at least twice, so that all calculations of CATIPO have been controlled by experienced physicians in a conventional manner. According to this experiences, a high quality of CATIPO calculations could be approved, if the therapy protocol is defined correctly.

CATIPO has not only the benefit that it can help to avoid mistakes it can also reduce the effort for deriving protocol-guided therapy plans, because each chemotherpy cycle can be used after its definition for several patients.

CATIPO provides additional tasks for supporting processes in clinical routine. First of all, the calculated therapy plans can be printed and they are used for administration and documentation purposes. The medical staff records the application of the calculated doses on the printed sheets and they will be filed in the patient record. Additionally, CATIPO prints labels and forms for ordering the drugs from the dispensary.

Limitations

The limitations of CATIPO are due to the fact that the basic idea was to have a simple and easy to use system. Therefore, the main task of CATIPO is just to derive a chemotherapy plan which fulfils the criteria of a therapy protocol. It is not yet possible to use it for computer-aided documentation. It may happen for example that the physician decides to change the calculated dosage, for example due to toxic reactions of the child. In this case CATIPO offers no possibility to record and store the actual applications electronically.

Additionally, CATIPO can currently only calculate a single chemotherapy cycle. It is not able to give an overview of the complete chemotherapy of a patient, or to include radiotherapy and surgery.

Often the integration of decision support systems in hospital information systems is mentioned as an important aspect in order to avoid multiple data entry ([15-17]). In the case of CATIPO the number of data that have to be entered after a protocol has been defined is rather low, so that the physicians have not yet regarded the lack of integration as a shortcoming of the system.

What are the reasons that CATIPO is really in routine use?

The most important aspect for the success of CATIPO is, that the demand for a system for computer-aided therapy planning came from the physicians working in pediatric-oncologic clinics. There was really a necessity of having a decision support of this kind. CATIPO was developed in close cooperation with the future users and is therefore well adapted to their requirements. The limitations of the system are well accepted by the users, because they enable that the system is easy to apply and easy to use.

Another important point is that by using CATIPO the physician does not have the feeling that the system is explicitly suggesting decisions. CATIPO just supports him with calculations on the basis of formally represented knowledge on therapy protocols. The physician is very well aware that he is responsible for the final decision. This can be shown with the help of an example: CATIPO is able to reduce the dosage of cytostatic drugs in comparison to the proposals of the protocol. But the decision that the cytostatic drugs should be reduced is up to the physician.

Up to now, the users did not ask for an additional kind of decision support.

Although CATIPO is in wide-spread use in Germany it has to be regarded, that there are still pediatric-oncologic clinics that do not use CATIPO for deriving patient-specific therapy plans. As the main reason they mention that knowledge acquisition is rather time-consuming and complex. A solution of this problem would be that the knowledge acquistion process takes place in the trial centers. This has not been done up to now, because normally all hospitals are using different drugs (with the same active agent) and are composing the infusions differently. It is now considered to distribute parts of the therapy protocols in CATIPO format, so that the pediatric oncologic clinics have only to modify certain parts with the help of the knowledge acquisition tool.

Which conclusions can be drawn from our experiences for the applicability of decision support systems in clinical routine?

To summarize, our experiences with CATIPO confirm the following criteria for the applicability of decision support in clinical routine:
- There should be a demand for decision support by the physicians.
- The decision support system should meet the requirements of the users.
- The system should be as easy to use as possible.
- The development of the decision support system should take place in tight cooperation with the users so that their feedback can influence further development.
- The benefit of the system in contrast to the effort for using the system must be obvious for the user.
- It should also be obvious for the user, that he is only supported with decisions. It can be assumed that a system is better accepted if it does not suggest decisions explicitly.
- The system must offer high quality decision support.

Perspective of CATIPO

CATIPO currently offers basic functions for decision support in pediatric oncology. A further benefit for patient care and research can be assumed by additional knowledge-based functions, although they are not yet explicitly demanded by the physicians. For example the protocol definition could be enhanced by knowledge on clinical actions that have to be taken besides the administration of drugs. At the time of deriving a patient-specific therapy plan, reminders could be given, when e.g. a laboratory examination has to be ordered, diagnostic material has to be send to reference institutions or a report on toxic reactions has to be transmitted to the trial center.

Knowledge-based functions can be the more effective, the more patient data can be taken into account. The functions of CATIPO are currently integrated in a computer aided clinical documentation system for pediatric oncology [18], so that a considerable amount of patient data will be available for decision support. Figure 2 shows the resulting architecture. But this offers also new perspectives for supporting the physician in his routine work. Then he will be able among others to

- record the actual applied therapy in comparison to the calculated therapy, so that it can be stored and provided for further patient care,
- generate reports about the therapy for filing in the conventional patient record,
- get an overview of the complete chemotherapy of a patient,
- add important therapy items automatically in a medical report or discharge letter,
- transmit research data to the trial centers electronically.

In the framework of integrating the therapy planning in the documentation system, the knowledge acquisition tool has been enhanced by the possibility to define sequences of chemotherapy cycles and to arrange them as a therapy arm of a protocol. Additional knowledge has been integrated about how therapy protocols can be composed of various therapy arms by stratification and randomisation.

We plan to evaluate the benefit and other consequences that will occur due to the integration of the therapy planning in a comprehensive documentation system.

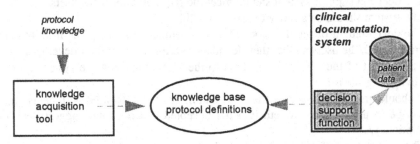

Fig. 2. Architecture of the therapy planning tools after integration in a clinical documentation system. The decision support tool of CATIPO is now an integrated part of the clinical documentation system. For deriving patient specific therapy plans the decision support function accesses the data base of the documentation system.

References

1. Kaatsch P, Kaletsch U, Michaelis J (1997): *Jahresbericht 1996 des Deutschen Kinderkrebsregisters Mainz*. Institut für Medizinische Statistik und Dokumentation.
2. Teich JM, Schmiz JL, O'Connell EM, Fanikos J, Marks PW, Shulman LN (1996): An Information System to Improve the Safety and Efficiency of Chemotherapy Ordering. In:

Cimino JJ: *Beyond the Superhighway: Exploiting the Internet with Medical Informatics. Proceedings of the 1996 AMIA Annual Fall Symposium (Washington).* Philadelphia: Hanley & Belfus. 498-502.

3. Hammond P, Harris AL, Das SK, Wyatt JC (1994): Safety and Decision Support in Oncology. *Methods of Information in Medicine*, 33, 371-381.

4. Bachert A, Classen C-F (1995): Wissensbasierte Chemotherapieplanung in der pädiatrischen Onkologie: Ein Beispiel zur Therapieunterstützung. In: Buchholz W and Haux R: *Informationsverarbeitung in den Universitätsklinika Baden-Württembergs.* Heidelberg: Hörning. 117-124.

5. Wirtschafter D, Carpenter JT, Mesel E (1979): A consultant-extender system for breast cancer adjuvant chemotherapy. *Annals of Internal Medicine*, 90(3), 396-401.

6. Friedman RB, Entine SM, Carbone PP (1983): Experience with an automated cancer protocol surveillance system. *Am J Clin Oncol*, 6(5), 583-592.

7. Enterline JP, Lenhard R, Blum B (1989). *A clinical information system for oncology.* New York, Springer.

8. Hickam DH, Shortliffe EH, Bischoff MB, Scott AC, Jacobs CD (1985): The Treatment Advice of a Computer-Based Cancer Chemotherapy Protocol Advisor. *Annals of Internal Medicine*, 103, 928-936.

9. Tu SW, Kahn MG, Musen MA, Ferguson JC, Shortliffe EH, Fagan LM (1989): Episodic Skeletal-Plan Refinement Based on Temporal Data. *Communications of the ACM*, 32(12), 1439-1455.

10. Bornhauser M, Schmidt M, Ehninger U, von Keller J, Schuler U, Ehninger G (1998): Computer-based quality control in high-dose chemotherapy and bone marrow transplantation. *Bone Marrow Transplant*, 21(5), 505-509.

11. Kaatsch P, Haaf G, Michaelis J (1995): Childhood malignancies in Germany - Methods and Results of a Nationwide Registry. *The European Journal of Cancer*, 31A(6), 993-999.

12. Müller R, Sergl M, Nauerth U, Schoppe D, Pommerening K, Dittrich HM (1997): THEMPO: A knowledge-based system for therapy planning in pediatric oncology. *Computers in biology and medicine*, 27(3), 177-200.

13. Müller R, Thews O, Rohrbach C, Sergl M, Pommerening K (1996): A Graph-Grammar Approach to Represent Causal, Temporal and Other Contexts in an Oncological Patient Record. *Methods of Information in Medicine*, 35, 127-141.

14. Soula G, Puccia J, Fieschi D, Bernard J-L, Le Boeuf C, Fieschi M (1998): Impact of the TOP-FORUM Hypermedia System in a Pediatric Oncology Care Unit. In: Cesnik B, McCray AT and Scherrer J-R: *MedInfo '98, Proceeding of 9th World Congress on Medical Informatics.* Amsterdam: IOS Press. 809-813.

15. Shortliffe EH (1993): The adolescence of AI in Medicine: will the field come of age in the '90s? *Artificial Intelligence in Medicine*, 5, 93-106.

16. Haug PG, Gardner RM, Tate KE, Evans RS, East TD, Kuperman G, Pryor T, Huff SM, Warner HR (1994): Decision Support in Medicine: Examples from the HELP System. *Computers and Biomedical Research*, 27, 396-418.

17. Brigl B, Ringleb P, Steiner T, Knaup P, Hacke W, Haux R (1998): An Integrated Approach for a Knowledge-based Clinical Workstation: Architecture and Experience. Methods of Information in Medicine. *Methods of Information in Medicine*, 37(1), 16-25.

18. Wiedemann T, Knaup P, Bachert A, Creutzig U, Haux R, Schilling F (1998): Computer-aided Documentation and Therapy Planning in Pediatric Oncology. In: Cesnik B, McCray AT and Scherrer J-R: *MedInfo 98, Proceedings of the Ninth World Congress on Medical Informatics.* Amsterdam: IOS Press. 1306-1309.

Experiences with Knowledge–Based Data Cleansing at the Epidemiological Cancer Registry of Lower–Saxony

Holger Hinrichs and Kirsten Panienski

Oldenburg Research and Development Institute for Informatic Tools and Systems
(OFFIS), Escherweg 2, D–26121 Oldenburg, Germany
holger.hinrichs@offis.uni-oldenburg.de

Abstract. In epidemiological cancer registries, extensive measures to clean data are inevitable. This is due to the heterogenity of reporting organizations, as for example hospitals, oncological centers, and physicians. Data cleansing ensures data quality, which is essential for epidemiological analysis and interpretation. By means of the software tool CARELIS, this paper shows that the process of data cleansing can be automatized to a considerable extent. CARELIS integrates a probabilistic record linkage method with knowledge–based techniques to minimize the effort of manual after–treatment of notifications transmitted to the registry. This paper focusses the discussion of experiences made by CARELIS users, usually medical documentation assistants.

1 Introduction

The main tasks of an epidemiological cancer registry are: population–based registration of cancer cases, differentiated monitoring, analysis of temporal and spatial trends, identification of risk groups and factors, and providing data for epidemiological studies [8]. These tasks can only be fulfilled with a complete and valid collection of cancer cases. Each case is to be stored in the registry only once, even if it is transmitted several times by different organizations (physicians, hospitals, pathologies, etc.). When recording, storing, analyzing, and interpreting cancer data, the registry has to take into account the so–called "right of informational self–determination of patients". The federal states of Germany are liable to establish epidemiological cancer registries by January 1st, 1999 [4].

In Lower–Saxony (some 7.3 million inhabitants), about 40.000 new cancer cases are expected per year (some 500 cases per 100.000 inhabitants). Assuming a registration that covers the whole area of Lower–Saxony, the local cancer registry [3] has to work up about 60.000 notifications from hospitals, 80.000 notifications from pathologies, and 87.000 death certifications (concerning all causes of death). This corresponds to a rate of multiple notifications of 3.5 (without death certifications).

Running an epidemiological cancer registry requires integration of data from different, heterogeneous sources. Usually, this is rendered more difficult by a number of data conflicts which have to be solved. Notifications on cancer cases typically contain information of varying quality and different representations; one often has to deal with redundant, incomplete, invalid, or inconsistent data. To increase data quality for epidemiological studies, information has to be corrected, standardized, and linked to related information. Several notifications referring the same patient or tumor have to be condensed to *one* explorable database record. The resulting record should contain the most reliable or most specific values of the single notifications. These steps (correction, standardization, linkage, and condensation) can be summarized by the term *data cleansing* [1, 2, 9]. Due to large data volumes and complex data processing, it has become inevitable to automatize the process of data cleansing as far as possible. Reaching this goal has been the driving force in developing the knowledge-based software tool CARELIS, which will be presented in the next section.

2 The Software Tool CARELIS

CARELIS (Cancer Registry Lower-Saxony - Record Linkage System) [6] is a knowledge-based, multi-user software tool for data cleansing at epidemiological cancer registries (Fig. 1).

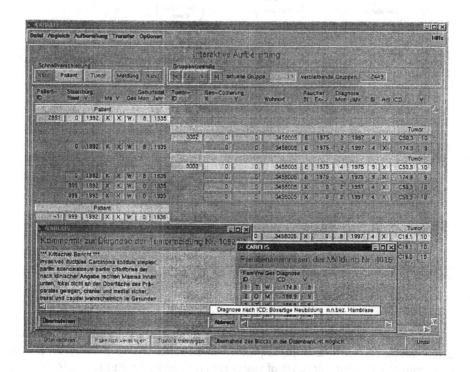

Fig. 1. CARELIS graphical user interface

A typical workflow using CARELIS is as follows (Fig. 2): first, knowledge-based consistence checks are done to discover incorrect or inconsistent values. Notifications that do not pass these checks have to be touched up manually. (In the future, this after–treatment will be partially automatized.)

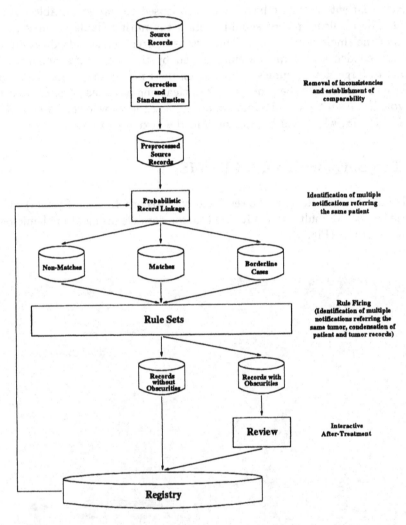

Fig. 2. CARELIS overall workflow

Following a standardization of data to establish comparability of values, a probabilistic record linkage [5] is performed between the preprocessed notifications and the current database of the registry, in order to find multiple notifications belonging to the same individual. A notification may match one or more other notifications and/or one patient record stored in the registry. It is also possible that no corresponding data can be found (non–matches) or that no obvious decision can be made (borderline cases). In either case, a knowledge–based after–treatment follows. The goal of this step is to attach a notification to a patient's tumor record (in case of a match) and to extract the most reliable and specific pieces of information out of the source data.

For automatic treatment of notifications, CARELIS accesses a number of rule sets. Rules typically have the form "if <condition> then <action>". These rule sets, which can be changed dynamically, are connected to the CARELIS workflow as follows (Fig. 3): first, CARELIS performs a fully automatic handling of a set of notifications that have been rated to belong to the same individual in the step of probabilistic record linkage. Apparently, in case of a non–match, the set contains only one member.

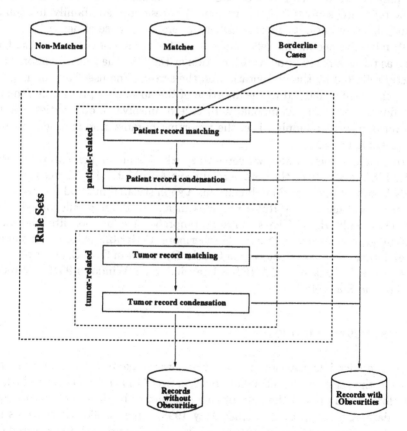

Fig. 3. CARELIS rule–based workflow

The various rule sets are initiated sequentially. First, matches between notifications and patient records are handled, followed by a condensation of patient data. The next rule set attaches notifications that have been classed with the same patient in the previous step to the respective patient's tumor records. Finally, the patient's tumor data are being condensed, too. Only if every single step of the described process has been finished successfully, the current set of notifications including the corresponding patient and tumor records will be stored in the registry's database, and the next set of unfinished notifications will be loaded.

On the other hand, if the application of rule sets reveals that an interactive after–treatment is necessary due to contradictory information, the CARELIS user has to review these obscurities. The same holds for borderline cases which resulted from the probabilistic linkage. In doing so, the user is being supported by a graphical user interface, dynamically adapting to the current constellation of notifications. Input of invalid values is avoided by automatic validity checks. The user may access various pieces of additional information (as far as transmitted by the reporting source), e. g. an anamnesis of residence and family, information about jobs, therapies, diagnoses, earlier tumors, and cause of death.

To minimize the manual effort of review, the results of the automatic treatment, as far as already under consideration at the time the rule sets aborted, are directly reflected by the presentation on the screen. The user is being informed about those rules that led to the abortion of the automatic process; he/she may then finish the treatment manually. In case of unsolvable obscurities, the user may initiate further inquiry, i. e. the reporting organization is asked to clarify the questionable case.

To conclude this section, we come to speak of some implementation details: CARELIS makes use of the commercial tools AutoMatch [7], ILOG Rules, and ILOG Views. While AutoMatch contains a sophisticated method for probabilistic record linkage, ILOG Rules provides means to develop rule–based expert systems. Finally, ILOG Views contains comprehensive function libraries for developing graphical user interfaces. Furthermore, CARELIS is based on the relational database management system Oracle. By means of ODBC, other relational systems can be attached. CARELIS is available for Windows 95/98, Windows NT 4.0, and Sun Solaris.

3   User Experiences

Since the epidemiological cancer registry of Lower–Saxony is being built up at the moment, the registration rates mentioned in Sect. 1 have not been reached, yet. Therefore, evaluation of the current rule sets had to be done on base of a quite small database. In particular, since May 1998, some 22.800 notifications have been transmitted to the registry, about 2.700 of which are still unprocessed (Fig. 4). Just now (November 1998), the registry's database contains about 11.900 patient records and about 12.500 tumor records. This corresponds to a current rate of multiple notifications of about 1.5.

At the moment, the CARELIS knowledge–base comprises about 100 rules, mostly for data condensation. 30 rules concern the treatment of patient–related values; 60 rules deal with tumor data condensation.

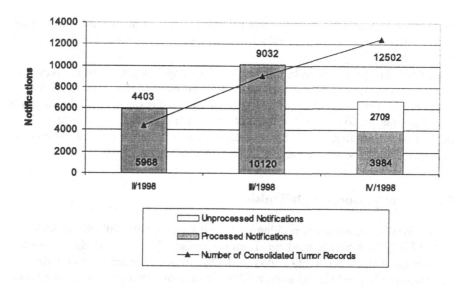

Fig. 4. Current extent of the registry's database

3.1 Automization Rates

First experiences have shown that approximately 70% of cancer cases can be processed automatically. However, this rate varies depending on the reporting sources. The so-called "Nachsorgeleitstellen" (clinical registries) usually transmit summarized data to the epidemiological registry. For this reason, CARELIS will find only a few additional matches in the step of record linkage. Preprocessing of data at the "Nachsorgeleitstellen" makes it possible to process up to 85% of records from this source automatically. On the other hand, pathologies usually transmit one record per histological examination. Aggregation of these data at the registry can cause data conflicts which have to be handled interactively. The same holds for matches between cases from different sources, where the degree of automation amounts to only 50%. Prospectively, continuous extension of rule sets will increase this rate in the future.

3.2 Rule Specification

In the beginning, specification of rule sets by the medical staff (1 physician, 2 medical documentation assistants) was difficult. We tried a graphical notation (a sort of decision tree), which proved to be impractical to represent medical knowledge because of ambiguous interpretation and costly transposition to the language of ILOG Rules. Next, we specified the rules using predicate logic. At first, the medical staff was unaccustomed to the strictly formal representation of knowledge. But after a while they got used to it and managed to do the rule specification successfully. Low effort was necessary to translate the specification into the target language.

The ability to extend rule sets in a flexible way has proved to be very profitable: an incomplete rule set is ready for use even if the portion of records that may be processed automatically by the rule set is quite low. The design of rule sets was based on a quite precautionary strategy, i. e. a case will only be processed automatically if there is really no doubt about the correctness of the decision. Otherwise an interactive after–treatment is inevitable.

3.3 Domain–Specific Difficulties

Apart from these notation problems, we had to cope with difficulties which resulted from the fact that medicine is an imprecise science, knowledge is developing continuously, and classifications are being revised regularly. For example, the classification ICD–O (International Classification of Diseases for Oncology) contains morphology codes with a specific behavior (degree of malignancy). Anyway, pathologies are allowed to transmit any conceivable combination of morphology and behavior which has to be accepted as a correct value. As a consequence, computer based quality management at cancer registries is limited.

In particular, for medical information there are no definite principles laying down which combinations of values are allowed and which are not. At least, it is possible to define probabilities of the appearance of combinations. In general, computer based validity checks of these probabilities may not prevent an unlikely combination from being saved, but may only put out a warning. Additional commentary of such a case by the reporting source will help the medical documentation assistants with their decision. Moreover, a history of earlier records referring to the respective tumor may provide better evidence for corrections than considering a single record. In spite of this, it is impossible to recognize every single miscoding.

To follow an international standard, our rule sets are based on [10]. This technical report defines groups of topography codes from the ICD–O (2nd edition) which refer to a single site. Besides, it describes groups of malignant neoplasms which are considered to be histologically different according to the definition of multiple cancers.

The knowledge–based component has been integrated into CARELIS lately. In doing so, we set great store by a homogeneous integration of the component into the existing workflow. The medical documentation assistants should not have to change their working habits, but should be preserved from monotonous activities and – where convenient – be supported in their decision–making. As a result, psychological effects could be observed, as for example increased working motivation and job convenience. Besides, there are economic advantages resulting from increased data throughput. Finally, increased data quality allows for a more reliable data analysis – one of the main tasks of population–based cancer registries.

4 Conclusion

Especially in case of multiple notifications referring the same tumor, knowledge–based techniques have turned out to be a considerable lightening of work. The rule sets allow for a systematic detection of data errors and for an automatic combination of consistent data. Consequently, the user may concentrate on exceptional cases.

In order to increase the rate of automization in the future, the degree of completeness of rule sets has to be improved. Of course, this goal could also be reached by a relaxation of the precautionary strategy of automization pursued so far, but only by putting up with a higher rate of wrong decisions and – as a consequence – a lower data quality.

References

1. Adamek, J.: Fusion: Combining Data from Separate Sources. Marketing Research: A Magazine of Management and Applications 6 (1994) 48–50
2. Agarwal, S., Keller, A. M., Wiederhold, G., Saraswat, K.: Flexible Relation: An Approach for Integrating Data from Multiple, Possibly Inconsistent Databases. International Conference on Data Engineering. Taipei 1995
3. Appelrath, H.–J., Friebe, J., Hinrichs, E., Hinrichs, H., Hoting, I., Kieschke, J., Panienski, K., Rettig, J., Scharnofske, A., Thoben, W., Wietek, F.: CARLOS (Cancer Registry Lower–Saxony): Taetigkeitsbericht fuer den Zeitraum 1.1.–31.12.1997. Technical Report (in German). OFFIS. Oldenburg 1997
4. Deutscher Bundestag: Gesetz ueber Krebsregister (Krebsregistergesetz KRG). Bundesgesetzblatt (in German) 79 (1994) 3351–3355
5. Fellegi, I. P., Sunter, A. B.: A Theory for Record Linkage. Journal of the American Statistical Association 40 (1969) 1183–1210
6. Hinrichs, H., Aden, T., Dirks, J.–C., Wilkens, T.: CARELIS – Record Linkage im EKN. Technical Report (in German). Epidemiological Cancer Registry of Lower–Saxony. Oldenburg (to appear)
7. Jaro, M. A.: Advances in Record Linkage Methodology as Applied to Matching the 1985 Census of Tampa, Florida. Journal of the American Statistical Association 84 (1989) 414–420
8. Jensen, O. M., Parkin, D. M., MacLennan, R., Muir, C. S., Skeet, R. G.: Cancer Registration: Principles and Methods. IARC Scientific Publications No. 95. International Agency for Research on Cancer (IARC). Lyon 1991
9. Kimball, R.: Dealing with Dirty Data. DBMS Magazine 9 (1996). http://www.dbmsmag.com/9609d14.html
10. Parkin, D. M., Chen, V. W., Ferlay, J., Galceran, J., Storm, H. H., Whelan, S. L.: Comparability and Quality Control in Cancer Registration. IARC Technical Report No. 19. International Agency for Research on Cancer (IARC). Lyon 1994

Author Index

Springer
and the
environment

At Springer we firmly believe that an international science publisher has a special obligation to the environment, and our corporate policies consistently reflect this conviction.

We also expect our business partners – paper mills, printers, packaging manufacturers, etc. – to commit themselves to using materials and production processes that do not harm the environment. The paper in this book is made from low- or no-chlorine pulp and is acid free, in conformance with international standards for paper permanency.

Lecture Notes in Artificial Intelligence (LNAI)

Lecture Notes in Computer Science